# GLOBAL JUSTICE AND AVAN
## POLITICAL AGENC_

Why should states matter and how do relations between fellow-citizens affect what is owed to distant strangers? How, if at all, can demanding egalitarian principles inform political action in the real world? This book proposes a novel solution through the concept of avant-garde political agency. Ypi grounds egalitarian principles on claims arising from conflicts over the distribution of global positional goods, and illustrates the role of avant-garde agents in shaping these conflicts and promoting democratic political transformations in response to them. Against statists, she defends the global scope of equality, and derives remedial cosmopolitan principles from global responsibilities to relieve absolute deprivation. Against cosmopolitans, she shows that associative political relations play an essential role and that blanket condemnation of the state is unnecessary and ill-directed. Advocating an approach to global justice whereby domestic avant-garde agents intervene politically so as to constrain and motivate fellow-citizens to support cosmopolitan transformations, this book offers a fresh and nuanced example of political theory in an activist mode. Setting the contemporary debate on global justice in the context of recent methodological disputes on the relationship between ideal and nonideal theorizing, Ypi's dialectical account illustrates how principles and agency can genuinely interact.

**Lea Ypi** is Professor in Political Theory at the London School of Economics and Adjunct Associate Professor in Philosophy at the Australian National University.

# Global Justice and Avant-Garde Political Agency

LEA YPI

OXFORD
UNIVERSITY PRESS

# OXFORD
## UNIVERSITY PRESS

Great Clarendon Street, Oxford, OX2 6DP,
United Kingdom

Oxford University Press is a department of the University of Oxford.
It furthers the University's objective of excellence in research, scholarship,
and education by publishing worldwide. Oxford is a registered trade mark of
Oxford University Press in the UK and in certain other countries

© Lea Ypi 2012

First published 2012
First published in paperback 2017

Published in the United States of America by Oxford University Press
198 Madison Avenue, New York, NY 10016, United States of America

British Library Cataloguing in Publication Data
Data available

Library of Congress Cataloging in Publication Data
Data available

ISBN 978-0-19-959387-3 (Hbk.)
ISBN 978-0-19-879866-8 (Pbk.)

*To Jonathan*

# Acknowledgements

Even though this project was initially intended as work in the history of ideas, hardly anyone reading the final product would doubt its ambition to contribute to debates in contemporary political theory. Such an intellectual journey was not exactly planned from the start, but if the transition turned out to be more enjoyable than expected, it is the merit of a number of friends and colleagues. I am particularly indebted to Chris Armstrong, Christian Barry, Clara Brandi, Geoff Brennan, Gillian Brock, Chris Brooke, Eamonn Callan, Simon Caney, Renato Caputo, Christine Chwaszcza, Helder De Schutter, John Dryzek, Dimitris Efthimiou, Lina Eriksson, David Estlund, John Filling, Katrin Flikschuh, Rainer Forst, Fabian Freyenhagen, Pablo Gilabert, Bob Goodin, Stefan Gosepath, Rob Jubb, Tamara Jugov, Patti Lenard, Catherine Lu, Raffaele Marchetti, Larry May, Sue Mendus, David Miller, Darrel Moellendorf, Peter Niesen, Claus Offe, David Owen, Stefano Petrucciani, Teresa Pullano, Wojciech Sadurski, Jörg Schaub, Henry Shue, Nic Southwood, Bo Stråth, Zosia Stemplowska, Annie Stilz, Marc Stears, Christine Straehle, Adam Swift, Laura Valentini, Nicholas Vrousalis, Peter Wagner, and Jonathan White for commenting helpfully on various parts of the book, for discussing ideas with me, and for invaluable suggestions on how to improve the work as a whole.

Drafts of different chapters were presented to audiences at the Italian Institute for Historical Studies in Naples, the European University Institute (EUI), the Australian National University (ANU), Princeton University, the London School of Economics, the Wissenschaftszentrum Berlin (WZB), the Wissenschaftskolleg Berlin, the University of Nottingham, the University of Essex, the University of Frankfurt, University College London, the Prague Critical Theory Conference, Luiss University in Rome, and the ECPR Joint Sessions in Helsinki. I would like to thank participants at these events for their critical remarks and suggestions. A first version was completed while holding a six-month fellowship at the Irmgard Coninx Stiftung at the WZB; special thanks go to Ingo and Sabine Richter, Sabine Berking, and Leo von Carlowitz for their friendship and generosity (as well as for indulging my attempts to defend its main arguments in stilted German). A good part of the material was prepared during two visits to the Australian National University: I would like to thank the EUI for sponsoring my travel the first time, and the staff and academics of the Research School of Social Sciences, especially Bob Goodin, for making my stay there incredibly pleasant and productive.

The final version of the manuscript was completed while I held a Post-Doctoral Prize Fellowship at Nuffield College, Oxford. I am particularly grateful to the college fellows, staff, and to my mentor, David Miller, for contributing to provide the best work environment one could hope for while writing one's first academic book. I would also like to thank the members of the Centre for the Study of Social Justice, of the Nuffield Political Theory Workshop, of the History of Political Thought Seminar, and of a small but extremely challenging Marxist reading group for making my intellectual experience at Oxford incredibly rich and stimulating. The late and much missed Jerry Cohen commented extensively on various chapters of the book; whilst he would probably still have much more to object in the final product, I believe that the work has significantly improved, thanks to his efforts and unfailing advice. In addition, I am very grateful to Dominic Byatt, Kok-Chor Tan, and another anonymous reviewer of Oxford University Press for their invaluable suggestions on the (almost) final draft of the manuscript.

Some core ideas of the book were first developed as part of my doctoral dissertation at the EUI in Florence. The years spent at the EUI have been among the most difficult of my life, and those who know the reasons also know that writing the thesis was the easy part. What they may not be fully aware of is how this latter task was only made easy thanks to their efforts and support. There is one friend in particular whose constant advice and support played an incredibly important role: Bob Goodin. I have inflicted on him more drafts of the book and more worries about life as an academic than it is reasonable to expect anyone to share. Had it not been for Bob, this project would not have been brought to completion, and my academic journey would have hardly started. I am also grateful to Peter Wagner who, in addition to being an extremely supportive supervisor at the EUI, is perhaps unaware that he saved me from abandoning the doctoral programme exactly halfway through.

In addition, I would like to thank Giulia Albanese, Migena Bregu, Adrian Brisku, Paola Caputo, Renato Caputo, Donatella Della Porta, Brett Goodin, Ross Goodin, Dana Goswick, Clarice Marsano, Massimo Montelpari, Ertol Muzina, Xhoana Papakostandini, Teresa Pullano, Mario Reale, Paola Rodano, Neila Sula, Françoise Thauvin, Shendi Veli, Ingela Walgrehn, as well as my wonderful friends at the 'Collettivo di Villa Mirafiori' of the University of Rome La Sapienza for being at my side in times of great need. John and Ann White have been extremely supportive during these first years in the United Kingdom. I am very grateful for their friendship, generosity, and invaluable help with the proofs. My mother, Lani, and Arbien deserve special thanks; they have often reminded me that one does not have just academic work to worry about and pleasantly distracted me from statist cosmopolitanism.

Finally, I will never find enough words to say how very grateful I am to Jonathan for being there when the whole world seemed to be falling apart. Meeting him at the EUI on my third day in Florence was without doubt the best thing that happened to me in the last few years. This book is dedicated to him.

Some of the material in the book is based on articles that have earlier appeared in print. I am grateful to the publishers for allowing me to adapt passages from the following:

'Sovereignty, Cosmopolitanism and the Ethics of European Foreign Policy', *European Journal of Political Theory*, vol. 7 (2008), 349–64. © Sage Publications Ltd.

'Political Membership in the Contractarian Defence of Cosmopolitanism', *The Review of Politics*, vol. 70, issue 3 (2008), 442–72. © Cambridge University Press.

'Statist Cosmopolitanism', *The Journal of Political Philosophy*, vol. 16, issue 1 (2008), 48–71. © John Wiley and Sons.

'On the Confusion between Ideal and Non-ideal in Recent Debates on Global Justice', vol. 58, issue 3 (2010), 536–55. © John Wiley and Sons.

'Politically Constructed Solidarity: The Idea of a Cosmopolitan Avant-Garde', *Contemporary Political Theory*, vol. 9, no. 1 (2010), 120–30. © Macmillan Publishers Ltd.

# Table of Contents

Introduction                                                                1

## PART I:  ON HISTORY AND METHOD

Chapter 1: The Historical Controversy                                      11

Chapter 2: Activist Political Theory and Avant-Garde Agency                35

## PART II:  DEFENDING THE STATE, DEFENDING COSMOPOLITANISM

Chapter 3: Politics and Associative Relations                             71

Chapter 4: Global Egalitarianism                                          88

## PART III:  STATIST COSMOPOLITANISM

Chapter 5: On Principles                                                  107

Chapter 6: On Agency                                                      131

Chapter 7: A Cosmopolitan Avant-Garde                                     154

Conclusion                                                               174

*Notes*                                                                   180
*Bibliography*                                                            208
*Index*                                                                   219

# Introduction

On an ordinary market day, Monday, 26 April 1937, Nazi units of volunteers from the German army and the German air force (the so-called Condor Legion) bombed the Basque town of Guernica in northern Spain. The attack, planned to support nationalist forces in the war against the Republican government, was extremely effective. Water mains were wiped out, roads and bridges were destroyed, countless houses were demolished. The Basque authorities reported that human casualties amounted to over 1600 civilians killed and around 900 wounded. In a little more than three hours, Guernica was razed to the ground.

At the time the bombing took place, the artist Pablo Picasso was in Paris preparing a mural commissioned by the Spanish Republican government for the international exposition dedicated to Art and Technology in Modern Life. After reading about the massacre, previous plans were abandoned and Picasso started working on a new piece of work entitled 'Guernica', soon to become one of the most poignant testaments to the horrors of the Second World War, and perhaps the best-known example of twentieth-century avant-garde art.

An anecdote illustrating the artist's perception of his own work at the time of the German occupation of Paris is indicative of the spirit in which the mural was composed. On one of the frequent visits Picasso used to receive from Gestapo soldiers (who pretended to admire his work but typically searched his studio for traces of collaboration with the Resistance), a Nazi official was shown a postcard reproduction of 'Guernica'. After a short pause observing the painting, the visitor allegedly asked: 'You did that, didn't you, Picasso?' 'No,' the painter apparently replied, 'you did it.'[1]

This anecdote is revealing of the attitude with which many pioneers of the early avant-garde perceived the relationship between art and reality, observation and creativity, reflection on existing states of affairs and subjective interpretation of their impact. It is also significant for introducing an issue that will occupy us extensively in the following pages: the relationship that those who engage in some kind of critical appraisal of social and political events entertain with the events themselves; how much they rely on a description of current features of the world and to what degree they must abstract and depart from them. From the time of its first public appearance in Paris to the present-day exhibition of a tapestry copy in the corridor of the United Nations Security Council chamber room, 'Guernica' has acted both as an icon of the devastation provoked by military technology and a symbol of the plea for peace; it has inspired in the public both a tragic sense of mourning for the slaughter of innocent civilians and a militant attitude of rebellion against the cruelty of human suffering. Its enduring legacy illustrates that, contrary to what is frequently assumed, effective avant-garde work (whether in art, politics, or society) is not reducible to the subversion of all existing canons, ways of life, and traditions of interpretation. It also ought not to be confused with the aspiration to abandon reality and create a radically different yet ultimately unintelligible world, a world populated solely by the artist's self-created dilemmas, fantasies, and ideals. Avant-garde work, one might venture to argue, is best understood as a kind of activity that aims to refine the lens through which reality is observed, to articulate and interpret the concerns and commitments of one's contemporaries, and to analyse current events with an eye to both critique and innovation. Only by doing so are those involved in it ultimately able to inspire viable forms of resistance, and coherent discourses of political, social, and cultural transformation.

Picasso's own impatient reaction when pressed to convey his views on the relation between art and reality seems to confirm these remarks. 'What do you think an artist is?' he is reported to have answered in the course of a 1945 interview for *Les Lettres Françaises*. 'A fool who has only eyes if he is a painter, only ears if he is a musician, only a lyre for all the chords of the heart if he is a poet, or even, if he is a boxer, only muscles? On the contrary, he is at the same time a political being, always wide awake on the face of the heart-rending bitter or sweet events of the world and wholly fashioning himself according to their image. How could he fail to take an interest in other people and by virtue of what ivory-tower indifference could he detach himself from the pulsating life they bring near him?' No, Picasso concludes. 'Painting is not made to decorate houses. It is a weapon of offensive and defensive war against the enemy.'[2]

Rhetorical emphasis aside, a view not too dissimilar from this one inspires this book's understanding of the vocation of the political theorist and the relationship between normative principles and political agency it tries to articulate. In what follows, a similar approach is called (for want of a better term) 'activist political theory'. A politically active theorist is, I argue, not very different from a politically engaged artist. Both seek to interpret the world around them as well as try to change it; both rely on observed facts as much as independent creative input to offer a critical reading of historical events; and both are constrained by particular standards (in one case of harmony and style, in the other of argumentative reasoning) in developing their critical reading of the world. But more importantly, in both cases their activity is not a solitary one. It forms part of a collective enterprise, informed by the practice of other agents in society, drawing from a common pool of conceptual resources, building and improving on the efforts of predecessors, and reacting or learning from their errors. A similar dynamic between innovation and preservation lies at the heart of any historically emancipatory discourse trying to elicit political (or social and cultural) reform.

All this is descriptively plain. The trouble consists in understanding how one could capture the development from a normative, and not purely explanatory, perspective. What kind of criteria can be adopted in assessing a plurality of views claiming to contribute to the theorists' emancipatory task? What method should one endorse when trying to develop progressive interpretations of the function and purpose of existing political institutions? Where do political ideals come from, and how do they relate to existing manifestations of political agency? What is the most appropriate way of understanding the link between causal empirical relations and normatively fundamental commitments? Under what conditions, if any, can moral principles become political obligations? How are political obligations motivationally sustained? What conception of political agency supports normative innovation and political transformation?

All these questions direct our attention, one way or another, to a larger issue concerning the purpose of normative theorizing, and the contribution of political activity in articulating that purpose. These are questions too large to address in the abstract. This book engages with them in the context of a familiar dispute in contemporary political theory: the so-called global justice debate. The starting question is familiar: the extent to which the reduction of *global* inequalities (however one conceptualizes their metric) ought to preoccupy political theorists, and the role of states with this regard. The positions are also relatively clear: cosmopolitans, it is well-known, object to the moral arbitrariness of the state; statists on the other hand object to the global scope of egalitarian principles. Their shortcomings, this book contends, have a common source: they stem from the confusion between ideal and nonideal categories in investigating the place of normative principles and their relationship to political agency. Remedying these shortcomings requires an alternative way of approaching that relation, one which is able to illuminate both the normative relevance of particular political obligations and to defend the global scope of egalitarian justice.[3]

The chapters that follow contribute to contemporary disputes in political theory at two levels: a methodological and a substantive one. From the point of view of the former, they articulate a way of pursuing political theory in an activist mode, trying to capture not just how appropriate normative views emerge and are endorsed to criticize the world but also under what conditions they can be invoked to change it. They rely on what I call a 'dialectical' way of approaching the relationship between principles and agency, one that seeks to place ideal and nonideal considerations at the fundamentally appropriate level of analysis. The method is sensitive to the circumstances under which interpretive accounts of the function and purpose of political institutions emerge, to the learning processes that inform agents' development of appropriate normative commitments, and to particular instances of political agency (what I call avant-garde political agency) in nurturing and completing this process. From a substantive perspective, a similar approach leads to an alternative position in the global justice debate: 'statist cosmopolitanism'. It also allows us to enter that debate with greater awareness of the proper place of issues of normative justification (asking what is the most appropriate interpretation of the function and purpose of global political institutions given current circumstances of global injustice) and issues of political practice (interested in what conception of associative relations supports political transformation in the world as we know it).

Many of these questions find their roots in debates on the relationship between cosmopolitanism and patriotism that appeared during the Enlightenment. The first part of the book explores some of these historical controversies as a way of introducing relevant methodological issues that will guide our assessment of current debates in the chapters that follow. A brief historical overview on some key figures of the Enlightenment illustrates how the idea of cosmopolitanism was both praised for cultivating a philanthropic interest in the equal well-being of every individual in the world and criticized for lacking an adequate conception of political agency able to justify civic political obligations. Teasing out the implications of this debate brings into sharper focus the necessity to distinguish issues of normative principle and issues of political agency and reveals the need for an activist conception of cosmopolitanism, one that is both appropriately justified from a normative perspective and able to motivate existing political action.

A similar account of cosmopolitanism, I argue, starts to emerge in the writings of Kant where the defence of state-based political relations at the level of agency supplements the defence of cosmopolitanism at the level of principle. The view is informed by a way of reading historical developments which is dubbed 'dialectical' and by a particular account of political agency: 'avant-garde' political agency. It focuses on the heuristic role of conflict for developing a normative account able to improve on its rivals both with regard to problem diagnosis and to its capacity to guide political transformation given existing political structures.[4]

The chapter that follows further explores these components of activist political theory (in particular the dialectical method and the concept of the avant-garde) by placing their analysis in the context of contemporary debates on the relationship between principles and agency. It illustrates how the dialectical method combines features from two prominent ways of understanding this relationship: an ideal and a nonideal approach. Defined as a method based on learning from the trials, errors, and successes of the past, dialectic assists theorists in identifying normative interpretations that aim to offer both a fundamentally appropriate analysis of conflict and to promote political transformation in the world as we know it. The method therefore seeks to reconcile the kind of first-order normative commitments that ideal accounts typically take to heart with the agency-oriented analysis of social and political practices central to nonideal accounts. Its capacity to deliver normative views able to adequately perform both roles, I argue, depends on the comparison between different available interpretations along three dimensions: diagnostic capacity, innovating role, and heuristic potential. Whilst the former helps identify the grounds and scope of existing conflicts, the second provides the positive body of normative content required to reform existing political institutions. Finally, the third is needed to continue the critical interrogation of how these institutions perform in the light of the concerns and expectations to which unforeseen developments give rise.

In the context of illustrating the process of moral learning informing the evolution of normative views, the idea of avant-garde political agency is introduced. At a first level we can think of avant-garde agents as those agents whose position in society renders them particularly vulnerable to the effects of specific political and institutional conflicts and therefore particularly relevant in informing the theorist's diagnostic enquiry. At a second level, however, and once an attempt to develop a fundamentally appropriate normative interpretation of the function and purpose of political institutions has been made, avant-garde agents join the theorists' activist effort to render normative views politically effective and motivationally sustainable. In this second, morally more relevant sense, avant-garde political agents are aware of their contribution to conceptual innovation and political change in a normatively mediated way. They provide essential support to the theorist's endeavours to render normative views politically effective and motivationally sustainable, and they contribute to preparing the ground for testing theories' heuristic potential by taking advantage of existing cultural, political, and social arrangements.

These issues are discussed at a more abstract level in the first part of the book, and applied to the global justice debate in the second and third parts. The controversy between statists and cosmopolitanism provides a fruitful philosophical terrain for exploring the relationship between principles and agency, and for understanding the contribution of avant-garde political agents in this regard. Many of the current disputes on the normative standing of the state and the scope of egalitarian principles, the book contends, would disappear if features from ideal and nonideal approaches were combined at the right level of analysis and a dialectical approach were endorsed. Yet existent theories of global justice often seem to confuse or misplace these categories in discussing the normative standing of states or the principles of global justice.

The main task of the second part of the book is therefore to illustrate how these errors occur. On agency, both statists and cosmopolitans tend to rely on false or idealized premises to reject or endorse the normative relevance of associative political relations but fail to ask what existing conception of political relations best supports political transformation. On principles, they tend to condemn the consequences of global poverty as self-evident moral wrongs without linking first-order normative commitments to an appropriately fundamental analysis of its causes. A different combination of ideal and nonideal categories, I suggest, would deliver a more plausible account of global justice, one that does not place exclusive moral weight on the facts of global poverty and on the principles associated with it, but that is able to analyse its causes within a normatively fundamental framework of inquiry. And it would also supply a different analysis of the role of states and of the relevance of associative political obligations, integrating their role within an avant-garde conception of political agency rather than letting current political constraints place restrictions on the scope of egalitarian relations.

The third part of the book further develops just such an account, called 'statist cosmopolitanism'. The dialectical method is here deployed to articulate a new relationship between principles and agency and to illustrate the theory's ability to improve on existing accounts of global justice with regard to all three dimensions deemed necessary to progressive political theorizing (capacity for diagnosis, innovation, and heuristic role). Its main components are, as far as principles are concerned, the need to combine normative and causal claims in identifying fundamental normative constraints and, as far as agency is concerned, a defence of associative political relations which supports cosmopolitan transformation.

The first of these questions is pursued in the fifth chapter. Here, the analysis of fundamentally appropriate principles of global justice is developed without any need to invoke the usual cosmopolitan premises on the arbitrariness of political membership. What matters for the theory is the causal link between absolute deprivation and relative deprivation and the role of this link in defending a particular version of global egalitarianism focused on the connection between poverty and inequality. As I argue in that chapter, by relying on a similar link with reference to a particular kind of goods, global positional goods, it is possible to illustrate that certain patterns of production and distribution are globally extended and that these patterns trigger global relational practices where a sharp distinction between sufficientarian justice (typically associated with statism) and egalitarian justice (typically associated with cosmopolitanism) is hard to justify. The argument therefore puts pressure on accounts of global justice limited to emphasizing the need for sufficientarian principles remedying absolute deprivation. It also illustrates how an egalitarian conception constitutes a more progressive, as well as diagnostically appropriate, account of the function and purpose of global institutional practices.

The next two chapters take up issues of agency and political transformation. The cosmopolitan principles defended in previous pages call for a political distribution of responsibilities which are in turn dependent on relevant (more or less radical) political and institutional reforms. For this kind of reform to be both politically feasible and motivationally sustainable, the role of existing associative relations appears to be crucial. Cosmopolitanism becomes politically effective by taking advantage of political mechanisms that allow citizens to transform collective institutions by putting constraints on each other's action. It may hope to be stably maintained by appealing to familiar learning processes, a particular sense of justice, and cultural resources that motivate existing moral agents. To clarify both points, the penultimate chapter invokes the concepts of popular sovereignty and civic education mentioned when exploring the tensions between cosmopolitanism and patriotism during the Enlightenment, and examines their application to the global justice debate.

Once we understand the nature of the relationship between principles and agency in this dialectical way, the question of how normative innovation and political change actually develops given current (more or less hostile) political circumstances becomes crucial. To analyse these issues, the final chapter returns to a concept introduced in the first part of this work, that of avant-garde political agency. As will be clear by now, in addition to the normative critiques cosmopolitanism encounters at the level of principle, an important part of the challenge is mounted at the level of agency. Those who seek to undermine an egalitarian interpretation of cosmopolitan commitments tend to emphasize its weak motivational force in the absence of special associative relations and without a shared ethos of global solidarity. However, the strength of analysing both issues of principle and issues of agency in the mode of activist political theory is that a similar perspective allows us to see the development of cosmopolitan commitments as a political and not just moral task. Such an analysis does not need to make heroic assumptions about what ordinary citizens will or will not be motivated to do when it comes to specific initiatives promoting cosmopolitan justice. It is enough to focus on particular political agents that are already exposed to and affected by inequalities of access to relevant global goods (in the case of our analysis: positional goods), triggering the diagnosis of the circumstances of injustice that we obtained in previous chapters. Once a basic normative framework for analysing these concerns and commitments has been developed, theory joins the innovating efforts of these political agents and we are able to understand the dynamic of cosmopolitan political transformations within particular associative relations.

The terms cosmopolitan and avant-garde therefore serve to designate all those individual citizens, civil associations and political actors relevant to our dialectical understanding of the relationship between principles and agency in the context of global justice debates. Starting with an analysis of how one should understand the concept of 'avant-garde', illustrating the usage of the term in the context of artistic activity and emphasizing the analogy between artistic and political innovation lead us to underline the creative aspects of avant-garde movements, their ability to critically interrogate but also deploy traditional resources to promote particular interpretations of existent relevant practices. We have already mentioned how the vision that motivates this book's account of activist political theory is similar to how Picasso perceived the role of engaged art. Exploring further the analogy in the final chapter takes us to a discussion concerning the role of avant-garde *cosmopolitan* agents and how their normatively inspired political initiatives might creatively intervene to transform the function and purpose of existing institutions compatibly with relevant principles of global justice. These agents, I argue, typically play a crucial role in sensitizing local publics to issues of transnational conflict and global inequality, and in enacting the learning process that gradually leads to challenging old categories and replacing available conceptual resources with new emancipatory discourses. In short, they constitute the engines of cosmopolitan political progress.

Although most of the reflections on justice and avant-garde political agency presented throughout these pages refer to only one amongst many debates in normative political theory (the global justice debate), and although they are deployed to strengthen the particular version of cosmopolitanism developed in this work (statist cosmopolitanism), some of the methodological concerns raised and some of the categories deployed might also apply more broadly. The way of understanding the relationship between principles and agency, the need to articulate normative principles at the appropriately fundamental level, and the analysis of categories through which the transformative potential of existing political relations could be conceptualized are issues that should be of relevance even to those who are not interested in the specific, substantive aspects of the controversy between statists and cosmopolitans. Many people believe that theory is not simply there to criticize the world, but also to try and change it. And many also think that political theory in an activist mode has not received the attention it deserves. To the extent that this is true, and regardless of the particular controversies we are concerned with, one might still find interest in this work. If that happens, the task of developing the central categories of the book so as to render them relevant to other debates in contemporary political theory will hopefully become a shared project.

# Part I

# On History and Method

# 1

---

# The Historical Controversy

## 1.1 A COSMOPOLITAN IS NOT A GOOD CITIZEN?

'*Un cosmopolite n'est pas un bon citoyen*,' boldly remarked in 1762 the fourth edition of the *Dictionnaire* of the French Academy. In a more moderate yet hardly unambiguous voice, the *Encyclopédie* of Diderot and D'Alembert also emphasized: 'On se sert quelquefois de ce nom en plaisantant, pour signifier un homme qui n'a point de demeure fixe, ou bien un homme qui n'est étranger nulle part.'[1] Both definitions suggest that, contrary to what is frequently assumed, the Enlightenment was as much the age of cosmopolitanism as of the aversion to it.[2]

This chapter explores the historical roots of the controversy between statism and cosmopolitanism during the Enlightenment.[3] It does so not in the spirit of providing a comprehensive (or even historically impeccable) account of all the positions and authors engaged in that debate, but of understanding the genesis of concepts and arguments that will occupy us in the following pages. Reflecting on some key intellectual figures of the Enlightenment illustrates how much of the disagreement between authors that we would now identify as statists and cosmopolitans is due to an under-theorized link between normative principles and political agency, a link that appears still neglected in contemporary political theory. A preliminary historical analysis of that relation provides a crucial tool for adjudicating between the relative merits of contending global justice theories, and for incorporating their commitments into a plausible alternative interpretation.

The first part of the chapter introduces two different ways of understanding the term 'cosmopolitan' that circulated during the Enlightenment, providing the reference points for both the critique and the defence of recent cosmopolitan accounts. The first is a negative one, associated with the attitude of citizens who ignore the special relevance of particular collective institutions and for whom any set of public laws is as good as any other. The second is a positive one, associated with the attitude of the 'sage' who makes his loyalty to a particular political community conditional upon its realization of a universal ideal of equality. The prevalence of either conception produces an oscillation from a sceptical or even hostile evaluation of cosmopolitanism on the side of authors such as Voltaire or Rousseau to the enthusiastic endorsement of it by others such as Leibniz and Diderot. Their arguments begin to reveal how the tension between the negative and positive understandings of cosmopolitanism arises from an under-theorized link between normative principles and political agency.

This issue is further developed in the second part of the chapter. By focusing in particular on Rousseau, an author often invoked by cosmopolitan-sceptics, the chapter analyses the evolution of his critique of cosmopolitanism from the *Discourse on the Origin and Foundations of Inequality among Men* or *Second Discourse* to *The Social Contract*. Starting with a more positive evaluation of cosmopolitanism, the idea is later considered by Rousseau, at best, morally indeterminate, at worst, politically disrupting. Cosmopolitanism re-presents either the attitude of a naïve virtuous hero or that of the indifferent citizen. In either case, it is limited to a more or less commendable individual attitude that appears far from encouraging a reform of political institutions.

The third part of the chapter shows how the persistence of this critique and the oscillation between the positive and negative understandings of cosmo-politanism lead to a conceptual turn in Kant's political writings. By focusing on Kant's philosophy of history and on his theory of right, one can see how an abstract and ill-defined concept, as cosmopolitanism is by the middle of the eighteenth century, becomes part of a more sophisticated analysis of the relationship between normative principles and political agency. Starting with a reading of historical events sensitive to the dynamic of moral progress, Kant is the first to see the possibility of reconciling statism and cosmopolitanism, a global conception of equality and the normative standing of associative political relations. Clarifying the relevance of Kant's statist cosmopolitan approach serves as an introduction to the rest of this work where an interpre-tation similar to the Kantian one is further developed and defended.

## 1.2 POSITIVE AND NEGATIVE COSMOPOLITANISM

'When he was asked where he came from he would say: "I am a citizen of the world".' Antiquity commentators (Greek and Latin) have invariably attributed the term *kosmopolitēs* to both Socrates and to Diogenes the Cynic.[4] Yet the spirit in which either (if any of them) would have pronounced the sentence is rather different, and different were also the models they inspired during the Enlightenment.

Socrates' teaching consisted in advising people to think for themselves, a maxim that Kant would later consider one of the founding principles of the Enlightenment.[5] For him, persons possessed equal moral status regardless of who they were and where they came from. Identified with a positive attitude of citizens committed to the equal welfare of all human beings, cosmopolitanism was also coupled with a firm political allegiance to native political institutions.[6]

In the case of Diogenes the Cynic – a character that Plato allegedly called 'Socrates gone mad'[7] – we confront a completely different meaning of cosmopolitanism. Diogenes' claim to be a citizen of the world carried no positive connotation; he recognized no attachment to anyone in the world, refused to abide by the polity's laws, and dismissed conventional politics. Loyalty to the world [*kosmos*] instead of a particular *polis* was a merely negative statement; it did not correspond to any *positive* assumption of responsibility extending to the *kosmos* the civic feelings of the polity. Diogenes considered living in harmony with the laws of nature the sole moral philosophy, yet never attempted to teach a similar doctrine. While rejecting all positive obligations to friends, family, or the polity, his emphasis on being a 'citizen of the world' merely intended to deride the assumption of any civic responsibility.

Both conceptions of cosmopolitanism – the positive and the negative one – resurfaced during the Enlightenment. Throughout the seventeenth and the eighteenth centuries, Europe appeared dramatically torn by political conflicts determined by the clash between diverse and apparently irreconcilable political and religious doctrines. A new world had started to emerge from the crisis of previous institutions which, having lost stability, exploited confessional hostility to ensure a contingent survival. The crisis of the Christian *res publica*, the emergence of Renaissance ideals, and a renewed interest in the study of Greek and Latin texts understandably brought cosmopolitanism to the fore. The Socratic ideal appeared especially apt to respond to the needs of this new age, promising as it did to maintain universal moral ideals and individual independence, earthly solidarity, and everyday tolerance. Yet the negative meaning of cosmopolitanism continued to be present in the attitude of irreverent individuals who declared themselves citizens of the world only as a means of denying responsibility to take part in any political controversy.

Leibniz was among the first to refer implicitly to the Greek 'positive' understanding of cosmopolitanism. 'Justice,' he claimed, is the virtue guiding affection to all human beings; 'the Greeks call it *philanthropy*'; it is 'a charity of the sage who follows the decrees (*dictata*) of wisdom and the dictates of reason'.[8] The exercise of justice should be considered unbound to national conventions and particular political circumstances because, he clarified, 'as long as something of consequence can be done, I am indifferent to whether it is done in Germany or France, I only wish the good of the human race'.[9]

Leibniz interpreted this cosmopolitan sense of justice as a universal instinct of compassion, a sociable feeling found in every human being that the exercise of reason had the duty to bring into light when obscured by opposing conventions or by selfish inclinations.[10] Yet he was sadly aware that the philanthropic attitude of single individuals was not enough for cosmopolitan projects to develop worldwide. One had to start from somewhere, seek support from this or that sovereign monarch, construct relevant social relations, and explore the potential of ideas in different political contexts. As he confessed to Peter the Great in 1712, while asking him to sponsor the project of an international Academy of Sciences, gathering researchers from all over Europe: 'as long as I can find the means and occasions to contribute efficiently to the common good on all these subjects – and here I make no distinction between nations and parties – I would rather see the sciences brought to flourish in Russia than see them cultivated in mediocrity in Germany. The country where this project will go best will be the one most dear to me, since the entire human race will profit from it and the real treasures will increase.'[11]

Leibniz's attitude was typical of several other philosophers throughout the Enlightenment. Thus Denis Diderot wrote to David Hume: 'my dear David, you belong to all the nations of the earth and you never ask a man for his place of birth. I flatter myself that I am like you, a citizen of the great city of the world.'[12] Again, in introducing the term 'citoyen du monde' in his *Encyclopédie*, Diderot approvingly reported Baron de Montesquieu's saying: 'If I know of anything advantageous to my family but not to my country, I should try to forget it. If I knew of anything advantageous to my country which was prejudicial to Europe and to the human race, I should look upon it as a crime.'[13]

This positive understanding of cosmopolitanism, which equated *philosophe* to *citoyen du monde* and rejected political chauvinism, was by no means the only one to circulate during the Enlightenment. Towards the middle of the eighteenth century, it was heavily contrasted by a *negative* conception, replicating the model of Diogenes the Cynic and indeed employing the very Greek word with which Diogenes allegedly introduced himself. It is possible to find this second use in the first eighteenth-century text where the term '*cosmopolite*' explicitly appears. Louis-Charles Fougeret de Monbron – one of the lesser-known French men of letters of the eighteenth century whom Diderot knew and despised – gave a rather unappealing definition of cosmopolitanism in his autobiography *Le Cosmopolite ou Le Citoyen du monde*.[14] The text, often described as having inspired Voltaire's *Candide*, narrates how the writer travelled everywhere without being committed to anyone because everything was indifferent to him:

> Tout les pays me sont égaux pourvu que j'y jouisse en liberté de la clarté des cieux et que je puisse entretenir convenablement mon individu jusqu'à la fin de son terme. Maître absolu de mes volontés et souverainement indépendant, changeant de demeure, d'habitudes, de climat, selon mon caprice, je tiens a tout et ne tiens a rien.[15]

In a somewhat similar tone, Raynal's *Histoire des deux Indes* has a cosmopolitan merchant declare his intentions:

Périsse mon pays, périsse la contrée ou je commande, périssent les citoyens et l'étranger...Tout les lieux de l'Univers me sont égaux. Lorsque j'aurais dévasté, sucé, extenué une région, il en restera toujours une autre où je pourrais porter mon or et en jouir en paix.[16]

The examples of Leibniz and Fougeret de Monbron reveal the two most relevant interpretations of the term 'cosmopolitan' over the course of the eighteenth century. Viewed positively, the idea appears morally plausible but politically and motivationally weak; it presents an admirable declaration of principles yet fails to be integrated by a positive conception of agency. Too fragile to inform a concrete political vision, the better versions of cosmopolitanism cultivated a mere academic fashion. It was the fashion of travellers, scientists, or writers whose communion of interests was embodied in the ideal of the *république des lettres*, but whose progressive moral intents struggled to find adequate political expression.

On the other hand, the negative interpretation of cosmopolitanism does not seem without political implications. Cosmopolitanism emerges here in dangerous opposition to particular political commitments and challenges individuals' loyalty to the institutions of the state. It threatens to disrupt an already fragile civic bond and it encourages individual anarchy and social dereliction. It leads to a sceptical and rather libertine attitude, stressing how the citizen of the world is in fact nothing more than an ironic and dismissive character that ignores local obligations and derides the development of political institutions.

Under no circumstances would the eighteenth-century *philosophes*, many of whom had put themselves at the service of enlightened monarchs in the hope of encouraging progressive political reforms, wish to be confused with these irreverent characters. Far from providing a remedy for selfishness and individualism, cosmopolitanism would in this case merely amplify those tendencies. Therefore, if, on the one hand, the positive contribution of moral cosmopolitanism was clearly appreciated, its unqualified opposition to statism would rather be suspected. The concept maintained this ambiguity for most of the eighteenth century until a new way of combining principles and agency emerged from such opposing considerations.


## 1.3 PATRIOTISM, THE STATE, AND THE *CITOYEN DU MONDE*

Voltaire does not mention the term 'cosmopolitanism' in his *Dictionnaire Philosophique* but the concept is present in an implicit and particularly revealing contrast to the entry *'patrie'* (homeland). As Voltaire defines the latter:

> A homeland is made up of several families; and just as you normally stand by your family out of pride (*amour propre*), when there is no conflicting interest, because of that same pride, you support your town or your village, which you call your homeland.[17]

Further down, the same point is made even more clearly:

> We all want to be sure of being able to sleep in our own beds without someone else arrogating to himself the right to tell us to sleep elsewhere. Everybody wants to be sure of his wealth and his life. With everyone thus having the same desires, it works out that the private interest becomes the general interest: when we express our hopes for ourselves, we are expressing them for the Republic.[18]

In sketching this Hobbesian hypothesis on the foundation of the state, Voltaire is hardly enthusiastic about the merits of patriotic feelings. Only a natural instinct of self-protection and the need to preserve their own life, he claims, nurtures people's attachment to collective political institutions. Here, as in the case of Hobbes, the necessity of a political authority leading to a civic union does not arise out of a common effort celebrating people's goodwill. On the contrary, if humans were naturally good they would not need to pay collective security at the price of individual liberty. They would not need a coercive force to suppress their natural instincts. Political power is not grounded on sociability but on conflict; common decisions are not due to tolerance but to reciprocal fear; association is not imposed by solidarity but by uncontained egoism. Far from grounding political community on humanitarian values and cosmopolitan feelings, state institutions arise precisely to compensate for their absence.

It is clear that, for Voltaire, human beings do not transform their character by entering the civic sphere. Subordinating themselves to political institutions hardly determines any qualitative transformation of people's natural instincts. Citizens support their homeland insofar as they support themselves, and they respect the community's bond insofar as this bond protects them from external threats. Such an attitude marks no progress from a purely individualistic and interest-maximizing attitude to something more authentic from a collective moral perspective. Not only do human beings fail to show deeper social feelings towards their fellows, but they may even actively harm them if personal or national security is endangered. In the words of Voltaire:

> It is sad that in order to be a good patriot one is very often the enemy of the rest of mankind. The elder Cato, that good citizen, always said when speaking in the senate: 'That's what I think, and let Carthage go hang.' To be a good patriot is to want one's city to prosper through trade and to be powerful through arms. Clearly, one country cannot win without any other losing, and it cannot conquer without making some people unhappy.[19]

Hence, individuals do not cure their *amour propre* by acquiring political obligations. The opposite is much more likely to occur; state membership risks having an amplifying effect on citizens' conflicting impulses and leaders might exploit human ambition to serve their own competitive passions. 'So that is the human condition,' stresses Voltaire, 'to want your own country to be great is to wish your neighbours ill.'[20]

Voltaire mentions the cosmopolitan spirit as a unique exception to this all-too-recognizable trend: 'The man who would want his homeland never to be larger, or smaller, or richer or poorer would be a citizen of the world.'[21] Yet he does not develop the issue further and it would be misleading to suggest that Voltaire is here embracing a cosmopolitan point of view. The *Dictionnaire Philosophique* does not go beyond a simple mention of the term '*citoyen du monde*' and an implicit appreciation for the inclusive motives that such an attitude reflects. This is because, in spite of his critical observations on *amour propre* as the main cause of rivalry among individuals and (by extension) among political communities, Voltaire did not consider it an obstacle to the enlightened progress of his age. In his own interpretation of history, selfishness and the bourgeois search for profit play a positive role in encouraging the expansion of wealth and civilization. For Voltaire, the age of Louis XIV was one of the most successful stages of human history since what really mattered were not greater freedom and the promotion of social justice, but military strength and the intensification of commerce and the arts.[22]

The centrality of commercial society for facilitating interactions between human beings, often coupled with a critique of the corrupting and degrading effects of the expansion of luxury and international trade, is one of the most familiar themes in Enlightenment political thought.[23] This is where Kant draws his conceptual resources for developing an interpretation of history and an analysis of cosmopolitanism that relies on conflict and cooperation (the idea of unsociable sociability) to arrive at an innovative account of the relationship between cosmopolitan principles and political agency. Before going into the details of his argument, however, it is worth considering a further development of the critique of cosmopolitanism in the writings of Rousseau, especially if one compares the use of the term in the *Second Discourse* and in *The Social Contract*. The ambivalent attitude towards cosmopolitanism is here similar to what we already observed with Voltaire, but the point of departure is radically different. While the latter considered *amour propre* to arise out of a natural instinct of self-preservation, for Rousseau the selfish character of bourgeois interactions generates society's evils and sets a limit to the development of an originally good nature. The role of history is also interpreted differently: in Voltaire, the evolution of science, commerce, and the arts represents a sign of human progress, whereas in Rousseau this very progress ultimately leads to the triumph of luxury, to the corruption of habits, and to what he calls society's 'glittering misery'.[24]

Voltaire particularly disliked Rousseau and ridiculed his *Second Discourse* as 'the philosophy of a beggar who wished that the rich be robbed by the poor'.[25]

However, it is interesting to notice that the term 'cosmopolitan' appears in the *Second Discourse* in a context very similar to Voltaire's discussion of patriotism. Here, Rousseau argues that even if one grants that political obligations within the state might succeed in solving citizens' conflicts, injustices re-emerge when we consider interactions between different states in a competitive international environment.

The Bodies Politic, he claims,

> thus remaining in the state of Nature among themselves soon experienced the inconveniences that had forced individuals to leave it, and this state became even more fatal among these great Bodies than it had previously been among the individuals who made them up. From it arose the National Wars, Battles, murders, reprisals that make Nature tremble and that shock reason, and all those horrible prejudices that rank among the virtues the horror of spilling human blood [...] more murders were committed in a single day's fighting, and more horrors at the capture of a single town than had been committed in the state of Nature for centuries together over the entire face of earth.[26]

Rousseau's complaint is obviously on a very different level from Voltaire's. Yet the context in which he mentions the cosmopolitan virtue of universal love for humanity, as opposed to states' competitive rivalry in the international sphere, is interestingly the same. As Rousseau puts it,

> Civil right having thus become the common rule of the Citizens, the Law of Nature no longer obtained except between different Societies where, under the name of Right of nations, it was tempered by a few tacit conventions in order to make commerce possible and to replace natural commiseration which, losing in the relations between one Society and another almost all the force it had in the relations between one people and another, lives on only in a few great Cosmopolitan Souls, who cross the imaginary boundaries that separate Peoples and, following the example of the sovereign being that created them, embrace the whole of Mankind in their benevolence.[27]

For Rousseau, the main virtue of cosmopolitan characters relies on a feeling people possess before entering into civil society: compassion. The description of such an attitude, which as Rousseau critically emphasizes has now been replaced by tacit conventions established for the sake of commercial interaction, is informed by a positive understanding of cosmopolitanism to which we also observed Leibniz refer. It is a feeling, Rousseau continues, which

> Hobbes did not notice, and which – having been given to people in order under certain circumstances to soften the ferociousness of his amour propre or of the desire for self-preservation prior to the birth of amour propre – tempers his ardour for well-being with an innate repugnance to see his kind suffer.[28]

This feeling is so natural to human beings and this virtue is so universal and useful that even Mandeville, 'the most extreme detractor of human virtues', was prepared to acknowledge its force. Cosmopolitan sympathy, Rousseau argues here, is the only remaining manifestation of an old natural virtue, threatened by the expanding corruption of human nature in civil society and by the diffusion of international animosity.

One would expect, given such a passionate praise of the moral purity of cosmopolitanism, to find it inspiring a new educative model or placed at the heart of a normative political project. Instead, nothing of this kind happens. Not only do particular examples of compassionate characters hardly make an appearance in Rousseau's successive writings but if we insist on investigating the fate of these 'great cosmopolitan souls', we will be surprised to notice a radically different approach. In the Geneva manuscript version of *The Social Contract*, the author complains that cosmopolitans 'boast of loving everyone' (*tout le monde*) so that 'they might have the right to love no one'.[29] In *Émile*, he goes even further and recommends one to 'distrust those cosmopolitans who search out remote duties in their books and neglect those who lie nearest'.[30]

It is important to understand what motivates this shift in the interpretation of cosmopolitanism from the *Second Discourse* to Rousseau's later political writings. If dedication to one's homeland means nothing more than amplified *amour propre*, why do characters once admired for their capacity to show compassion towards all other human beings now emerge as some kind of impostors indifferent to any moral constraint? Why has Rousseau decided to make a target of his critique the negative conception of cosmopolitanism rather than maintain the positive one he initially embraced? In order to answer this question, we need to analyse the role that the acquisition of political obligations plays in Rousseau's successive political writings and to assess his understanding of the relationship between principles and agency in the context of political transformation.

In the *Discourse on Inequality*, the analysis of the state of nature and the critique Rousseau directs to the institutions of the state play a diagnostic rather than normatively constructive role. At the root of present-day conflicts lies the emergence of private property, an institution that continuously undermines natural equality and prevents the establishment of a comparatively just distribution of resources.[31] Given the historical circumstances that have determined its emergence, a political union of the kind modelled by previous social contract theorists, Rousseau argues, is unable to restore peace and preserve justice. The contractual union has no other purpose than to consolidate an arbitrary process of acquisition and transfer by ascribing to it the appearance of rightful action. Society and its laws, claims Rousseau, change a 'skilful usurpation' into an 'irrevocable right', and 'for the profit of a few ambitious men' subject 'the whole of Mankind to labour, servitude and misery'.[32] Blind selfishness and unrestrained will for power cultivate the rule of the strongest. When the foundation of the state rests on a similar set of interactions, and when its laws are distorted by the unilateral interests that *amour propre* generates, the conflicts and inequalities developed with the expansion of civilization can only be expected to escalate.

The question appears deeply transformed in *The Social Contract*. 'Man is born free, and everywhere he is in chains. How did this change happen? I do not know. What can make it legitimate? I believe I can show it.'[33] It is possible to notice, from the initial pages of the book, how the diagnostic problem of identifying the roots of an allegedly unjust initial distribution ceases to preoccupy Rousseau at this point. His primary concern lies in the remedies that could be offered to justify a civil order working in the interest of all: theory no longer tries to simply criticize the world but is positively interested in transforming it. Returning to a state of nature in which human beings enjoyed peace and disposed of infinite resources available is far from representing a realistic prospect. Political society, whatever its limits, appears as the most plausible framework for social interaction; political activity is the only means through which one might hope to contain human corruption and to restore social equality.

In *The Social Contract*, the issue of political obligation ceases to be part of a historical investigation seeking to identify the origins of unjust acquisition. Rousseau's own account of political activism is developed through an analysis of the institutional arrangements necessary to tackle social conflict. According to his newly developed (and widely familiar) theory of the state, sacrificing unrestrained individual freedom is indispensable to ground the collective exercise of popular sovereignty. Once certain political mechanisms are in place, citizens' mutual obligations of obedience are internalized in particular learning processes, and can be tempered through civic education.[34] *The Social Contract* does not merely re-propose a sum of singular individual wills (*volonté de tous*) but qualitatively transforms this common force into a unitary entity capable of serving the common good of all (*volonté générale*). Conflicts cannot be solved through the efforts of individual moral agents, who are always at risk of encountering epistemic limits (by failing to identify the roots of particular problems) or of displaying motivational weaknesses (by indulging their selfish inclinations). It is the dynamic of the union of all and the kind of obligation this generates that establish the possibility of overcoming the particular inclinations of the pre-political man (of the *bourgeois*) in a rational determination of interests carried out by the same subject as *citoyen*.

Popular sovereignty and civic education confer on the Rousseauean theory of the state a special normative standing. Its strength derives from the collective participation in democratic practices that arise not simply out of the common recognition of mutual normative constraints. As Montesquieu had already emphasized, the efficiency of laws and their motivational sustainability are tightly bound to the uses and mores of a particular political community, to its historical development, its major virtues, and to its dominant vices. Rousseau emphasizes the relevance of cultivating this learning process in one of the most important parts of *The Social Contract*. Morals, customs, and above all opinion, he argues, constitute the secret attendance of a great legislator while he appears to restrict himself to particular regulations 'which are but the ribs of the arch of which morals, slower to arise, in the end form the immovable Keystone'.[35]

Rousseau therefore agrees with the sceptics that no individual moral will is sufficient to establish universally binding political obligations, all the more so if one reflects historically on the emergence of the latter. This does not imply, however, that renouncing the idea that a community of citizens could, with time and across several generations, give rise to various expressions of political agency by virtue of which normative principles are promoted. Of course, politics does not arise out of morally good intentions but to compensate for their absence. However, if the general will succeeds in progressively establishing limits to self-interested inclinations, if learning processes are effective in determining the historical transformation of shared institutions, associative political obligations can also be seen as a vehicle for further social and political emancipation.

Similar considerations on the function of the social contract and the relationship between individual and state, universal and particular, led Rousseau to a different evaluation of cosmopolitanism. It is now easier to understand why, in his later writings, cosmopolitanism is judged only negatively and dismissed as the attitude of rootless individuals who ignore the essential civic bond though which political obligations are discharged. The ideal model of a community of moral and social equals cannot be realized through isolated acts of individual human beings and by appealing to their perhaps sincere but nonetheless contingent sense of justice. Natural kindness cannot be a substitute for political activism. What modern society needs is not promoting compassion but reinforcing justice. As long as the *citoyen du monde* claims to overcome with his all-inclusive compassionate feelings particular political boundaries, he is essentially placing himself outside the moral and political context where political agency is expressed, at best failing to understand his fellow citizens' concerns and commitments, at worst reducing his share of responsibility in undertaking collective political transformations.

Rousseau's observations invite one to seek a solution to the emergence of social inequalities by scrutinizing the power-relations and political–institutional context upon which the general will is grounded. *The Social Contract*, however, leaves essentially unanswered the further question of conflict in the *international* sphere that the *Discourse on Inequality* had so perceptively raised. This issue appears crucial if we examine Rousseau's theory of political obligation in the context of relevant global circumstances where the effort to pursue the common good of members in one particular state might threaten citizens in another. This was not a hypothetical scenario, even for Rousseau. The impact of international trade and colonial expansion on the rise and fall of various European and non-European countries was too familiar a component of political development for much of the eighteenth century to be ignored by Enlightenment theorists.[36] Rousseau makes no exception, and even though *The Social Contract* does not directly raise any of these questions, subsequent writings seem to give them at least some attention.

One prominent example is Rousseau's remarks with regard to the project of perpetual peace designed by the Abbé de Saint Pierre. If the social order, he writes here,

> were really, as it is pretended, the work not of passion but of reason, should we have been so slow to see that, in the shaping of it, either too much, or too little has been done for our happiness? That each one being in the civil state as regards our fellow citizens but in the state of nature as regards the rest of the world, we have taken all kinds of precautions against private wars only to kindle national wars a thousand times more terrible? And that, in joining a particular group of men, we have declared ourselves enemies of the whole race?[37]

In the pages that follow these remarks, Rousseau lends support to the idea that the only rational alternative to the principle of balance between powers is extending to the international order political commitments analogous to those one finds in the domestic sphere. He defends Saint Pierre's proposal for a European political federation which, although not requiring states to renounce their national sovereignty, aims to preserve territorial security by seeking their collective agreement on matters of common interest. As Rousseau puts it,

> if there is any way of reconciling these dangerous contradictions, it is to be found only in such a form of federal government as shall unite nations by bonds similar to those which already unite their individual members, and place the one no less than the other under the authority of the law.[38]

Yet one can easily note that, despite the relevance of this federative project for promoting perpetual peace, the motivation for the project is prudential rather than principle-based. The creation of a political community capable of overcoming the international state of nature does not express the general will of *citizens* considered as members of an international community but the common interests of their *states*. The realistic tone of Rousseau's discussion suggests that the project for a future European federation is not guided by normative principles and moral intentions but by a purely rational calculation founded on states' utility maximization.[39] Here, the need to reach an agreement on the organization of global interactions preserves the normative standing of particular political communities; no superior tribunal is allowed to question the moral legitimacy of their interests, neither are they entitled to be placed under coercively enforceable political obligations.

There are good reasons to remain sceptical of states, judged from this selfish and interest-based perspective. But, as we have seen, there are also good reasons to suspect the cosmopolitan individualist attitude, especially its dangerous oscillation between moral flamboyance and political passivity. Is there a way of combining the principled commitments of cosmopolitanism with political agency expressed through membership in the state? Rousseau's reflections, as we have seen, offer a number of conceptual resources on the basis of which one could develop an answer to this question: the centrality of conflict in articulating claims of justice and equality; the need to reflect on the causes of these conflicts from a perspective which is historically sensitive as well as normatively inspired; the role of collective political agency in the dynamic transformation of shared political institutions; and, finally, the support of popular sovereignty and civic education in rendering certain principled commitments politically effective and motivationally sustainable. These are precisely the elements on which Kant's theory relies in developing an innovative interpretation of how principles and agency should be analysed so as to promote a fundamentally appropriate ideal of cosmopolitan emancipation.

## 1.4 FROM A HISTORICAL PERSPECTIVE TO A PRINCIPLE OF JUSTICE

It is no exaggeration to argue that in Kant's work the shift from an individualist conception of cosmopolitanism (associated, as we have seen, either with hopeless moral utopia or with a dangerous anti-civic sentiment) to a politically active normative theory becomes fully intelligible. In order to understand this shift, deeply influenced by Rousseau's analysis of the concept, it is important to begin with Kant's essay: *Idea for a Universal History with a Cosmopolitan Purpose*, published in 1784. The very title of the essay and the fact that cosmopolitanism is linked to a 'purpose' orienting the historical interpretation of events reveal two Kantian innovations in the use and understanding of the concept. The first one is Kant's attempt to isolate the term from its Cynic individualist meaning and turn it into a normative category used to question the performance of present social and political institutions. The second innovation consists in the development of an interpretive approach that combines normative principles and political agency in a dialectical exploration of the role of conflict and its relationship to human progress. Let us consider them in turn.

Like Rousseau, Kant starts from the problem of conflict in the international sphere and examines the performance of social and political institutions in the light of their ability to respond to it. 'What is the use of working for a law-governed civil constitution among individual men, *i.e.*, of planning a *commonwealth*?' he asks. 'The same unsociability which forced men to do so gives rise in turn to a situation whereby each commonwealth, in its external relations (*i.e.*, as a state in relation to other states), is in a position of unrestricted freedom. Each must accordingly expect from any other precisely the same evils which formerly oppressed individual men and forced them into a law-governed civil state.'[40]

Yet Kant is far from limiting the purpose of political obligations to the protection of interests found within particular states. Whilst sharing Rousseau's diagnostic view that the expansion of civilization and the development of commercial relations do not necessarily resolve (and might in fact exacerbate) the problem of inequality among human beings, his essay on universal history attempts to construct a narrative of human progress whereby social antagonism acts as a vehicle for political transformation. As Kant puts it, desire for honour, power, and property leads a human being to seek status among his fellows, 'which he cannot *bear*, yet cannot bear to leave'. Through this process, skills are developed, and 'by a continued process of enlightenment, a beginning is made towards establishing a way of thinking which can with time transform the primitive capacity for moral discrimination into definite practical principles'. In this way 'a pathologically enforced social union is transformed into a moral whole'.[41]

What we find here is an attempt to link a backward-looking, diagnostic interpretation of the emergence of social conflicts to a forward-looking account of how normative views seeking to resolve them can be incorporated into a larger moral project at the service of human progress. The presence of conflict encourages people to modify their interactions and find means of coping with common problems, whether in the form of creating joint political institutions or in that of engaging in activities cultivating their sociable dispositions.[42] From an initial stage of antagonism characterized by the assertion of aggressive instincts of self-protection, a kind of calculating rationality, utilitarian in scope, emerges. For Kant, one is not entirely free insofar as practical action is oriented by selfish interest. However, decision-making at this stage is not entirely determined by natural instincts either; human beings are able to calculate their advantages and rationally choose among different options. The creation of joint political institutions and submission to a public coercive authority guarantees that similar claims are channelled in a way that avoids mutual destruction. Such an attitude is distinctive of that historical age of human development in which human beings are divided between the call of natural necessity and that of practical reason, where egoism is associated with a capacity of choice unknown to animals though not fully developed. Instrumental motivation can therefore be put at the service of practical reason, provided relevant social and political mechanisms contributing to that task are identified.

Kant shares with his Enlightenment predecessors the idea that focusing on conflict represents a crucial step for understanding the transition from nature to civil society and the state. He also seems to agree with the view that the genesis of associative political obligations in the pursuit of unilateral and selfish inclinations does not preclude the future promotion of morally good intentions, in Rousseauean terms, of the general will. For Kant, as for Rousseau, political agency is the means through which the sources of conflicts can be publicly articulated and common problems are eventually addressed. Emphasizing the role of 'unsocial sociability' among human beings helps understand the mechanisms of transition from a state of injustice and the expansion of social inequality to one in which appropriate forms of political activity represent a vehicle for introducing practical imperatives in civic life. It is precisely on this idea that the justification of loyalty to particular states lies.

However, all this is not enough. Kant is acutely aware that overcoming socially produced inequalities will hardly be complete without a common effort to attain 'civil society which can administer justice universally'.[43] Once we shift the emphasis from the descriptive point of how political obligations emerge and justify the authority of the state to the prescriptive question of how they can be invoked to promote a more inclusive ideal of justice, new questions start to arise.

If taking seriously political obligations requires establishing a collective political authority capable of administering justice universally, the persistence of conflicts where similar obligations are absent continues to represent a normative problem. As Rousseau and others had already emphasized, the development of morally good intentions is threatened not only by the antagonism between unsociable individuals but also by the ongoing presence of competitive interactions between states, as reflected in commercial rivalries, colonial expansion, or the harmful effects of international trade on indigenous populations.[44] Hence, Kant says, until the spirit of mediation and the collective effort in promoting 'united power' and 'deliberation according to laws of a unified will' is able to guarantee peace and develop freedom for all human beings, history will be marked by stages of destruction followed by contingent progress. But what is the alternative?

Here the Kantian project starts to emerge clearly, developed further in his essay on *Toward Perpetual Peace* and in the *Doctrine of Right*. It is related to the planning of a 'great political body of the future' which,

> although it exists for the present only in the roughest of outlines, nonetheless seems as if feeling to stir in all its members, each of which has an interest in maintaining the whole. And this encourages the hope that, after many revolutions, with all their transforming effects, the highest purpose of nature, a universal *cosmopolitan* existence, will at last be realised as the matrix within which all the original capacities of the human race may develop.[45]

This is precisely the point at which the cosmopolitan concept, defined in Leibniz, Voltaire, and Rousseau as part of an ethical doctrine referring to the attitude of single individuals who think of themselves as citizens of the world, starts changing its original meaning. Cosmopolitanism ceases to be associated with abstract sentiments of love for humanity and a vague sense of justice, and emerges as the central category through which we interpret international conflicts and reflect on their transformative potential. The latter task for Kant requires establishing an institutional order where political obligations are universally distributed and every state may obtain security 'not from its own power or its own legal judgement', but only from 'a united power and the law-governed decisions of a united will'.[46] It is a task that can only be brought to completion if one is able to capitalize on previous social and political achievements, and put these at the service of new transformative political projects.

Interpreters usually converge on the opinion that in the development of his thought from the *Idea for a Universal History* to the *Doctrine of Right*, Kant may have progressively abandoned this original idea of a single political body with coercive powers in favour of a less demanding but pragmatically more appealing project of a voluntary association of states. An ongoing scholarly debate focuses on the reasons motivating Kant's oscillation from the former to the latter, thus raising the question of the enforcement capacities of a free league of states.[47] However, the difference between the 1784 essay and Kant's later political writings may not lie in the modification of the substantive proposal but rather in the systematic role of the principles of cosmopolitanism and in the different conceptualization of the agents required for their promotion. The more interesting question therefore concerns the method that Kant assigns to his new cosmopolitan theory, a method which is both sensitive to past history and the learning processes this makes available to human development, and concerned with forward-looking expressions of political agency able to accomplish this emancipatory project.

In *Idee zu einer allgeimener Geschichte (Idea for a Universal History)*, cosmopolitanism constitutes a point of view from which to interpret the antagonistic development of human interactions in the light of a teleological conception whereby nature itself acts as a guarantee of moral progress. This theory is developed with the help of a historically sensitive method centred on learning processes by virtue of which, as Kant puts it, 'after many revolutions, with all their transformative effects', normative principles become gradually action-guiding. However, in the writings after the French Revolution, the emphasis shifts from how nature contributes to the development of human beings to what human beings themselves acquire in the course of interacting with nature, and among themselves.[48] This significantly reduces the degree of dogmatic faith in progress one might associate with the earlier teleological conception of history. It suggests a much more critical reading, where appeals to past history only act as a heuristic device guiding our analysis of how normative principles interact with current expressions of political agency (a reading we will also invoke in assessing the possibilities of political transformation in the context of current global justice debates).

For Kant, cosmopolitanism can be rendered politically effective and motivationally sustainable by paying attention to the role of innovating political agents who already act in the present to exit particular circumstances of injustice. The guarantee of the cosmopolitan proposal (in Kant's words whether this proposal might have 'objective reality') is provided by existing manifestations of political agency. One important example, in the case of Kant, is provided by the contribution of what he calls a 'powerful and enlightened people', i.e. citizens participating in the events of the French Revolution. Their attempts to promote appropriate principles of justice so as to establish the 'highest political good' are precisely what renders perpetual peace a credible project.[49] Of course, even in this case there is no guarantee that such activist efforts will always succeed in transforming existing political institutions compatibly with cosmopolitan principles. But the knowledge and experience one acquires in the course of attempting these transformations contribute to refine the normative tools and enrich the stock of political resources from which future generations can draw to consolidate their efforts.[50]

The shift in the use of the term 'cosmopolitanism' from a category associated with the conduct of single individuals to a politically relevant interpretation of justice can also be illustrated if we consider the association cosmopolitanism – philanthropy. In the earlier essays, Kant understands cosmopolitanism as a 'universally *philanthropic* attitude' in exactly the same way as Leibniz. However, in *Perpetual Peace*, he seems to have abandoned this individualist conception of cosmopolitanism and argues, in striking contrast to Leibniz, that cosmopolitanism 'is not a question of philanthropy but of right'.[51] Along similar lines, the opening section on cosmopolitanism in the *Doctrine of Right* declares that the rational idea of a 'peaceful, even if not friendly, thoroughgoing community of all nations on the earth that can come into relations affecting one another is not a philanthropic (ethical) principle but a principle having to do with rights'.[52] The solution to the question of the state of nature in the international domain is investigated here in the spirit of *The Social Contract* where principles of justice, instead of being presupposed in the assertion of moral categories, provide the condition of possibility for their further development. By breaking with philanthropy, cosmopolitanism is offered as a fundamentally appropriate interpretation of the function and purpose of political institutions orienting political action in the world. It is grounded in the political life of states and provides a normative goal on the basis of which to seek internal political reform. The conflict between cosmopolitanism and patriotism is thereby resolved not by opposing the former to the latter but by rendering the cosmopolitan union an internal political end of states.[53]

## 1.5 IUS GENTIUM AND IUS COSMOPOLITICUM

The reflections above lead precisely to what Rousseau in his observations on Saint Pierre's project for peace had failed to provide. Analogously to Rousseau, Kant grounds political obligation on the relationship between the distributive will of all and the collective general will but gives it a further universalist spin. In the *Doctrine of Right*, the *ius cosmopoliticum* stands as a separate normative category orienting political agency in present circumstances of injustice and is distinguished by both the rights of citizens within a state (*ius civitatis*) and the right of nations (*ius gentium*).[54] The need for it emerges out of a diagnostic analysis of the sources of conflict in the international sphere, and in light of the persistence of global relations of injustice that are neither accounted for in existing international arrangements nor reducible to domestic factors. The specificity and all-encompassing relevance of cosmopolitan right is deduced by the global extension and reciprocal influence of interactions among people who 'all stand *originally* in a community of land'.[55] This is, as Kant clarifies, a 'community of possible physical *interaction* (*commercium*)' in which each member may offer 'to engage in *commerce* with any other, and each has the right to make this attempt without the other being authorized to behave toward it as an enemy because it has made this attempt'.[56] The extension of global relations of dependence among human beings and the conflicts that their competitive interactions bring about create the need for a new normative category requiring political obligations to go beyond the domestic sphere.

However, it is worth noticing that in Kant's *Doctrine of Right*, cosmopolitanism does not replace statism. It does not abolish the right of states to territorial integrity and autonomous decision-making; it rather complements it with a normative interpretation that appeals to the political contribution of their citizens to establishing just global political relations.[57] Cosmopolitanism integrates traditional conceptions of *ius gentium* with a political duty to transform shared institutions in a way that facilitates non-exploitative forms of international exchange (including trade) and which ensures that global interactions do not end up harming worse-off people in worse-off societies. Kant alludes to this duty in the very definition of the concept: 'this right, since it has to do with the possible union of all nations with a view to certain universal laws for their possible commerce, can be called *cosmopolitan right* (*ius cosmopoliticum*)'.[58] Far from denying the relevance of state-based associative obligations, this right protects vulnerable groups of citizens from inequalities determined by violent or manipulative moves of powerful countries seeking to appropriate their resources or to establish unfair commercial contracts.[59]

Kant's preference for internal mechanisms of political change and his scepticism towards the creation of a unitary political body with coercive powers are not due to concerns about the empirical feasibility of the project, as might appear from a superficial reading of the *Doctrine of Right*.[60] Instead, they are consistent with two strong arguments on the basis of which the relationship between principles and agency is brought into sharper light and the frequently invoked analogy between individuals in the state of nature and the anarchical condition of the international order ultimately collapses. The first refers to Kant's remarks on the undesirability of a sovereign enforcer of cosmopolitan justice and is linked to his insistence on the role of history as a learning platform contributing to moral and political progress. The *Doctrine of Right* emphasizes that a single political body, globally extended and with coercive powers, would be impossible to govern, might soon degenerate into despotism, and establish an irreversible anarchy.[61] In *Toward Perpetual Peace*, Kant comments on a similar issue with an observation that reminds one very much of Rousseau's discussion on patriotism. 'The more the social bond stretches,' Rousseau noticed, 'the looser it grows.' Kant seems to quote this passage implicitly when he emphasizes that 'as the range of government expands, laws progressively lose their vigour'.[62] As Rousseau had emphasized, unlimited territorial extension would undermine patriotism by turning citizens into strangers who share nothing but a coercively imposed allegiance to laws. Without popular sovereignty being integrated by civic education, without the possibility to refer to shared historical experiences, normative principles would be neither politically effective nor motivationally sustainable. For Kant too, the diversity of cultures and religions – even if it may initially give rise to conflict – allows for a 'gradual approach of human beings to greater agreement in principles'.[63] Cosmopolitanism is in this case 'produced and secured' not merely through the coercive use of forces but 'by means of their equilibrium in the liveliest competition'.[64] By referring to existing concerns and commitments, and by interacting with pre-existing schemes of understanding, emerging normative interpretations can rely on a much more sophisticated (and endurable) relation between principles and agency.

The second argument relates to Kant's explicit emphasis on the difference between the conflicts between individuals in the state of nature and institutionally mediated antagonism. As he clarifies with reference to the latter, 'such a state of affairs cannot be pronounced completely unjust since it allows each party to act as a judge in its own cause'. When citizens are bound by collective political obligations, they cannot be said to face the same 'lawless' condition as that of individuals in the state of nature. For, as to states, Kant claims, 'they already have a rightful constitution internally and hence have outgrown the constraint of others to bring them under a more extended law-governed constitution in accordance with their concepts of right'.[65] Hence, one need not consider the role of states arbitrary in analysing the problem of cosmopolitan justice. The superiority of public right over any ad-hoc mechanism for resolving conflicts between private individuals produces a shift away from any easy analogy of the international order with the domestic state of nature. For Kant, as for Rousseau, justice is realized through citizens' participation in collective political practices of deliberation, through the exercise of popular sovereignty coupled with civic education. It is very important not to undermine this process and instead build on its strengths whilst attempting to bring about political transformations. *Ius cosmopoliticum* represents a necessary 'supplement to the unwritten code of the right of a state and the right of nations'; it indicates the emergence of a new normative interpretation of the function and purpose of shared institutions whilst at the same time acknowledging the relevance of existing political obligations.[66] It constitutes the condition of development of the *ius gentium* but it neither leads to an exercise of power with juridical rule – which is always statual or inter-statual – nor does it require a substitution or vertical dispersion of sovereignty.[67]

While replacing the individualistic features of cosmopolitanism with a project of global justice, which pays particular attention to the historical development of the relation between normative principles and political agency, the moral concern of cosmopolitanism is transformed into a political demand, vindicating the need for a commitment which is not limited to the critique of political institutions but actively tries to change them. However, Kant's *ius cosmopoliticum* does not abolish the preceding *ius gentium*; instead, it constitutes its historical–universal condition of development. This seems to be a relevant element to take into account while discussing the link between principles and agency in a theory of global justice. Within the Kantian paradigm, *ius cosmopoliticum* acts as a regulative principle orienting historical and political initiatives with global inspiration. Realizing such a principle requires mobilizing political agency *within* the state because only here the relevant political, social, and cultural conditions necessary to an effective allocation of political obligations may be found.

## 1.6 STATISM, COSMOPOLITANISM, AND THE AVANT-GARDE

Kant's way of reconciling statism and cosmopolitanism may appear naive, relying as it does on existing political communities to provide the most appropriate associative framework for developing cosmopolitan political agency. Cynics might object that states always seek to promote their own interests and that there is no reason why their citizens should take seriously cosmopolitan concerns and commitments, especially if such commitments challenge them to relinquish the benefits they presently receive. Kant acknowledges the strength of the objection. 'Admittedly,' he argues, 'if there were no freedom and no moral law based upon it and everything that happens or can happen is instead the mere mechanism of nature, then politics, as the art of making use of this mechanism for governing human beings) would be the whole of practical wisdom.'[68] Interactions between states would rely on selfish interest, and the whole concept of cosmopolitan justice, indeed of justice altogether, would be 'an empty thought'.[69]

Yet, as Kant's normative analysis of politics and history illustrates, morality does seem to exercise an influence on internal political change; it grounds the general will, and raises the concept of right to 'a limiting condition of politics'.[70] How exactly that transformation is to be understood requires a more detailed analysis of the intervention and role of particular political agents, agents who act within the state to introduce progressive views of the function and purpose of shared institutions. Kant calls these agents 'moral politicians', and argues that they are able to take seriously the principles of prudence yet succeed in reconciling them with the requirements of morality. Similar agents, Kant claims, will act *within* the state in a way that promotes cosmopolitan justice. They will intervene in political circumstances on the basis of the principle that 'once defects that could not have been prevented are found within the constitution of a state, or in the relations of states, it is a duty [. . .] to be concerned about how they can be improved as soon as possible'.[71] For even though it would be absurd, and indeed contrary to both prudence and morality, to require that 'those defects be altered at once and violently', it seems possible (and plausible) to ask moral politicians to 'take to heart the maxim that such an alteration is necessary'.[72] It is precisely on the role of these agents, able to put existing concerns and commitments at the service of normative innovations, that a theory of cosmopolitan justice might rely on becoming both politically effective and motivationally sustainable.

The following pages will return to the relevance of similar agents (what I shall call the cosmopolitan avant-garde) who make it their duty to act within the state in conformity with cosmopolitan principles of justice. Here it seems important to stress some significant elements on which Kant's brief remarks on the intervention of moral politicians seem to rely in explaining the possibility of their politically transformative role. The first is to see how the intervention of these agents is located at the point in which, as Kant puts it, 'defects that could not have been prevented are found in the constitution of the states and in the relations between states'. That is to say, their activity is linked to a kind of diagnosis necessary to critically reflect on the performance of current institutions, to identify conflicts to which these seem (at present) unable to respond, and to investigate roots of these conflicts and features contributing to their expansion. A normative theory seeking to establish fundamentally appropriate principles for political transformation has a necessary diagnostic component, and the validity of its principles will depend at least in part on the balance between its diagnostic capacity and its potential for innovation.

This point leads us to the second feature Kant emphasizes when analysing the role of similar political agents: their willingness to act on the basis of obligations compatible with required principles of right. Once problems are detected, Kant seems to argue here, the duty of political agents consists in identifying principled remedies to existing conflicts and reflecting on viable routes toward necessary political transformations. Even though the realization of such desired ends might be obtained through a gradual rather than sudden process, it is unlikely to be achieved if moral politicians fail to internalize these fundamentally appropriate normative principles and guide political action compatibly with them. Whilst these transformations occur, ordinary citizens will become 'gradually susceptible to the influence of the mere idea of the authority of the law',[73] and if they are coercively enforced their process of civic education will be more and more complete.

The moral politician therefore plays a crucial innovating role in taking the necessary political steps designed to bring political reality closer to the requirements of right. How exactly this innovating task unfolds and in what way first-order normative principles (in this case of cosmopolitan right) are integrated into the political life of particular states are not issues that Kant explores in sufficient detail.[74] To be sure, he discusses the importance of creating a republican constitution which respects the principles of freedom, equality, and independence, and therefore contains progressive laws conducive to cosmopolitan right. Yet a normative analysis of the mechanisms of political change that contribute to the emergence of such progressive laws is absent at this point.

Completing the answer to this question is an issue that will extensively occupy us in the chapters that follow. As far as Kant is concerned, it is possible to obtain some insights into the method according to which it is possible to reflect on the dynamic of political change by emphasizing the importance of learning from historical experience. Appealing to past history, Kant claims, constitutes an important heuristic device for thinking about how present generations ought to try and perfect the efforts of previous ones, what kind of skills and views they should appropriate, and how they might distance themselves from mistakes made in the past. This process of learning from trial, error, and success has important implications when it comes to assessing the performance of current institutions and judging between various courses of action in different political circumstances. The fallibility of human judgement, even when individuals act according to their best intentions, means that those who operate in contingent circumstances have to take into account both the normative desirability *and* the political viability of particular normative views. Theirs are not decisions that can only be informed by abstract considerations, a feature that perhaps serves to explain why rendering cosmopolitan principles politically effective and motivationally sustainable is not a task one can lightly absolve. To accomplish it, human beings need several elements: 'a correct conception of the nature of a possible constitution, great experience tested in many affairs of the world, and above all else a good will prepared to accept the findings of this experience'. However, Kant insists, 'three factors such as these will not be easily found in conjunction and if they are, it will happen only at a late stage and after many unsuccessful attempts'.[75] A historically sensitive analysis of the associative political conditions in which such attempts are to take place and an account of the processes and agents through which a similar task can be accomplished are of the foremost importance for a theory that invokes cosmopolitan principles not merely by virtue of their critical function but in an action-guiding mode.

## 1.7 CONCLUSION

It seems difficult to circumscribe Kant's contribution to a normative theory of global justice to the explicit formulation of 'cosmopolitan' principles, as many authors seem to suggest.[76] Taken literally, Kant's idea of cosmopolitanism is a rather limited one, restricted to conditions of 'universal hospitality' and ruling out (for the most part) any more demanding principles of justice. The real Kantian contribution to the global justice debate is unfortunately the one that has been most neglected. Kant was the only philosopher of the Enlightenment able to go beyond both the moral optimism of his cosmopolitan predecessors and the political pessimism of their statist adversaries. He could combine a cosmopolitan view of principles with a state-based conception of agency, focusing on a diagnostic analysis of conflict and stressing the role of active political initiative in determining conceptual and political change. He did so not merely out of scepticism on the possibility of finding a global political authority able to enforce cosmopolitan justice but on grounds of a deeper critique to the limits of any political theory that detaches abstract reflection on normative principles from an analysis of the political circumstances in which they can be realized.

Cosmopolitanism in Kant is not only a product of his theory of right and of the project of perpetual peace but also, importantly, a regulative idea of history, guiding the progressive introduction of fundamentally appropriate normative principles in collective political practices. Endorsing certain first-order ideals does not suffice to bridge the gap between valid moral imperatives and concrete political initiatives. Only the internal, conflicting development of each political process, and the practice of relevant agents committed to normatively oriented transformation can gradually convert selfish interests and prudential considerations into a set of collective attitudes receptive to valid moral and political imperatives.

The difficulties of realizing cosmopolitanism cannot be avoided by simply appealing to an ethics of the categorical imperative in politics. A complete theory of global justice must take into account the relationship between first-order values and contingent circumstances, between principles and agency, the latter promoting moral ends appropriate to each political stage and the former conferring clarity on these ends by expounding their normative implications. This is also the essence of the frequently invoked maxim that theorizing about politics should take people as they are and laws as they should be. This chapter's historical overview tried to illustrate how state-based political relations neither set an arbitrary limit to the principles of global justice (as many contemporary non-cosmopolitans insist) nor may be easily dismissed or replaced by alternative agents (as their cosmopolitan rivals wishfully think). It also introduced some important elements (e.g. conflict and the heuristic role of history, the importance of a particular account of political agency) that are indispensable to understand in what way associative political obligations can be put at the service of cosmopolitan principles in a fundamentally appropriate account of global justice. The task of unfolding these arguments in more analytical detail belongs to the remaining chapters.

# 2

## Activist Political Theory and Avant-Garde Agency

### 2.1 ACTIVIST POLITICAL THEORY

The Enlightenment maxim that any reform of social institutions must start with people as they are and think about institutions as they should be is not without appeal. Our goals ought to reflect theoretically rigorous principles on what an ideally just society should look like; yet our strategies for achieving them must take account of how society actually is, its nonideal agents, and its existing political structures. We observed in the last chapter how, in constructing the relationship between cosmopolitan ideas and domestic political relations, Kant emphasized that when a certain institutional order is confronted with unforeseen kinds of political conflict, a subset of the civic body (for Kant: the 'moral politicians') acquires responsibility for working towards its solution. Let us call a similar attempt to construct the relationship between principles and agency by placing emphasis on the normative relevance of such political agents an 'avant-garde conception of political agency'.

This chapter examines how political theory (if interested in changing the world rather than simply interpreting it) should reflect on the link between principles and agency, and the role of avant-garde political agents in doing so. I shall call a similar mode of engaging with political reality 'activist' political theory. And I shall call the particular methodological approach of political theory in an activist mode a 'dialectical' approach.

Whether a similar mode of political theorizing exhausts the theorist's task more broadly conceived, or whether there is something else to be said in defence of the truth-seeking (in addition to action-guiding) function of political theory, is an issue that far exceeds the scope of this work. What matters for present purposes is the claim that mainstream political theorists have, on the whole, paid little attention to a certain aspect of the relationship between normative theory and political agency: its politically transformative aspect. This tendency appears even more troubling in an area such as the global justice debate where the relevant questions are often said to emerge in response to upsetting empirical facts (e.g. facts regarding the impact of globalization on the material conditions of citizens in different states or from different social classes), calling for urgent, principle-based political transformations. An essential part of my subsequent critique of both statists and cosmopolitans invokes the distinction between principles and agency to expose some weaknesses in their analysis of the role of the state and the principles of global justice. But the way in which these errors arise in the global justice debate is an interesting consequence of a much larger and perhaps more pervasive neglect of the activist mode in political theory more broadly conceived.

## 2.2 MAPPING THE FIELD

The role of this chapter is to explore the foundations of an avant-garde conception of political agency and to articulate the particular method we adopt when doing so. I have dubbed that method 'dialectical' and I shall introduce it after exploring stylized interpretations of two alternative views, what I shall call 'ideal' and 'nonideal' approaches. Although current political theories differ significantly in the consistency with which these methods are applied, and the elements borrowed from each of them, my aim here is not to go into their detailed analysis but only to explore common assumptions found in general across the debate. Stressing the relevance of the ideal approach often leads to underlining how the priority for normative theory is to figure out what justice requires as a matter of ideal principle, and only in a second stage to reflect on the way in which its principles can be brought to bear on political practice.[1] On the other hand, those who insist on the relevance of the nonideal approach tend to emphasize how, rather than seeking to identify highly abstract and indeterminate principles, political theory ought to enable us to guide political action here and now.[2]

   The dialectical approach introduced below challenges this division of labour and proposes an integrated framework. But it is important to emphasize that, when engaging critically with defences of the ideal and nonideal approaches, my primary aim is not to deprive either of them of potentially legitimate spheres of application. The point is to integrate their strengths and to illustrate their weaknesses when exploring a different way of articulating the relation between principles and agency, and when revealing the transformative potential of that relation. This work, and this chapter in particular, emphasizes both what is lost when we proceed in the dualist way I shall describe and also suggests another way of constructing the relationship between principles and agency. After a critical assessment of some familiar components of ideal and nonideal approaches, the dialectical alternative, central to the avant-garde account of political agency, is introduced. This alternative, it is argued, makes space for a more dynamic reading of the relationship between political ideas and political practice. It also allows us to bring into sharper focus the normative relevance of avant-garde political agency, which (as we shall see in the following chapters) is crucial to a politically effective and motivationally sustainable development of particular conceptions of global justice.

To say that political agency plays an important normative role in discussions about justice is to say that certain instances of political practice (what I will call 'avant-garde' ones) contribute significantly to the emergence, articulation, revision, and development of a particular family of normative political theories: those that seek to change the world rather than simply interpret it. The role of these theories, as already anticipated, is to give prescriptions on how political societies *should* be arranged, how agents *ought* to behave, and what politically effective and motivationally sustainable steps *could* be taken to transform existing social and political relations. The analysis of political agency, this chapter argues, is a crucial component of these normative theories, at least when they are pursued in an activist rather than purely speculative fashion. This is in the sense that an important part of the concepts we invoke in activist political theory are informed by relevant (avant-garde) instances of political practice, and also in the sense that the activity of theorizing about politics is itself an expression of a certain way of engaging with our political reality.

But that is not controversial at all – some might argue. In fact, who would deny that political theory is informed by political practice? So let us suppose that this objector is right; let us grant that the issue is not controversial. In this case, it appears all the more surprising to find so little discussion on the normative relevance of transformative political agency, to see how rarely the issue is analysed, if only to emphasize the theorists' common ground. This chapter could then be seen as an attempt to fill the gap by explaining how political agency contributes to the process of normative theorizing in an activist mode, at what stage it intervenes, and how.

To argue that political agency is a necessary component of political theory is not the same as saying that the interpretation of political practice exhausts the tasks of political theory. The process of normative theorizing is distributed at different levels, and might serve different functions. It is plausible to think that the analysis and interpretation of political agency are but one component of that larger enterprise. Nevertheless, if we aim to construct theories that seek to guide political action rather than simply discover the normative truth (assuming that can be done), the methodological premises of such theories ought to be fully spelt out. In articulating an avant-garde account of political agency, it is crucial to understand what features of a certain theoretical construction ought to be informed by political practice, in what relationship they stand to each other, and how we should proceed in integrating these features into a fundamentally appropriate normative account.

I have argued that much contemporary political theory sees the process of answering normative questions as characterized by a division of labour between an ideal and a nonideal approach. The genesis of the distinction is commonly associated with Rawls,[3] but the recent literature on the topic has since departed from his account in many ways, not least the fact that the definitions of 'ideal' and 'nonideal' tend now to be cast in much more general terms.[4] In this chapter, I shall adopt a distinction between ideal and nonideal which pays particular attention to the way the relation between principles and practical agency is constructed, both with regard to the method and to the aim of each type of approach. As far as the method is concerned, in ideal approaches, principles are considered unconstrained by how agency is expressed in the real world; they can be constructed with reference to false, abstract, or counterfactual circumstances, and often explicitly rely on an intentionally distorted picture of the world.[5] As far as their aim is concerned, ideal approaches try to identify and establish a fundamentally appropriate analysis of first-order normative principles, regardless of whether these principles can meaningfully guide action in the real world.[6] Nonideal approaches, by contrast, aim to develop principles able to guide agency in empirically contingent circumstances. More-over, as far as the method is concerned, they take agency to play a constitutive role in the premises that contribute to the identification of relevant principles, and consider these principles importantly constrained by features of current social and political practices.[7]

This way of casting the distinction between ideal and nonideal may well be controversial. One reason appears to be that, despite some of the evidence, we might find it hard to identify normative accounts that fit perfectly within either of the stylized interpretations of ideal and nonideal approaches offered above.[8] More likely, and as the following chapters illustrate, many contemporary political theories will tend to display features of both, in varying degrees and at various levels. The trouble consists in establishing how insights from ideal and nonideal approaches should be combined, which elements of a normative account ought to be influenced by either of them, and why. The task will hopefully appear less burdensome once the basic contours of the dialectical approach are clarified, and for that some degree of generalization of the alternatives is necessary. So let us for now proceed with the simplified definitions introduced above. And let us limit ourselves to underlining that views (or aspects of these views) which attempt to identify what a maximally just society would look like, on the basis of assumptions unconstrained by how agency is expressed in the real world, fall *mostly* within the ideal camp. On the other hand, theories that seek to guide us in the normative evaluation of existing states of affairs, and produce principles that are constrained by the function and purpose of current expressions of practical agency, fall *mostly* within the nonideal camp.

At a first glance, a division of labour in the tasks of ideal and nonideal approaches might seem appropriate. Some issues may be better tackled through an ideal approach, others through a nonideal approach. One of the reasons one might give for this way of proceeding is that if theorists start with assumptions that rely heavily on existing practices, material conditions, and contingent empirical circumstances, they might end up formulating very concessive accounts of what ought to be done. If we let present expectations inform our views on what is, say, perfect justice, we will end up formulating a theory that is much less demanding compared to what we might have obtained had we assumed away some psychological, material, or social constraints burdening our account of justice.

On the other hand, those who defend the significance of a nonideal approach often emphasize the irrelevance of ideal prescriptions when it comes to reflecting on the concerns embedded in existing patterns and practices. The fact that ideal approaches are able to instruct us on the principles according to which a perfectly just society should be arranged means very little when we are required to guide action in more or less just contingent political circumstances.[9] This appears especially relevant when existing states of affairs fail to display the kinds of properties required for an ideal approach to have its principles interpreted and endorsed in any determined and meaningful way.

Now, one way to avoid the contrast between these views is to emphasize that even if ideal and nonideal approaches are hard to reconcile, there may be reasons to engage separately with both: ideal theorizing as a kind of pure intellectual exercise and nonideal theorizing as a contribution to addressing the problems of the real world. But it is worth noticing that a similar division of labour would not have great appeal when pursuing political theory in an activist mode. If we are interested not in simply identifying first-order normative principles but also in how these principles could be rendered politically effective and motivationally sustainable, isolating the ideal approach is unlikely to take us very far. On the other hand, if we seek to avoid principles of justice that simply reflect what existing agents and institutions are already committed to and if we intend to criticize current practices with a view to transforming them, the flaws of nonideal approaches will also probably emerge. Whether a similar dualist approach is the most valuable way of addressing both the 'status-quo' bias that threatens nonideal political theory and the 'irrelevance' charge faced by some forms of ideal theorizing remains, at best, an open question.

In what follows, I shall not take issue with that question. I shall simply develop some lines of critique to ideal and nonideal approaches in order to illustrate an alternative way of proceeding, one that promises to reconcile insights from ideal theory with an analysis of the conditions under which first-order principles identified with its help can be interpreted and endorsed.

## 2.3 INTRODUCING THE DIALECTICAL APPROACH

What would the alternative way of pursuing normative theory in an activist mode look like? Let me outline one way of reconciling ideal and nonideal features within an avant-garde conception of political agency by introducing what I earlier called the dialectical approach.

Dialectic is a much-abused term, but in its simplest and more accessible formulation we can think of it as the method of learning from trial, failure, and success.[10] Activist political theory, we emphasized, is concerned not merely with interpreting the world but also with changing it. It typically seeks to identify certain first-order principles *and* to combine them with an interpretation of conflicts and commitments existing in particular social practices.[11] The goal of activist political theory, remember, is not simply to satisfy intellectual needs; it also tries to promote normative views in a way that speaks to concerns arising in the real world. On the face of these concerns, theorists (assisted by other social and political actors) start with a number of general assumptions, identify ways of combining these assumptions in inferential statements, develop analogies and contrasts between different available theories, identify tensions in them, and come up with specific interpretive categories able to render more determinate first-order principles identified with the help of ideal theory. Of course, as time goes by and relations between agents evolve, the nature of political institutions also changes. New problems are likely to emerge and new interpretations of political practice are required to articulate them, giving rise to new combinations of principles and agency. Some of the categories deployed in these interpretations will be related to old ones. Other categories and the concepts necessary to frame them will be invented anew, in response to unforeseen kinds of problems.

Later in the chapter, I shall refer to the agents that contribute to the development and articulation of these new interpretive categories with the term 'avant-garde political agents', and I shall try to illustrate at what level of activist political theory we should analyse their contribution. What matters at this point is clarifying the method by which decisions on how to interpret concerns and commitments embedded in particular political practices are made, and to clarify on what grounds these decisions can claim validity in a way that is both normatively appropriate and politically relevant. Dialectic is a heuristic method aiming to provide an authoritative account of how the relation between preservation and innovation of principles unfolds given particular practices: it helps to clarify, for example, which conceptual categories of the past are eliminated or shown to be morally problematic, and which ones are emphasized, updated, or invented from scratch. In short, dialectic is concerned with the kind of learning processes that take place in the course of adapting a certain reflective apparatus to the development and needs of a particular historical age. It is precisely this feature of the dialectical method that renders it apt to promote a normative theory that is, at the same time, fundamentally appropriate, politically effective, and motivationally sustainable.

Described in these terms, dialectic may appear both plausible and unsurprising. No one would want to deny that agency expresses itself through various social and political institutions. Likewise, it is uncontroversial that the relations between agents and such institutions always reflect their normative commitments, that individuals give reasons to each other as occupants of particular social roles: as representatives of particular social classes, as citizens, as members of the public, and so on. However, the dialectical method tries to do more than simply provide a genealogy of the emergence and evolution of these reasons. It attempts to confer on historical development a crucial heuristic function; it claims that an appropriate philosophical reflection on past historical processes can be put at the service of a normative account relevant for orienting present political action. One example that helps to illustrate this pattern is how (as explained in the previous chapter) Kant sees the idea of cosmopolitanism as both supported by a certain evolution of past interactions between human beings (e.g. the empirical account of unsocial sociability combined with the development of individual moral dispositions) and playing a pivotal role in orienting the political transformation of existing institutions and practices.

According to the dialectical way of thinking, history exhibits a clearly discernible (some might even say rational) development of the relationship between principles and agency. It is possible to try and express this relationship in very general terms. The circumstances of particular conflicts and the analysis of existing sociopolitical practices lead theorists and other agents occupying relevant social roles to reflect on them and to articulate specific interpretations of the concerns and commitments they express. After various stages of revision and having obtained some basic level of plausibility, these interpretations are combined with certain first-order values and give rise to fundamentally appropriate theories, theories that are in turn invoked to guide political action. If and when these theories are endorsed (both politically and motivationally) – if and when they succeed in transforming political institutions compatibly with their requirements – the main social and political institutions will be arranged in accordance with them. However, as these institutions develop and transform their character, so too does the nature of interactions they serve to mediate alter its shape: new problems emerge, new institutional and social roles are occupied, and new principles for political reform are required. Due to these unprecedented forms of interaction, institutions will both retain something from the old patterns and practices and also profoundly modify them. Capturing these relevant transformative moments, reflecting on the nature of the problems they try to articulate, and identifying in what relationship the present stands to the past, for example, what commitments are retained, what concerns persist or emerge anew, and what sorts of interpretations seeking to conceptualize them arise, are some of the prime challenges of the dialectical enterprise.

Admittedly general, this way of describing the relationship between principles and agency seems to fit most patterns and practices.[12] An issue worth noticing at this point is that given the nature of normative commitments, once we move beyond the acknowledgement of highly abstract normative aspirations, the particular relationship between principles and agency is subjected to multiple evaluations and might give rise to a wide range of candidate theories and interpretations. It would therefore be naïve to think that in any given set of problematic circumstances only one account of what should be done to bring these first-order ideals to bear in particular political circumstances is likely to emerge. Agents will interpret claims in distinctive ways, they will assign differential weight to the values upon which their judgements are grounded, and the conclusions they will reach will also be significantly different.[13] So we might end up with a wide range of theories trying to interpret the world and to provide guidance for political action. The question then becomes: which of these theories (or families of theories)[14] is better able to combine principles and agency in a fundamentally appropriate but also politically effective and motivationally sustainable way?

In answering this question, activist political theory is assisted by the dialectical method. The latter is crucial for understanding the contribution of avant-garde political agents to the selection of appropriate interpretations of the function and purpose of specific political practices. As I shall explain in what follows, conceptualizing avant-garde political agency requires understanding the relationship between the political activity of certain historically situated agents and the way in which the learning process we have been describing unfolds. It is easy to see that the function of the dialectical method is here not purely descriptive. Sensitivity to past achievements is extremely important for developing both a negative heuristics which facilitates the elimination of certain, normatively problematic, accounts of the relationship between principles and agency, and for exploring a positive heuristics which enables the emergence of new, fundamentally appropriate interpretations and candidate theories. This emphasis renders the dialectical account particularly sensitive to the dynamic of political transformation and especially relevant to capture conceptual change. It also provides adequate space for being more receptive to the genealogy of theory emergence and to the development of appropriate interpretive frameworks by avant-garde political agents.

Before going into more detail on these issues, we need to consider some objections to the allegedly most controversial feature of the dialectical method. This is the idea that in the process of learning from the trials and failures of the past, we can hope to develop interpretations that both preserve some normative commitments of earlier institutional relations and contribute to the emergence of more sophisticated but also more and more progressive results. The critique has been for a long time at the core of many ferocious attacks on the dialectical method, especially in its Hegelian variant.[15] Indeed, the objection goes, even if we grant that dialectic is the kind of method that provides us with the resources needed to engage in an internal critique of existing institutions, and to observe dynamic changes in their purpose and function, why should we conclude that whatever theory emerges from this process at any given point is 'better' than what we already had? Why assume that what survives the confrontation between alternative conceptions is conducive to improved results rather than something which is simply different but equally problematic?

Taken as a statement about the internal logic of these transformative processes, the critique might indeed seem to have force. If one claims that the dialectical method captures the objective motion of powerful but partly inscrutable developments of certain historical events, that these events follow a particular internal logic, and that the logic relies on the rejection of the principle of non-contradiction, objections become understandably hard to avoid.[16] But it is important to point out that the learning process implicit in the method of trial and failure plays only a heuristic role. It contributes to the normative assessment of future states of affairs guided by practical experience and by the theoretical knowledge obtained through reflection on past courses of action. The method of trial and failure is not a purely descriptive one, and dialectic is not a way of seeking to reproduce the development of the inevitable. It may yet have an important role to play as a heuristic device for identifying relevant interpretations, supported by what we know about human agency, by previous accounts of how ideal aspirations have informed social and political transformations, and by the development and self-correction of individual and institutional relations. The potentially progressive tendency involved in the critique of existing institutions becomes plausible when we consider that moral reflection and historical performance are related to each other.[17] The link to the past guarantees continuity with previous normative commitments and allows us to grasp the conceptual innovation introduced at the new level of reflection.

Rather than being fully developed or rejected in purely theoretical space, activist political theories emerge and operate in concrete political circumstances. That is to say, they rely for the articulation of specific interpretations of existing concerns and commitments on agents whose position in society renders them politically suited and morally motivated to bring about changes compatible with their ideal requirements: avant-garde political agents. The challenge is of course to understand in what way the dialectical method can be deployed to select among various candidate interpretations all who purport to contribute to political progress in this way. As I shall argue in what follows, some interpretations of the function and purpose of political institutions might be considered more appropriate than others if they perform better than their competitors in the following three tasks.

The first one is what we may call the 'diagnostic' task. Interpretations that outperform their competitors in the diagnostic task are able to assess the grounds and scope of a particular conflict at the appropriate level of analysis, to account for the empirical evidence relating to that conflict better than its competitors, and to identify agents and commitments affected by these conflicts in a way that is immune to the status-quo bias. So, for example, as we shall see in the second and third part of the book, a suitably modified egalitarian theory of justice develops an analysis of the circumstances of global injustice able to capture all these features better than its rival, statist accounts.

The second task is what we may call the 'innovating task'. In articulating particular conflicts, an interpretation (or family of interpretations) could be said to outperform its rivals if it is able to formulate principles that preserve all the normative benefits of its predecessors whilst avoiding their failures. This, as I shall also illustrate in the second part of the book, can be achieved if an interpretation is able to combine normatively fundamental and causally fundamental claims in a way that eliminates commitments that appear morally problematic and preserves others that survive critical scrutiny in new circumstances of justice. So, for example, a global egalitarian theory of justice which combines normatively fundamental and causally fundamental claims at the appropriate level of analysis is able to preserve the statist commitment to global sufficientarianism whilst avoiding the problematic consequences of the restriction of global equality to the domestic sphere.

Finally, we would have reason to prefer one normative interpretation over another if this normative interpretation also displays what we might call 'heuristic potential'. As already anticipated, any innovating interpretation of particular concerns and commitments will produce principles conducive to extensive reforms of current institutions. It is reasonable to expect that similar reforms will reshape agents' position in society, the current understanding of their social roles, and the kinds of obligations and aspirations related to newly emerging expectations. In this sense, a particular interpretation of existing concerns and commitments is able to perform better than its rivals when its combination of innovating principles with conceptual categories already available contains also some guidelines for anticipating new, unforeseen questions and challenges. In other words, an interpretation displaying heuristic, in addition to diagnostic and innovating, capacity is able to improve our analysis of the function and purpose of existing practices and also to raise new (normative and empirical) questions concerning the development of institutions reformed according to its requirements.

If new interpretations manage to satisfy the three criteria laid out above (and for as long as they do so), they are likely to succeed in rendering the commitments implicit in them politically effective and motivationally sustainable. But if they seem to fail, profound and pervasive conflicts will erupt, and if more promising alternatives emerge in the meantime, they will be eliminated. These other alternatives will be endorsed and the cycle is likely to begin again. Dialectic is the method that captures this ongoing process: the elimination of some interpretations which progressively lose their relevance in addressing the issues with which they were initially confronted, the supersession of these interpretations by others which seem to fare better (at least for a time), and the possibility of anticipating potential future challenges.

This is all rather sketchy and I will say more below on each of these points. For now, however, it might be worth emphasizing that, if it can be defended, the dialectical method displays great potential in combining features from the ideal and the nonideal approaches, whilst avoiding some of their flaws. Indeed, it seems able to reconcile first-order values with an analysis of existing political concerns, to articulate at a fundamental level the grounds for conflicts that historically situated agents appear to encounter, and to deliver innovating principles able to guide political transformation. Such theories have ideal elements because they are able to preserve the appeal of certain first-order normative commitments and to illustrate their development in time. But they also contain nonideal features in that they seek to render these commitments determinate and relevant within existing social and political practices. Focusing on the differences between the dialectical method and each of these approaches (if endorsed on their own) is helpful in order to expose how it avoids both the 'irrelevance' charge faced by defenders of the ideal approach and the 'status-quo' bias faced by partisans of nonideal accounts. Let us first consider how.

## 2.4 IDEAL APPROACHES AND THE CHARGE OF 'IRRELEVANCE'

Ideal approaches, we emphasized, seek to construct first-order normative principles unconstrained by how agency is expressed in the real world. The validity of arguments rests on the weight and plausibility of specific premises, combined with each other by using theoretical generalizations usually referred to as idealization and abstraction.[18] We begin by asking, for example, what values should, ideally, inspire people's relation to each other? Or what normative principles would govern society in the absence of any epistemic, natural, or social impediments? The search for first-order normative principles is conducted by invoking false and/or general assumptions which present the world, for purposes of theoretical re-description, as simpler than and different from how it really is.[19] This is not to deny that theories deploying the ideal method will construct and combine these premises following different routes. Some accounts will confer significant relevance on intuitions, taken either in a very basic or in a more generalizable form. Others will construct their principles by relying on allegedly self-evident moral judgements, judgements such as, for example, 'avoid harm'. Some might insist on the ability of specific inferential sequences to generate agreement among a community of rational interlocutors. Others still might pay attention to their ability to stand in reflective equilibrium. But it is worth noticing how in all these cases practical agency will play a marginal role in the reconstruction of background circumstances: it will only be explicitly invoked at the stage in which its principles are applied to the real world, rather than at the stage in which they are developed.

Now, one of the most trenchant critiques of a similar way of proceeding has traditionally been that the theories it inspires are insufficiently sensitive to controversial empirical facts. Given the character of their generalizations (both in the form of abstraction and in that of idealization), these theories, as it has often been put, tend to '*shape* and *order* the facts' and 'can therefore be retained come what may'.[20] Given the nature of background circumstances, there is a danger that if the theory starts with arbitrarily chosen (but intuitively plausible) counterfactual premises, it might end up with an incomplete or indeterminate selection of problems and factual instances.[21] The tendency will be either to produce very partial forms of theorizing or to deliver highly indeterminate principles that will only answer the kinds of highly abstract and idealized questions for which the theory has been initially designed.[22] The theory might in this case both underestimate its internal limits and disregard other sets of problems. All that might be achieved is a partial theorization of a phenomenon, with the conclusions reached crucially determined by which part of the phenomenon one chooses to theorize, and no internal authoritative mechanism for deciding why the choice has fallen upon this rather than another part.[23]

The problem, notice, is also familiar in the sciences. Consider an example of planetary misbehaviour, where an analysis similar to the one that inspires ideal approaches might make it very difficult to assess the relevance of the theory in different sets of empirical circumstances to the ones initially conceived:

> A physicist of the pre-Einsteinian era takes Newton's mechanics and his law of gravitation, ($N$), the accepted initial conditions, ($I$), and calculates, with their help, the path of a newly discovered small planet, p. But the planet deviates from the calculated path. Does our Newtonian physicist consider that the deviation was forbidden by Newton's theory and therefore that, once established, it refutes the

theory *N*? No. The physicist simply says there must be an unknown body causing the deviation from the predicted path. If present telescopes are unable to discover that unknown body, bigger and better ones are built. If they are not adequate to discover the unknown planet, satellites are launched. And if they are unable to discover the unknown cause of the 'deviation', the scientists invent other reasons why the unknown body cannot be discovered.[24]

This example illustrates how one can persist in ignoring important complications by constantly rendering more sophisticate the reflective apparatus on the basis of which the search for particular principles is conducted. By selecting its problematic background in the way we have described, the theory ends up assessing principles that may be irrelevant or too indeterminate to interpret other important cases. Given the development of its premises, and confronted with evidence challenging the significance of its principles, the ideal approach will have no internal resources to deal with their assessment in many alternative empirical circumstances. Analogously to the scientist who continues to postulate the existence of different (as yet unobserved) planets in order to maintain his conviction of the truth of Newtonian physics, the ideal theorist might be tempted to introduce more and more new assumptions when testing our intuitions in the search for desired principles, rendering interpretive constraints different from the ones presented in the real world.

The last point will be familiar from cases that are regularly invoked in normative theory to test our intuitions about the 'intrinsic' relevance of specific values – say, the value of equality. Consider, for example, the thought experiment in which we are asked to reflect on the relevance of equality by imagining a society (call it Beverly Hills) populated by different groups of well-off individuals (call them rich and super-rich) and where the choice situation concerns the distribution of luxurious goods (e.g. fine wine).[25] Or a second thought experiment, this time borrowed from the global justice debate, in which we are asked to consider reciprocal obligations holding between societies whose development occurs in conditions of complete autarchy.[26] Finally, think about cases in which considerations of distributive justice are meant to arise in circumstances where the world (or the universe) is considered divided and where half of its population is taken to be unaware of the other half. Similarly to the scientific case mentioned above, the ideal theorist predicates false properties of existing states of affairs. He does so in order to remove the conflict between competing values (e.g. equality and sufficiency) and to test our intuitions about the intrinsic relevance of only one among them. What these examples share is the reconstruction of circumstances of justice helped by false or idealized assumptions. But if the initial construction of the thought experiment is partial and indeterminate in this way, the final outcome is also likely to suffer. By removing the kind of conflicting circumstances that complicate our assessment of the relevance of one rather than another particular value, we are far from crystallizing our judgements when it comes to giving more determinate interpretations of these principles of justice.[27] After all, and notice that many defenders of ideal theory would agree with this point, there is no guarantee that the choices we make when we inhabit a simplified and embellished normative universe will (or should) coincide with those emerging when we enter the real world and competing considerations return.

It is very plausible to think that all these considerations have nevertheless some role to play when we are pursuing normative analysis in a purely abstract, truth-seeking mode. But they would be devastating when exploring the contribution of ideal approaches to activist political theory, the kind of theory interested not merely in a range of *possibly* valid principles but also in how they can be effectively combined with existing expressions of political agency able to guide action in the real world. Suppose, to go back to our previous thought experiments, that through those thought experiments we discover we care about equality *in itself*. What will this tell us about the world in other relevant cases, where all the other previously excluded and competing considerations will also be at stake? Does it mean we will embrace the orthodoxy of equality, no matter what? Or will the findings we obtained in our hypothetical world now serve to override all other existing concerns?

Not surprisingly, many of those who believe in clarity of mind obtained in this way will hardly admit that this is the right way to go.[28] It is of course plausible to postulate that some future (real) world might resemble the one imagined in the thought experiment so that the principles identified in our hypothetical case *will* be directly relevant to assess *that* future state of affairs. But even if we grant that this might turn out to be the case, it will not be the case because the first-order principles isolated through our ideal approach have action-guiding force *on their own*. That state of affairs might come about because such first-order principles were correctly combined with a fundamentally appropriate analysis of existing circumstances of injustice and the real-world manifestations of political agency that these circumstances generate. By divesting themselves of factual constraints in elaborating their premises, many ideal approaches rely on false and idealized examples endorsed to identify moral judgements that should guide reflection in necessarily hypothetical cases. But since assumptions are selected without paying attention to how they relate to existing commitments and concerns, the theory runs the risk of trading on remote moral dilemmas – dilemmas that have no immediate bearing on our normative interpretation of conflicting circumstances in the real world.

It is plausible to think that the motivation behind similar examples is to present us with conditions under which our judgement cannot be biased by relying on familiar conceptions, personal experience, political history, or social background. The risk is, however, that in doing so individuals are so estranged from their experiential knowledge that they start losing any common ground, coming up with principles that relate to no clear, intelligible analysis of existing problematic circumstances.

To see this point, imagine a theory centred on the importance of some coherently identified and plausible value, for example, the value of chivalry. Think about Cervantes' Don Quixote. Quixote is both a tragic and a comic character. He is tragic because he is in a way right: his beliefs, although out of date, are not mutually inconsistent. But he is also comic because, albeit consistent, the principles to which those beliefs lead are very remote from reality: having aged historically, they fail to relate in any meaningful way to his contemporaries' commitments and concerns. The questions fellow-Castillians try to answer are not the same as his, and vice versa, the problems he identifies are unlikely to preoccupy any of them. What renders Quixote's principles troubling is not only that they fail to orient his actions but also that they corrupt his mind. Of course, this may not be quite the case with many defenders of ideal theory. But a similar difficulty remains: when applied to particular political circumstances, ideal approaches can hardly tell us what to do or even what to think in any determinate way. If one fails to establish their limits, they run the risk of turning the answers to important political con-troversies into battles against windmills. Moreover, just as in the case of Don Quixote, they might render us unable to follow historical change and less useful for political transformation.[29]

It is plausible to think that just as in the sciences, any new discovery of natural laws changes the way individuals perceive the world, in political theory, any new political transformation should bring them to revise their understanding of previous social relations and try to establish constructive links between normative principles and concrete expressions of political agency. But it is not clear how adopting an ideal method that proceeds in the way we have described could facilitate this task. By placing too much weight on counterfactual circum-stances and hypothetical inferential sequences, the ideal theorist might end up isolating himself from contingent historical and political events, and create a different language, unaffected by practical commitments and concerns. There is a risk that one removes from fellow-interlocutors the ability to invoke shared social and political understandings and to appeal to past experiences in evaluat-ing future courses of action. This, some have ventured to argue, ultimately amounts to an arbitrary exercise of intellectual power, depriving others (espe-cially those who are not trained normative theorists) of meaningful ways of communicating.[30] But that is not the basic problem. The basic problem is that by counterfactually modifying the context of problems in which practical judge-ment (the application of practical reason to particular cases) develops, we are led to unfamiliar territory where the coherence and strength of a particular sequence of justification is measured by no other authority than individual skills in ordering and presenting certain logical sequences. One could of course exonerate this way of proceeding if the aim were simply to contribute to political theory in a purely exploratory mode. But, as far as activist political theory goes, critical thinking and the orientation of political action are not only unlikely to benefit but are also in danger or being distorted.

But if the ideal approach is not sufficient, by itself, to orient activist political theory, what is the alternative? One familiar way of proceeding, lying at the heart of rival, nonideal accounts, is the following. In engaging with normative problems, we start by interpreting the nature of the practice to which we want our principles to refer. We are asked to come up with a sufficiently uncontroversial description of such practice, to articulate its function and purpose, and to choose between interpretations that best reflect the normative commitments implicit in it. The next section assesses a similar way of proceeding, explores a number of critiques typically associated with it, and prepares the ground for introducing the 'dialectical' approach.

## 2.5 NONIDEAL APPROACHES AND THE 'STATUS-QUO' BIAS

Contrary to ideal approaches, nonideal approaches are importantly constrained by practical agency in assessing the ability of theories to articulate social and political problems from a normative perspective. According to this family of theories, the aim of normative principles is to guide action in existing circumstances, both by orienting the evaluations of problematic states of affairs and by indicating a path to adequate principled reforms. Important differences between the two approaches emerge also when we consider the issue of method. In the case of ideal approaches, the validity of specific principles is established by idealizing background circumstances, comparing intuitions, inferring considered judgements from them, and evaluating the plausibility of these judgements as premises of an inferential sequence trying to persuade those engaged in rational argumentation. In the case of nonideal approaches, it is the interpretation of specific social and political practices that provides the first step with reference to which the normative territory is explored and principles are further articulated. An informed analysis of concrete states of affairs signals, for example, that some principles might be incompatible with the function and purpose of given social practices; it alerts us to their inability to capture the concerns and commitments of real-world agents, and to articulate normative interpretations responsive to their claims. Examining the function and purpose of existing practices plays a crucial role in constraining the reasons given for endorsing (or rejecting) principles compatible (or incompatible) with them. It allows theorists to critically reflect on a relevant unit of analysis, indicate what kinds of subjects are involved, illuminate the types of claims they advance, and offer a background interpretation which prepares the way to fundamentally appropriate principles for political reform.[31]

To understand these points, it pays to consider more carefully the way in which nonideal approaches proceed. The basic assumption is that since social and political institutions fundamentally modify the nature of relations between agents, the nature of such institutions also influences the reasons these agents might have for endorsing or rejecting principles designed to regulate their reciprocal relations.[32] It is for this reason that appropriate principles of, say, justice are considered those that could be supported by a satisfactory interpretation of the existing patterns of practice. Where there is no match between postulated principles and concrete states of affairs, agents lack persuasive reasons for endorsing the principles contained in the theory as meaningful to articulate their competing claims. Hence, the theory's ability to produce politically effective and motivationally sustainable principles is significantly undermined.

The point here is not that specific normative principles are proven wrong if agents do not succeed in realizing them here and now. The point is that if these principles fail to reflect the kind of agency embedded in particular social and political practices, they are also unable to articulate and give coherent shape to the concerns that trigger the need for normative theory, and to capture the reasons agents might have for endorsing its principles. As some scholars put it, the justification of any particular normative conception requires an interpretation of the 'point and purpose of the institutions that the conception is intended to govern and of the role principles are intended to play in them'.[33] Existing relations and practices therefore undermine principles that fail to reflect and critically relate to the 'point and purpose' of such practices. If a particular fit with given social practices is absent, principles lack determinate content and application.

To illustrate the argument, let us take one example from the global justice debate, which will extensively occupy us in the following chapters. Consider the argument on the moral arbitrariness of one's place of birth to which cosmopolitans often refer in defending their favourite (egalitarian) conception of global justice. Following the reasoning above, the view is considered too vague, underspecified, or counter-intuitive to trigger desired global egalitarian principles. A similar conception, critics argue, does not fit with the concerns implicit in particular practices, for example, practices of joint citizenship and the associative relations in which fellow citizens stand to each other. The global egalitarian principles that cosmopolitans tend to infer from the moral arbitrariness argument are undermined by a more appropriate interpretation of the function and form of current (intra- and interstate) social and political practices.[34]

This is not the place to go into a thorough critique of this particular argument.[35] What matters at this point are its methodological premises. In assessing the virtues and limits of nonideal accounts, a great deal seems to depend on the plausibility of their interpretation of existing practices and the analysis of concerns and commitments embedded in such practices. In other words, the identification of the function and purpose of existing institutions plays a pivotal role in orienting our search for desired normative principles. But where does the authority of that identification come from? And what directs the choice of the unit of analysis, for example, the practices that we select as meaningful to scrutinize?

In trying to clarify this point, theorists have referred to the activity of those seeking to interpret the function and purpose of existing practices as one of 'constructive interpretation', consisting of three different stages: pre-interpretive, interpretive, and post-interpretive.[36] In the first, pre-interpretive, stage, we are concerned with the identification of the raw data of interpretation, for example, providing an uncontroversial description of the basic features of a specific practice in need of being articulated and criticized.[37] In the second, interpretive, stage, those engaged in rational critique seek to offer a plausible account of the function and purpose of the practice previously identified as the relevant unit of analysis. Finally, in the third, post-interpretive, stage, critics come up with specific normative principles for reforming the practice and seek to do so in a way that best expresses its function and purpose.

It is important to notice the crucial relevance of the first two stages in determining the principles established in the final one. At first, the enterprise is presented as essentially observational: we are merely concerned with the identification of what we might call basic, uncontroversial, sociological facts in need of critical scrutiny and interpretation.[38] At a second step, those reflecting on these basic facts come up with a moralized reading of the function and purpose of the commitments and concerns reflected in them. Although normatively laden, the concepts identified in this second stage are not a matter of pure idealization. Their moralized characterization relies heavily on views that are part of a generally accepted understanding of those practices, as revealed by the public views of participants and also (as appropriate) by historical texts, important legal documents, or reflected in other relevant institutional arrangements. The process is guided not by the use of false assumptions but by an attempt to observe particular practices and to identify normative commitments that follow general patterns. So to take one prominent example, Rawls' interpretation of the basic structure of a well-ordered society as characterized by social cooperation is grounded on the 'public political culture of a democratic society' and implicit in the 'political institutions of a constitutional regime and the public traditions of their interpretation (including those of the judiciary), as well as historic texts and documents that are common knowledge'.[39]

But what is the guarantee that collective normative commitments and the boundaries that separate one set of practices from the other have been correctly identified? And how does the interpretation linking these factual observations to a general account of the function and purpose of the practices in which they are found become an authoritative one? It is not difficult to notice that the reliance of nonideal approaches on observed social facts is here affected by a peculiar methodological problem: there seems to be no sharp boundary between a descriptive account and an interpretive one. Any observed account of factual evidence that can be offered to support specific interpretations is itself theoretically laden.

An analogy with science, where the problem is also familiar, might help here. Galileo's refutation of the Aristotelian theory of flawless celestial spheres was supported by what he claimed to be observed facts: the existence of mountains on the moon and spots on the sun.[40] However, the authority of this account was not in itself derived from further observed features, and supported by the unaided senses. On the contrary, Galileo's observations relied on the use of telescopes and the optical theory of telescopes, which was hugely contested at the time. And even now, although most interpreters tend to converge on the main assumptions of Galileo's system, they often also emphasize inaccuracies in many of his observations (e.g. how he seems to have mistaken Saturn's rings for moons and how he confused optical illusions with craters on our own moon).[41] In this sense, one could interpret the controversy as being not between a theory unsupported by the facts (such as the Aristotelian one) and one which could claim factual evidence (such as Galileo's method), but between two sets of observations, each of which is supported by plausible theoretical arguments. The basic facts invoked to support a certain direction of research are themselves informed by theoretical assumptions.

A similar problem affects, in possibly even more dramatic forms, both the pre-interpretive and the interpretive task of the normative theories we have been describing in this section. Far from being simply observed in reality, the units of analysis are chosen, and that choice reflects a precise theoretical commitment. The selection of contexts and practices in need of being scrutinized, and the emphasis on specific concerns and commitments reflected by these practices, are themselves a matter of theoretical controversy. However basic, our understanding of sociological facts and their impact on human life is not simply given to us and cannot be observed without theoretical lenses. The kind of factual evidence that is considered relevant reflects the interpreter's own preference for a particular way of understanding human affairs, a specific analysis of the claims and agents under consideration, and a particular ordering and ranking of the commitments expressed by the institutions that affect them. If one is blinded to the way in which the selection of the raw material of interpretation occurs, and if one fails to see how normatively laden the identification of the function and purpose of existing practices already is, one's post-interpretive activity and the selection of appropriate principles for reforming such practices will be influenced by the first two stages, and will suffer from the same potential bias. At best, the interpretations emerging might neglect important social phenomena that are not captured by a particular interpretive 'telescope', a telescope which might itself require more careful critical scrutiny. At worst, these interpretations might produce principles for reform that fail to depart in significant ways by rather uncritical observed features.

Of course one might answer here that we are overstating the role that the pre-interpretive and interpretative stages play in the overall construction of action-guiding normative principles. One might want to distinguish, for example, between a conventionalist approach that simply takes cultural beliefs and practices as given and makes the final outcome dependent on them, and an alternative institutional approach, which only uses this material as the starting point of the investigation but may ultimately reach sufficiently critical principles.[42] But unless one is content with a rather unsophisticated understanding of what a culture is, and what it means to take seriously existing expressions of beliefs and practices, it is hard to see how the distinction could make a significant difference. If we understand culture in non-restrictive terms as a collective form of self-understanding, characterized by the search for a certain degree of coherence in both the symbolic and functional representation of various spheres of human activity, we come to see that political institutions are only one small subset of a larger pattern of activity and cannot be isolated from it.[43] Separating the analysis of political institutions from the kind of cultural norms at the heart of the so-called conventionalist approaches reveals a very simplistic account of the interplay between such institutions and other spheres of human life.[44]

All this goes to show that in both conventionalist and institutionalist interpretations of social practices, the problem of authority in the selection of the unit of concern remains. How do we know that the choice of relevant social facts that plays a foundational role in establishing the fit with particular normative principles is not biased in favour of the status quo? As we already observed, in both variations of the nonideal approach, it seems insufficient to claim that participants and critics exhibit a significant degree of overlap in the concerns and commitments of particular forms of agency, and in their understanding of the function and purposes of the practices in which they are expressed. For, as we have already illustrated, our analysis of that overlap is theoretically laden and could itself be a result of fairly uncritical assumptions.

One might try to answer this question by endorsing a version of the account where particular practices provide the interpretive material relevant to normative principles but grant that these practices only *condition* and do not *determine* the content of these principles.[45] For example, one might acknowledge the force of first-order normative principles, such as the idea of moral equality between persons, which do not themselves depend on a particular interpretation of specific practices. This would then provide a standard against which we test the critical resources intrinsic in existing beliefs and practices, condemning the ones that clearly violate first-order moral principles and saving those that are consistent with them.

But notice that a similar response to the status-quo objection concedes to the ideal approach more than a nonideal theorist might want. This has important implications for the endorsement of the nonideal method of enquiry as an alternative in itself. Once we grant that the nonideal approach depends on first-order moral principles to obtain critical bite, the argument that such first-order principles are too vague and indeterminate to orient our concrete judgements regarding existing states of affairs turns out to be simply false. If the principles really were indeterminate, we would not be able to invoke them in saying *anything* about the justice or injustice of existing states of affairs. If we resort to them in order to condemn practices that seem inconsistent with certain normative commitments, it means we are ranking them above any reason agents embedded in particular social practices might bring to justify such practices, with regard to both clarity and capacity for guidance in concrete political circumstances. These practice-dependent reasons and our interpretation of the concerns and commitments expressed in them seem to neither determine nor condition the content of our principles. They do not determine it because our interpretation of social practices is not alone in informing the content of these principles; we clearly refer to other first-order moral norms. But they also do not condition it because, as we saw in the example above, the authority of first-order moral norms can be invoked to rule out all those practice-dependent reasons that are inconsistent with it.

Before introducing an alternative way of tackling these questions, let me summarize what has been argued so far. Our dissatisfaction with some elements of the ideal approach, in particular those lacking internal resources for answering the 'relevance' charge, brought us to consider a second strategy: one which assigns practices and existing expressions of political agency a pivotal role in the identification of relevant normative principles. Our observation and interpretation of such practices inform the reasons agents have for endorsing principles that respond to the concerns and commitments expressed in them, and for rejecting those that seem to depart from them. This in turn raises a dilemma concerning the choice of the unit of analysis: how do we make sure that the general assumptions informing our interpretation of social practices are not status-quo biased? On what does the interpretation that informs our identification, description, and reflection on such units rely in order to be justified?

To answer these questions, one needs to give more careful thought to the way the ideal and nonideal approaches reciprocally interact. The previous considerations reveal that, at least when engaging with political theory in an activist mode, ideal and nonideal methods cannot orient reflection if pursued separately from each other. And since neither the ideal approach nor the nonideal approach can carry the burden on its own, it is important to explore a third possibility which combines elements from both: the dialectical approach.

## 2.6 IDEAL, NONIDEAL, AND DIALECTICAL

The previous section illustrated two main problems affecting nonideal approaches that seek to link normative principles to a particular interpretation of the function and purpose of existing practices. Firstly, they seem to lack uncontroversial criteria for selecting the unit within which existing normative commitments can be observed. And, secondly, they fail to provide a persuasive internal account of what makes a specific interpretation of these practices authoritative and non-biased. Even though the nonideal approach aspires to bring us some way towards the identification of normative interpretations that appear more responsive to relevant political concerns, the way it perceives the relation between principles and agency needs to be refined.

The dialectical method has resources to contribute to this refinement. To see this point, recall our earlier definition of dialectic as the method of learning from trial, failure, and success. Whilst, as already observed in the previous pages, it may be very difficult, if not impossible, for any theorist to appeal to the observation of basic social facts without always also providing an interpretation of them, it is plausible to think that a combination of first-order normative principles with carefully selected internal constraints might lead to a more authoritative endorsement of one kind of interpretation rather than another. The method of trial, failure, and success helps in the identification of these internal constraints. Moreover, it does so in a way that seems to avoid the status-quo bias of nonideal accounts. Let me explain.

One way in which nonideal approaches seek to interpret the function and purpose of existing practices is by trying to identify general normative commitments expressed in the dominant institutions and public culture constituting similar practices. Theorists in this case try to identify some kind of basic, uncontroversial consent involving the moral norms that both participants and observers see reflected in the practices with which they engage.[46] But practices are dynamic, and interpretations of their function and purpose may vary depending on how we construct the unit of analysis and on where we decide to concentrate attention, both geographically and temporally. Our interpretation of them will be governed by different ways of thinking about fundamental issues, for example, the sort of institutions observers should analyse, how these institutions interact with each other, what kind of questions can be asked about them, what method is legitimate in answering these questions, and so on. The trouble with nonideal approaches as described is that they lack internal criteria concerning the selection of one rather than another set of interpretations as relevant and authoritative in guiding political transformation.

The dialectical method, on the other hand, has resources to do so. Recall that we defined dialectic as a method based on learning from the trials and failures of the past. One first advantage of this way of approaching normative questions is that it enables us to concentrate not on the construction of consent around the institutions that define particular practices but on the moments of crisis. In other words, in seeking to interpret the function and purpose of particular institutions we focus first of all on contestation: on the position and claims of agents that seem to be in contrast with commitments expressed by existing institutional arrangements. We try to reflect critically on the kind of conflict this contestation expresses, the different concepts prota-gonists invoke to render it meaningful, the kinds of theories that they deploy to explain its occurrence, and on the interpretive paradigms upon which a combination of all these features eventually relies.

History, as already mentioned, is crucial for the assessment of similar claims. A historically informed analysis of particular social and political practices reveals how first-order principles inform concrete expressions of political agency in ways that are relevant to fight institutional injustices. Yet this is not a purely descriptive exercise; the method contains important heuristic resources to direct future activities. Learning from previous accounts of how similar ideals were interpreted in concrete historical circumstances allows us to invoke these experiences in addressing present political concerns. The findings derived from such a historically informed approach can be applied cross-contextually, for example, to undermine the strength of claims supportive of social orders that the pursuit of these first-order principles has historically led to supersede. One such example is the demise of slavery: once the conflict between the fundamental material interests of slaves and those of slave owners has been exposed, the injustice revealed by that conflict and the social order that its abolition brings about strengthens our reasons for endor-sing theories that militate against any attempt to revive it.[47]

All this can be achieved without necessarily restricting the application of these moral lessons to the same geographical location where socially discre-dited institutions were first challenged. Invoking past history need not be contextually delimited in this way. Once a certain (more progressive) inter-pretation of the function and purpose of existing institutions enjoys wide-spread support, we can appeal to the reasons adduced in its favour in future analogous circumstances, where agents face similar tensions and require-ments. I shall return to the question of how we can determine the extent to which a particular interpretation is able to contribute to progress in a moment.

For now, it is worth recalling the three dimensions with reference to which comparisons between different candidate interpretations are established: what I earlier called the diagnostic, innovating, and heuristic tasks. It is easy to see that an interpretation offering to contribute on all three levels need not be contextually restricted. If the nature of conflicts faced is such that geographically limited interpretations of the function and purpose of particular practices seem to struggle with their analysis, this signals the need for a theory able to contribute at the diagnostic stage, regardless of where the various elements informing that theory come from. In developing this theory, an assessment of the historical performance of previously available interpretations is necessary. No normative attempt to articulate existing concerns and commitments develops from scratch: one typically retains features of previous accounts that remain unchallenged by the new conflict (e.g. its abstract, first-order principles) and seeks to integrate them with new, emergent, conceptual categories and discourses. This is where the innovating potential of an interpretation begins to unfold. The process of moral learning, exemplified in the course of readjusting normative expecta-tions to the emergence of alternative concerns and commitments, progres-sively reshapes and improves our understanding of the function and purpose of specific practices. Once a new interpretation has obtained a certain level of plausibility, it interacts with existing expressions of political agency to generate more specific normative principles, principles that in turn display heuristic potential and guide political transformation.[48]

In the next pages, I will explore in greater detail how we might more concretely think about this process of rupture and transition, in what way alternative interpretations of specific social practices emerge, and how first-order principles interact with particular expressions of political agency (e.g. avant-garde political agency) to innovate existing paradigms and interpretive discourses. I shall also give a few examples of historical cases where we can observe a similar pattern, and emphasize its implications for the methodolog-ical point I am trying to make, as well as illustrate its relevance to the global justice debate. But now let us consider in more detail the criteria that the dialectical method endorses when comparing and assessing the adequacy of different interpretations.

Let us start with the question of diagnosis. One of the advantages of focusing on moments of crisis and contestation rather than consent surrounding existing political institutions is that this allows a more careful assessment of how available interpretations may account for anomalies arising in the practices to which they apply, both at a normatively fundamental and at a causally fundamental level. Even when the match between interpretation and practice is not perfect, it is reasonable to expect that efforts will be made to ensure that interpretations are appropriately modified to take emerging claims into account. However, if conflicts persist even after several attempts at readjustment, different candidate views might be expected to arise. This will produce alternative interpretations of existing concerns and commitments, with different core assumptions, focusing on different units of analysis, raising new questions to be asked, and constructing a new relation between principles and manifestations of political practice.

This leads us to the second, innovating, stage and to raising the question of how the dialectical method might contribute to assessing the progressive potential of emerging interpretations. As already emphasized, the method is guided by an attempt to identify those families of views able to capitalize on the advantages of previous theories whilst also addressing their anomalies and developing new interpretations of existing commitments and concerns. We could call an account conceptually static when it seeks to articulate existing conflicts by resorting to old concepts, discourses, and principles, without being able to integrate first-order normative principles with an analysis that opens up avenues for political transformation. We could call it conceptually progressive when it is able to revise and add normative content to existing interpretations of specific social practices, and to eventually generate remedial principles that are politically effective and motivationally sustainable. To better clarify these points, let me go back to an example that will connect to some of the issues emphasized in the previous chapter and that will also resurface in the rest of this work: cosmopolitanism and its articulation in Enlightenment political thought.

As already emphasized in the first chapter, the progressive contribution of Enlightenment theories of cosmopolitanism starts to emerge with the shift from an individualistic understanding of cosmopolitanism, taken to be in striking contrast to patriotism, to one in which the cosmopolitan idea inspired a political model compatible with patriotism but offering supplementary principles for overcoming interstate tensions. Recall that the seventeenth- and eighteenth-century accounts of political obligation, and the contractual model associated with them, were only able to identify a just normative framework for relations between fellow citizens, yet had very little to offer when exploring relations between citizens of different states. Kant's cosmopolitan theory could improve on existing views in several dimensions, all of which illustrate how a normative account should combine ideal normative principles with existing background interpretations of social practice in order to be considered progressive.

Firstly, Kant's theory was able to contribute at a diagnostic level by identifying the roots of political antagonism in the intensification of global commercial relations and the degree to which trade relations fostered both interaction and conflict between citizens of different states. Of course, many of the elements of Kant's theory were not new to Enlightenment theorists of the eighteenth century. However, Kant was the first to doubt that a normative interpretation centred on principles of humanity and exclusively focused on state-based political obligations could address, at the appropriately fundamental level, the claims of emerging political agents and articulate the grounds and scope of injustice present in global relations. This scepticism, in turn, provided additional resources for responding to many of the challenges that earlier theories of political obligation had been unable to properly integrate in their conceptual apparatus, yet it managed to preserve commitment to the same first-order principles of freedom by which they were also characterized.

Secondly, by placing the category of cosmopolitanism at the heart of a system of rights including both the claims of fellow citizens and those of citizens of different states, a new interpretation was available for conceptualizing relations between states beyond the realist paradigms available to previous theories of political obligation. In short, Kant's theory was able to both incorporate first-order normative principles (e.g. the idea of moral equality) and the conceptual innovations of his predecessors (e.g. the notions of popular sovereignty and civic education) without sacrificing their emancipatory potential. It developed new normative categories, for example the idea of cosmopolitan right as holding between all human beings, and linked the latter to a different analysis of global circumstances of injustice. The theory could therefore claim to have produced a novel and, allegedly, more progressive interpretation of the function and purpose of familiar political practices.

Finally, the theory could also be seen as contributing to the emergence of new questions with its principles containing what we earlier called heuristic potential. Once the necessity to understand relations between citizens of different states from a cosmopolitan perspective is established, new questions concerning the more specific principles and institutions necessary to enact this just framework of interaction seem to arise. They are not questions that could be anticipated within the conceptual apparatus of previous theories. To be sure, they are also not questions to which we will find fully satisfying answers in Kant's own cosmopolitan account, given both the minimalism of its criteria and, more importantly, the fact that if dialectical heuristics holds, the theories developed ought to tailor their interpretive principles to changes in the world. Indeed, once we move beyond first-order ideals, the search for more determinate principles and the analysis of how they reflect or depart from existing practices become crucial and will extensively occupy us in the chapters that follow. The key point to understand here is that once an interpretive paradigm is in the process of being replaced by an allegedly more progressive alternative, the normative space is open for raising other questions and conceiving new principles for political reform. Such questions and principles could not have been envisaged earlier and arise only when previous interpretative frames are fundamentally challenged.

As already emphasized, this process of appropriation of old background interpretations, analysis of how they reflect the claims and concerns of existing political agents, and replacement with alternative discourses and principles, seldom involves theorists in isolation from the rest of society. Kant, as we saw in the previous chapter, emphasized the importance of 'moral politicians' in both identifying claims and conflicts embedded in existing institutions and advancing new discourses for articulating the grounds and scope of these conflicts. In a somewhat less restrictive way, I have called agents engaged in this process of critique, revisiting old patterns of interaction and advancing new ways of conceptualizing the relationship between principles and agency, avant-garde political agents. The next section discusses the role of such agents within a dialectical account.

## 2.7 AVANT-GARDE POLITICAL AGENCY

One of the distinctive strengths of the dialectical method compared to an *exclusively* ideal or *exclusively* nonideal approach when pursuing activist political theory is its focus on political conflict and the possibilities this forecloses for the promotion of progressive normative accounts. The method, as we already observed, is both historically informed and forward looking. On the one hand, new interpretations of the function and purpose of political institutions inherit from previously available ones part of the conceptual apparatus deployed to articulate normative concerns. On the other hand, historical trends and the unforeseen development of particular institutional relations lead to the emergence of new expressions of political agency, advancing novel claims and demanding inclusion within a reformed institutional configuration. Depending on the nature of these claims, and on how the theories accounting for them relate to their predecessors, activist political theory will more or less support political transformation.

I have called the attempt to understand the progressive role a certain kind of political agent plays in the articulation of new theories an avant-garde account of political agency. We can distinguish three stages in the analysis of that role: the first two contribute to what we earlier called the diagnostic part of activist political theory, and the third to its innovative part. In the first stage, the theorist's enterprise combines evaluative and observational features. We analyse particular political conditions and circumstances of injustice with a view to determining the kind of conflict they reveal, whether there is a pattern to this conflict, whether its effects are profound and persistent for a significant amount of time, and what kinds of agents appear most affected by it.[49] The second stage is characterized by an attempt to reflect on this conflict based on available interpretations of the function and purpose of current institutions. If these interpretations are inadequate or unable to capture emerging claims and concerns, the groups who are most affected by the conflict will contest the meaning of conceptual categories associated with them. They will furthermore attempt to appropriate these categories and to interpret them in a different way – a way that tries to link them to first-order ideal principles and seeks to promote an alternative set of claims. It is at this point that the third, innovative, stage of the process begins to unfold.

In this third stage, the normative theorist is in the position both of spectator and of active participant; he attempts to articulate theories appropriate for new forms of political agency but is also an active supporter of them. He is a spectator in the sense that the raw material on the basis of which new interpretations of the purpose and function of political institutions are advanced is not found in any hypothetical world but based on a critical diagnosis of existing circumstances of injustice and on how available normative views are able to cope with them. Assisted by the dialectical method, the political theorist will interrogate categories familiar through tradition, analyse what assumptions on justice and political legitimacy exist, to what symbols and principles they refer, in what conceptual language and by what form of argument they are advanced, and, finally, how they could be endorsed and updated so as to formulate more specific normative principles able to respond to the conflicts at hand. But the theorist is also in the position of participant who takes sides in the battle of ideas. His theoretical works can themselves be seen as political interventions expressive of new forms of political agency; they interact with the everyday claims of real-world political agents, they support their practices of contestation, and they bring coherence to their efforts to innovate by introducing new interpretations.

The role of activist political theory so understood is to guide practice by putting familiar intuitions to new uses, by scrutinizing and ordering the concepts available in tradition, by showing the inadequacy of old categories, and by bringing coherency and persuasiveness to emerging ones.[50] Yet it is vital to insist that the theorist's endeavours are here informed and inspired by the practical activity of real-world political agents. Unsatisfied by the kinds of principles that existing normative commitments deliver, these agents will seek to undermine existing institutions in a way that, if successful, will contribute to the promotion of different interpretive paradigms. In short, their claims and concerns will serve as a lens through which to observe anomalies displayed by existing institutional arrangements and to assess the ability of available interpretations to account for these anomalies. The theorist tries to analyse to what extent the concerns of these agents have progressive potential, whether their claims preserve some of the positive features of old theories, and in what respect they illustrate their flaws. The negative heuristic implicit in the dialectical method serves to eliminate candidate accounts that seem to either merely repeat the findings of their predecessors or, worse still, constitute nostalgic returns to previous, morally problematic interpretations[51] without offering any potential for innovation. The positive heuristic on the other hand serves to choose between candidate interpretations with excess content over predecessors, to select appropriate assumptions, and to orient the search for principles inspired by them. Dialectic as the method of trial, failure, and success orients the way theorists engage with real-world political conflicts. It guides their interaction with the individuals and groups expressive of new political claims in the light of a historically determined process of collective moral learning.

If we place emphasis on the activity of theorizing about politics linked to the emergence of contestation of existing political institutions, we start to understand better what I mean by avant-garde political agency. We are also able to grasp the strength of a methodological approach (such as the dialectical one) which places at its heart a normative analysis of avant-garde political agents. The principles of this account are both interpretive and action-guiding, and the theorist finds himself both in the position of conceptualizing the avant-garde and of being an active part of it. A critical approach to history and existing social practices puts emerging interpretations of the function and purpose of political institutions at the service of political emancipation. Similarly to the nonideal account we examined, activist political theory is sensitive to existing interpretations of the function and purpose of current social practices. However, its focus on moments of contestation rather than agreement contains more critical potential and might be able to deliver principles that avoid being hostage to the status quo. Moreover, similarly to the ideal theories we examined, it can be committed to very demanding, first-order normative principles in orienting political action. But unlike these theories, the method is not indifferent to the relationship between principles and agency and manages to avoid the 'irrelevance' charge associated with it. The account is open to social practice informing normative constructions at a fundamentally appropriate level, including providing a diagnostic account of how new interpretations develop in response to different historical circumstances and assessing the ability of theories to contribute to progressive political action.

The method is therefore both backward looking and forward looking; it takes account of the past whilst seeking to formulate normative principles in the course of engaging with new expressions of political agency. In the diagnostic stage of the process, theorists scrutinize existing manifestations of political practice, try to understand the attempts of political actors to emphasize the limits of existing interpretive discourses, and observe their use and efforts to innovate on available conceptual discourses. It is important to emphasize that in doing so they do not start with individual intuitions or personal normative assessments. As in the nonideal case, they start with some general assumptions, factual assumptions about the kind of society to which their political theory applies. Some of these assumptions are available through a study of the main currents of a public political culture, an analysis of its dominant economic arrangements, the recourse to ideological assumptions invoked by political actors in the public sphere, the observation of prevailing religious beliefs, the critique of relationship patterns with foreigners, an understanding of the way in which current institutions reflect or react to particular historical episodes, and so on. The concepts used to articulate particular interpretations of the point and purpose of existing institutions borrow elements from all of the above. What are presented as intuitively plausible starting points reflect the degree of social and political awareness that participants in a particular practice share with each other. However, contrary to nonideal theorists, those who endorse a dialectical method focus on moments of challenge rather than agreement surrounding these shared assumptions. In other words, what interest them are the historical stages in which such shared understandings start being contested, the emergence of groups that seek to appropriate existing conceptual categories, and their efforts to innovate and place these categories at the service of new claims and alternative interpretations.

Therefore, those who rely on the dialectical method concede that political change has a passive element. Theory can change the world insofar as it speaks to existing political conflicts, insofar as it tries to articulate the claims and concerns of real-world political agents, and insofar as it takes into account pre-existing understandings and shared social features. The material and social conditions of particular groups in society are often a consequence of especially profound and pervasive institutional patterns whose roots are to be found in even deeper principled commitments. When that is the case, claims contesting these institutions, even if initially expressed by particular political agents, may be a symptom of the malaise that has affected society in general and concerns potentially everyone.[52] The fact that existing institutions fail to live up to their normative commitments reveals the need to rethink their relationship to agents affected by them, and to conceive new principles distributing social roles and orienting political reform.

The history of political thought is replete with examples in which similar interpretations can be seen to emerge in response to the crisis of previous accounts of the function and purpose of political institutions. These theories both inherit part of the old conceptual apparatus and contribute alternative discourses inspired by the emergence of new expressions of political agency. So, for example, as many authors have emphasized, Machiavelli's civic humanism emerged as a *political* response to the crisis of Florentine republicanism; it sought to integrate some of the assumptions found within a Christian understanding of the polity with an interpretation of legitimacy based on the revival of the Aristotelian 'science of virtue' and a more secular conception of the good society.[53] Hobbes' conception of the state as an 'artificial person' can be seen as a political intervention in English Civil War debates on political allegiance, challenging traditional royalist accounts of political legitimacy and offering support to political actors endorsing the idea of 'de facto' rule.[54] What is important for our purposes is that the thought of these authors does not mature in isolation from the attempts of other agents in society; on the contrary, it is both inspired by the political struggle of their contemporaries and provides further support and a more coherent normative articulation of it.

I have called the agents whose place in society renders them a particularly significant source for the analysis of political conflicts avant-garde political agents. But the designation of 'avant-garde' is not without normative implications. It is important to emphasize that it can only be conferred at a stage of the process in which the theorist has ceased to be a mere spectator and assumes a politically active role. As already noticed, the critical, observational stage of the process is followed by a more constructive one, in which theorists have to make decisions about which claims and discourses are more likely to contribute to political emancipation, and therefore should be supported, and which ones represent mere defences of the status quo.

Avant-garde political agents are here similar to those creative scientists or artists who put existing knowledge and techniques at the service of fresh experiments, developing new perspectives, asking unprecedented questions, and paving the way for the development of alternative paradigms. As far as activist political theory goes, their role in society seems to place them in a crucial position for reflecting on the symptoms of a certain crisis, revealing potentially significant sources of conflict, and articulating the kinds of claims to which existing institutional arrangements prove unresponsive. Avant-garde agents are therefore also both rooted and forward looking. Prompted by their material and social conditions, they initiate political change by contesting the meaning of familiar terms of reference and the way political institutions perform. If the nature of their claims promises developments that depart from old, morally discredited discourses, their role is crucial in supplying the theorist with the raw material on the basis of which a novel interpretive paradigm can emerge.

How does the normative theorist interact with the avant-garde? A previous theory or family of theories which offered principles of political reform able to resolve certain historically specific conflicts is unable to do so any more. The claims of particular groups in society act as a lens through which to observe the consequences of this collapse. On the one hand, their emergence reveals how institutions are failing to live up to their normative commitments. On the other hand, it signals the need for new theories able to articulate fresh, less deficient interpretations of their function and purpose. But it is important to clarify that an agent or set of agents cannot really be called 'avant-garde' unless the dialectical method is invoked to scrutinize the nature of their claims and how they might contribute to political progress. At this point the theorist's intervention is crucial; it clarifies the terms of the debate among contemporaries, contributes to a clearer diagnosis of the conflict at hand, and gives an active and coherent voice to the claims of the avant-garde. In this sense, neither activist political theory nor the avant-garde could exist without each other. We might go as far as saying that the avant-garde is the *ratio essendi* of activist political theory but activist political theory is the *ratio cognoscendi* of the avant-garde.

## 2.8 CONCLUSION

This chapter explored an avant-garde conception of political agency and introduced an alternative way of proceeding in the pursuit of activist political theory: the dialectical approach. It introduced the dialectical approach as the method of learning from the trials, failures, and successes of the past; tried to explain how it relates to current methodological approaches; and what independent resources it has for coping both with the 'irrelevance' charge that affects ideal accounts and the 'status-quo' bias displayed by many nonideal rivals. It also sought to clarify how the dialectical approach offers to activist political theory a historically sensitive method for distinguishing progressive and regressive claims to political change. In particular, it argued that one or more interpretations of certain practices contribute to political progress if they display diagnostic, innovating, and heuristic potential. This means that such interpretations perform better than their rivals if they can articulate existing concerns and commitments at a fundamentally appropriate causal and normative level; if they can reflect on the function and purpose of political institutions in a way that preserves and adds content to the positive normative commitments of previous theories whilst avoiding their morally problematic aspects; and if they can raise new, unforeseen questions related to the development of political institutions reformed in accordance with their requirements.

In analysing these points, the chapter also tried to analyse how political agency plays a constitutive role in the development, articulation, and revision of activist political theory. Illustrating the dialectical method has shown that, when trying to overcome the 'status-quo' bias, the task of the normative theorist is inextricably linked to the emergence and development of new forms of political agency and to an understanding of how these challenge existing institutions. It requires scrutinizing claims and concerns symptomatic of current institutional (but principle-based) anomalies, explaining how normative theory can be used to critically assess these manifestations of political agency, and also examining how it might be considered an active expression of them. I called the kinds of political agents that stand in a similar relationship to the development of progressive normative theories, 'avant-garde' political agents. I explained that those are agents whose position in society renders them particularly relevant for giving rise to the claims that cultivate politically active normative enquiry. At this level, such political agents are ahead of others (avant-garde) not in a moral sense but simply because their institutional or social activity expresses in a particularly deep and revealing way the sorts of conflicts that give rise to new concerns for political theory. In other words, the claims of avant-garde political agents supply political theorists with the raw material on the basis of which progressive theoretical constructions can be developed. But at a second level, these agents are also crucial in joining the theorist's endeavours to articulate and revise political principles responsive to particular conflicts and are able to provide progressive interpretations of the function and purpose of existing institutions. In this second and morally more relevant sense, an avant-garde political agent is aware of its particular position in society in a normatively mediated way. It supports the theorists' efforts to disseminate and render more coherent and persuasive emerging attempts to combine, say, freedom and equality, and it contributes to the overall establishment of new interpretive paradigms.

There are many historical examples of how theorists and avant-garde political agents have historically interacted in the ways I have described. I shall return to the issue and its relevance for the global justice debate in the third part of this work. Before that, however, it is important to illustrate in what ways the dialectical method introduced here can be applied to that debate, and how it reconciles ideal and nonideal features in assessing the normative standing of states and the defence of global egalitarian justice.

# Part II

# Defending the State, Defending Cosmopolitanism

# 3

## Politics and Associative Relations

### 3.1 THE CONFUSION BETWEEN IDEAL AND NONIDEAL IN RECENT DEBATES ON GLOBAL JUSTICE

Activist political theory seeks to integrate principles and agency by dialectically combining insights from ideal and nonideal approaches at the appropriately fundamental level of analysis. This issue has important implications for assessing the normative role of the state and the justification of global egalitarian principles. It allows us to perceive what is normatively problematic when we neglect the state, and also how acknowledging the normative relevance of the state does not limit the scope of egalitarian justice. It also prepares the ground for a more politically engaged, as well as normatively coherent, analysis of questions arising in the debate on global justice.

A cursory look at the existent literature shows how both rival theories in the global justice debate – statism and cosmopolitanism – have insufficiently examined these issues at the methodologically appropriate level. The problem is in part determined by the confusion and misplacement of assumptions from ideal and nonideal approaches in the reflective apparatus of each. When exploring the relationship between principles and agency, statists and cosmopolitans tend to endorse features from each but in the wrong places. On agency, they discuss the moral relevance (or irrelevance) of states from an ideal perspective, instead of considering how existing political agents might act to render politically effective and motivationally sustainable first-order normative principles. On principles, they are nonideal and condemn the facts of global poverty as self-evident distributive wrongs, rather than placing their analysis in an appropriately fundamental theoretical framework.

This chapter focuses on the first part of the problem. It argues that both the defence of the state and the cosmopolitan alternative to it are conducted at the ideal level where they ought to incorporate more elements from a nonideal perspective. Statists defend the relevance of specific associative relations from an idealized perspective but overlook the crucial question of which conception of political association supports transformation in the world as we know it. Cosmopolitan counterarguments fail to engage their adversaries at the appropriate level of analysis. Instead of criticizing statists for confusing or misplacing ideal and nonideal considerations, cosmopolitans endorse their methodological premises in debating the nature of associative duties, thus contending the same normative territory.

It is worth exploring in more detail how these errors arise. A clear analysis of how both cosmopolitans and statists confuse or misplace ideal and nonideal considerations should pave the way to understanding the dialectical reconciliation attempted in the rest of this work. Once we have explained at which stage of normative theorizing on global justice ideal or nonideal considerations ought to prevail, the virtues of a dialectical framework will emerge more clearly. At that point, the normative defences of both cosmopolitanism and the state should also be easier to reconcile. Clearing the ground from such methodological confusion on both sides will therefore also prepare the reader for the (hopefully) more sophisticated way of combining insights from ideal and nonideal approaches in our third part.

## 3.2 WHAT'S IDEAL ABOUT ASSOCIATIVE RELATIONS?

The first point of controversy between cosmopolitan and statist approaches to global justice concerns the nature of states in relation to the scope of distributive equality. Statist accounts take particular distributive obligations (including obligations of an egalitarian kind) to be grounded on special associative relations. These associative relations are usually conceived in either a cultural–conventionalist or in a political–institutionalist fashion. As far as cultural relations are concerned, it is often claimed that distributive justice requires a bounded political community where social goods are equally valued and in which citizens share common sympathies motivating them to take relevant distributional responsibilities.[1] As far as political relations are concerned, it is emphasized that the cooperative or coercive nature of state institutions places on those institutions higher burdens of justification with regard to the relative well-being of the people they represent.[2]

Cosmopolitans tend to emphasize that, on both points, statists rely on controversial assumptions as to why distributive equality represents a serious concern only within particular political communities. With regard to the first argument, cultural conventionalists are criticized for romanticizing the national community and for mischaracterizing the patterns of identification possible to observe in it. These authors, so the argument goes, fail to consider, for example, how common sympathies might be lacking in culturally heterogeneous societies or overstate the extent to which they follow territorial lines rather than, say, ideological or group-based ones.[3] With regard to the second, political, argument, it is often emphasized how the view arbitrarily restricts the sphere where relevant associative relations of coercion and cooperation might be found. These, it is often said, hardly ever characterize *only* institutional relations mediated by the state and might also be present in sub-state or supra-state units affecting individuals' life more broadly conceived. Hence, so the cosmopolitan argument goes, there seem to be no plausible reasons for taking seriously the normative relevance of states, and for narrowing down the scope of distributive equality.[4]

To answer this objection, statists typically emphasize how they intend their theory of global justice to be *ideal* at this level. The real issue, they argue, is not so much verifying whether any existing collection of individuals really exhibits all the relational properties associated with cultural conventionalism. No one, certainly not liberal theorists, would deny the existence of fundamental disagreement on comprehensive moral doctrines or build consent around a substantive theory of the common good.[5] Yet an ideal account of global agency does not need to imply that any existing society actually fulfils the criteria statists ascribe to it. The relevant question is instead whether the notion of common sympathies constitutes a sufficiently desirable form of human social organization to serve as the basic unit of the global society, not whether it realistically describes any actually existing political form.[6]

But once this argument is granted, it tends to invite another cosmopolitan question. Even if one decides to take seriously the ideal argument in favour of culturally homogenous entities, cosmopolitans still tend to press their rivals on why such entities should differ along territorial lines. If we are merely interested in ideal possibilities, some cosmopolitans insist, gender, religion, or social class – to give only a few examples – are equally relevant units of aggregation compared to the statist reification of bounded political communities.[7] Indeed, precisely because we start with ideal premises which need not reflect an existing partition of the world, we could redraw political boundaries so that collective loyalties are vertically dispersed.[8]

This cosmopolitan objection is problematic too, and I shall examine it more carefully in the next section. But it is striking to see how the methodological confusion we are exploring prevents statists from confronting it at the right level of analysis. Their response takes the form of an attempt to elaborate an alternative view on the relevance of particular associative relations, one that sets aside special cultural relations and focuses instead on special institutional ones.[9] Contra cosmopolitans, their rivals emphasize how justice has a specifically political character. They argue that the priority of state-based relations as grounding distributive concerns does not need to rely on principles of justice that apply to individual conduct or are based on any morally comprehensive account. Instead, it relates to the presupposition of a particular kind of associative relation that justice requires in order to be exercised. The point, they claim, is not so much identifying normative principles that may, after all, fail to provide much guidance in particular associative circumstances. It is not about how the world would look if its basic social institutions were redesigned from scratch. It is about how we could justify the existence of such institutions to the specific agents they serve to represent. In the version of this argument relevant to the debate on global justice, principles of an egalitarian kind presuppose the existence of a collective body that reciprocally acknowledges, cooperatively endorses, and coercively imposes a particular institutional framework.[10] That is where these egalitarian principles start, and that is where they stop.

The analysis, one cannot but observe, is informed by important assumptions implicit in the nonideal approaches examined in the previous chapter. However, and this is where the confusion becomes troubling, one will be puzzled to find defenders of a similar position insisting that the view is no less part of an 'ideal' account of justice.[11] But one might ask why collective political agency should be idealized at this stage. And how does this idealization affect the choice of relevant normative principles in the case of debates on global justice?

As we insisted in the previous chapter, it is easy enough to agree that activist political theory requires that a specific set of political relations be in place for normative principles to become politically effective and motivationally sustainable. But this does not necessarily imply that the validity of these principles depends, all things considered, on the presence (or absence) of such state-based associative relations. The selection of the unit of analysis and the distribution of boundaries separating one set of practices from the other has so far remained unjustified. The statist argument seems to rely on a crucial (but, at present, methodologically arbitrary) shift from the question of what kind of relations and practices ground valid distributive claims and should be included in a normative assessment of the principles of justice to what kind of relations would need to be in place for such an ideal to be considered politically and motivationally viable. From the point of view of the former, we are interested in a fundamentally appropriate account of the relations necessary to articulate certain demands on the patterns of production, distribution, or rectification applying to relevantly placed parties (e.g. parties in particular circumstances of justice). This is a matter of principle. From the point of view of the latter, we are interested in the way agents interact with each another to develop politically effective and motivationally sustainable interpretations of these demands when faced with specific associative constraints and a distribution of responsibilities reflecting these constraints. This is a matter of agency.

Issues of principle and issues of agency must not be confused, but they should also not be isolated from each other. Both are crucial to the avant-garde account of global justice. Both form an essential part of our attempt to construct an activist political theory interested not merely in how agents should interact with each other but also in how to transform the world compatibly with normative requirements. Applying the dialectical method to the global justice debate allows us to establish constructive links between principles and agency, but it does so in a way that places ideal and nonideal considerations at a fundamentally appropriate level of analysis. As the following chapters try to explain, as a first step we should seek to develop an interpretation of the function and purpose of political institutions which is satisfactory at the diagnostic level, that is, links normatively fundamental constraints with a causally appropriate analysis of concerns and commitments identified in particular circumstances of *injustice*. The principles delivered by such an account should also contain more innovating and heuristic potential compared to other available interpretations. As a second step, the theory should make space for nonideal assumptions, and reveal particular sensitivity to the politically relevant criteria that constrain transformative collective initiatives (e.g. feasibility, legitimacy, stability). It should also pay particular attention to the agents and institutions through which these initiatives are more likely to succeed.

As we acknowledged in the previous chapter, the decision on which kind of relations to focus on when developing a particular normative view (in this case a particular interpretation of global justice) is itself normatively laden (and controversial). Applying the dialectical method allows for a more plausible account to be advanced, avoiding the irrelevance charge of many ideal approaches but combining their commitment to certain first-order values (say, the ideal of moral equality of all human beings or the entitlement to access basic standards of material well-being) with an analysis of how existent practices fail to live up to related normative expectations. Conflict and the circumstances of injustice provide here the relevant starting points. But it is necessary to emphasize that in the initial stage of theory construction the agents finding themselves in particular circumstances of injustice and those guiding political transformation may not always and clearly coincide. It is only activist political theory and an avant-garde conception of political agency that can bring them closer to each other, a point to which I shall return.

It is also crucial to bear in mind that some kinds of relations (e.g. relations of competition for access to specific goods) that are relevant for articulating particular principles of global justice may not be identical to the relations that obtain normative priority when issues of agency are discussed (e.g. relations of shared cultural and political membership). Prioritizing state-based associative relations at a stage at which normative demands are articulated runs the risk of excluding, at the level of principle, other relevant forms of institutional relations. The move threatens, for example, to ignore how citizens and non-citizens alike might interact in the same global processes of production, exchange, and transfer, and how they might be equally affected by structural economic and political injustices. Endorsing premises from the statist account of agency at the stage at which principles are articulated runs the risk of promoting an unduly limited and exclusionary interpretation of the circumstances of injustice.

Notice, however, that tracing such a distinction between principles and agency does not necessarily lead to considering political membership an arbitrary feature as several cosmopolitans maintain. We can afford to concede that there will always be special sympathies bringing closer to each other particular groups of people, or that the boundaries and configuration of special (state-based) institutional relations matter for the allocation of political responsibilities. What we need to emphasize is that where such associative relations obtain particular significance is at the stage of the theory at which the issue of agency obtains prominence. All the arguments usually advanced by statists to defend the normative standing of states become crucially relevant at this point. Coercion, for example, is necessary to guarantee feasibility; reciprocity is necessary to guarantee legitimacy; and cooperation is necessary to guarantee stability. Yet it would be as wrong to prioritize such criteria and the relations informed by them already at the level of principle as to ignore them altogether. If the statist analysis of associative relations is wrongly pitched at an exclusively ideal level, the same occurs with current cosmopolitan proposals trying to undermine its validity. As the next section illustrates, despite an admirable attempt to focus on relevant circumstances for the articulation of global justice principles, the cosmopolitan alternative idealizes these circumstances to an unnecessary degree. Here again, the inadequate application of ideal and nonideal considerations deprives the position of its potential strengths, and leads to a new confusion between issues of principle and issues of agency.

## 3.3 THE ARBITRARINESS ARGUMENT AND THE CIRCUMSTANCES OF JUSTICE

The previous section emphasized how statist accounts (both in their conventionalist and institutionalist versions) focus on the relevance of states as a matter of ideal construction, instead of emphasizing the role of particular associative relations at the level of transformative political agency. Cosmopolitan counterarguments are prone to an equivalent mistake. Their failure to distinguish at what level of the theory political membership becomes particularly relevant cultivates a simplistic and uncompromising emphasis on its 'morally arbitrary' nature and an equally problematic understanding of the relation between political change and individual moral agency. A similar cosmopolitan approach has important repercussions for the tenability of the theory when pursued in an activist mode. To begin with, it unnecessarily complicates the background interpretation of relevant circumstances of injustice. More importantly, it deprives the theory of essential resources when it comes to addressing questions of transformative political agency. Let us start by examining the first.

The cosmopolitan critique of the relevance of political membership typically starts with an attempt to place at the heart of the theory individuals rather than alternative collective agents such as associations or states. A well-known thought experiment invites us to imagine different individuals placed in specific counterfactual circumstances (e.g. a global original position) confronting their competing conceptions of justice with the aim of establishing relevant principles of global cooperation.[12] Since, as one scholar puts it, 'one's membership in one nation as opposed to another, and the natural inequality among nations may be as morally fortuitous as any other natural fact', all individuals are entitled to be included in this initial thought experiment.[13] Political membership, another cosmopolitan insists, is 'just one further deep contingency (like genetic endowment, race, gender, and social class), one more potential basis for inequalities that are inescapable and present from birth'.[14]

The attempt to extend the justificatory framework to normative relations that are not necessarily limited by the bonds of shared citizenship is itself an admirable enterprise. Whether a similar extension also requires to be coupled with a critique of the arbitrary nature of political membership remains to be seen. One reason typically advanced to motivate the cosmopolitan project is that if we abstract from contingent and allegedly arbitrary features in articulating the fundamental principles of justice, what would remain are individuals for whom the only relevant criterion of membership in global circumstances of justice is a moral one. In other words, the account of agency that cosmopolitans typically endorse in searching for the appropriate principles of justice is one where individuals, regardless of who they are, possess only the two essential powers of moral personality: the capacity for a sense of justice, and the capacity to form, revise, and pursue a conception of the good.[15]

It is worth asking whether, without distinguishing between the different levels at which the critique (if at all plausible) operates, a similar analysis is needed. Why does the cosmopolitan account need to idealize the nature of agents placed in relevant normative circumstances? And what are the implications of these idealizations? One difficulty with the proposal is that by moralizing the nature of individual agency one runs the risk of obscuring potential sources of conflict and failing to see the distinctiveness of problems in response to which demands for justice typically arise. Despite the best cosmopolitan efforts to model their normative enterprise after Rawls' original position, the difference between these and his analysis of the circumstances of justice remains striking here.[16] Whilst embracing a Humean definition of the subjective circumstances of justice, Rawls' theory of justice (whatever its other limits) has the virtue of directing attention to two empirically plausible features that create a special need for particular principles of justice: individual selfishness and moderate generosity.

As we saw in the first chapter, this attempt is by no means unprecedented. Rousseau and Kant also emphasized the relevance of conflict, of unsocial sociability, in triggering particular normative claims. Justice is a virtue of practices characterized by competing interests and intersubjective disagreements, where individuals vary in their analysis of the function and purpose of particular institutions and feel entitled to press claims against each other.[17] As David Hume has memorably put it: 'encrease to a sufficient degree the benevolence of men, or the bounty of nature, and you render justice useless, by supplying its place with much nobler virtues, and more valuable blessings'.[18] If moral dispositions really were a reliable feature of human cooperation, justice would become superfluous.

The cosmopolitan proposal modifies this account of agency by idealizing the normatively relevant features agents in particular circumstances must possess for the right principles of justice to emerge. The model of association envisaged in this case tends to overlook political conflict and the extent of intersubjective disagreement, and is built upon values that are taken to be genuinely shared.[19] Agents placed in particular relational circumstances represent moral persons for whom the rationality of global distributive principles is justified with reference to a baseline of moral equality.[20] It is not difficult to see that agents so conceived are very different from those central to the account of circumstances of *injustice* introduced in the previous chapter, where the starting point was conflict rather than agreement on particular values. Whilst the point of departure for that mode of enquiry was the existence of agents pressing contrasting claims against each other, and the need to select between different interpretations of the function and purpose of institutions affecting their lives, in the cosmopolitan case the starting point is provided by a moralized account of individual agency with much of the rest being postulated away.

The difficulty with a similar position is that by idealizing agents placed in relevant normative circumstances, cosmopolitanism relies precisely on that for which justice is required. What differentiates this version of cosmopolitanism from the activist political account introduced in the previous chapter (and developed in the rest of this book) is that the latter need not assume that politically relevant principles of justice result from moral agreement on particular distributive conceptions. On the contrary, it emerges as a result of theorists' attempts to develop justified normative principles through a critical analysis of concerns and commitments present in existing circumstances of injustice. The way of proceeding in that case, we argued, echoes Rousseau's enquiry on whether there can be 'a legitimate and reliable rule of administration in the civil order taking men as they are and laws as they can be'.[21] In other words, without necessarily assuming that all parties naturally possess a sense of justice, activist political theory justifies the necessity of political transformation without losing sight of disagreement on how general moral principles should be reflected in particular institutional relations. That theory starts with agents embedded in existing political conflicts and enquires about the principles necessary to interpret and address these conflicts at the appropriately fundamental level of analysis. In doing so, it follows Rousseau's critique of the moralization of circumstances of justice and his defence of the necessity of political transformation: 'in order for an emerging people to appreciate the healthy maxims of politics [...] the effect would have to become the cause; the social spirit, which should be the result of the institution, would have to preside over the founding of the institution itself, and men would have to be prior to laws what they ought to become by means of laws'.[22]

The upshot is that one can hardly expect individual moral agency to be placed at the heart of political transformation. It is precisely because of the unilaterality of individual judgements and the indeterminate nature of individual commitments that justice is required. As I tried to show in the first chapter, Kant also insists on the issue while discussing the role of political activists in promoting moral progress. As he puts it, 'it is not the case that a good state constitution is to be expected from inner morality; on the contrary the good moral education of a people is to be expected through a good state constitution'. In fact, Kant adds, by relying on morality alone 'nothing will be achieved'.[23]

This understanding of moral capacity as a collective disposition which needs to be politically developed marks an important, though little noticed, difference from the versions of cosmopolitanism we have discussed in this chapter. It also connects more appropriately with the activist political theory defended in the previous one. Far from raising an obstacle to the manifestation of moral powers, as in the cosmopolitan theories we are examining, sharing particular political practices allows individuals to articulate opposing concerns and commitments in a way that contributes to their shared political emancipation. 'It is only by entering into a civil constitution,' Kant emphasizes in his early essay on universal history, 'that moral dispositions can be fully developed.'[24] This is extremely relevant to illustrate the dialectic between moral progress and transformative political agency that will occupy us in the chapters that follow.

In the alternative account of global justice developed in this work, agents in relevant normative circumstances confront each other with conflicting concerns and commitments. Theory emerges as a result of the efforts of activist political theorists to articulate these commitments in conjunction with a fundamentally appropriate analysis of particular circumstances of injustice. But theorists are not alone in undertaking this task: they are prompted by larger patterns in society to diagnose the source of particular problems and they interact with other relevant political agents in contributing to conceptual innovation. A very different approach animates the cosmopolitan theories we are examining. The two relevant starting points considered sufficient to produce particular principles are here the idea of individuals as free and equal moral persons and a thought experiment from which all morally arbitrary factors should be excluded.[25] As with Leibniz's humanitarian cosmopolitanism examined in the first chapter, the parties are here individual moral agents whose natural sense of justice leads them to favour specific global distributive principles.[26] This issue is, however, controversial: if we could rely on such ideal agents, on individuals' altruism and epistemic ability to come up with determinate principled requirements, one would have difficulty explaining how conflict occurs and claims of justice have initially emerged.

One response might be of course that justice is simply required for reasons of coordination rather than conflict resolution, in order to support a particular distribution of benefits and burdens and without being threatened by any unintended consequences of social interaction. But even granting that this might be the case, and even assuming that the task exhausts the intervention of political theory more broadly conceived, what is gained by the argument on the arbitrariness of political membership? If anything, starting with agents considered as members of different political associations might facilitate rather than hinder the partial resolution of coordination problems. Referring to a set of institutional mechanisms and channels of communication through which the claims of citizens occupying particular social roles can be exposed and analysed benefits social coordination rather than raising an obstacle to it.

Cosmopolitans need neither idealize individual moral capacities nor prove that states are arbitrary entities in the construction of circumstances of justice. Illustrating conflicts characterizing relations between citizens belonging to different states and occupying particular institutional roles is possible even granting the relevance of political membership. The advantage of such a view is that we need not start from dubious assumptions about the degree of moral awareness individuals in circumstances of injustice must already possess – a feature which turns out to be crucial at the stage of the theory at which issues of agency are typically addressed. It is sufficient when discussing the need for specific principles of justice to start with an appropriate diagnostic analysis of the grounds of certain conflicts, a plausible reconstruction of the relevant unit of analysis, and the commitment to first-order values as they are identified when reflecting on the process of adaptation of social institutions to various forms of human cooperation. The following chapter will examine in more detail whether and how all this can be achieved without making any problematic assumptions on the arbitrariness of political membership. Before that however, and having illustrated how idealized premises complicate unnecessarily the interpretation of the circumstances of injustice, it is important to explore the second part of the issue mentioned at the outset of this section:

how these assumptions deprive the theory of essential resources needed for the analysis of agency when discussing political transformation.

## 3.4 IDEALIZING THE SENSE OF JUSTICE

To justify their idealized focus on individual agency and the shift away from circumstances of justice characterized by the clash between conflicting concerns and commitments, cosmopolitans tend to emphasize the purely *hypothetical* nature of their assumptions concerning individual moral agency. A similar response is consistent with another thought experiment typically considered to produce appropriate principles of global justice: the use of the veil of ignorance. Here too an idealizing tendency intervenes, and it unsurprisingly involves the wrong theoretical categories. We are asked to bracket off all contingent information about the real nature of agents placed in relevant circumstances of injustice, and to adopt specific false assumptions designed to bring attention to the moral character of individual motives. This section examines some implications of this idealization, illustrates its shortcomings when applied to issues of political membership, and explains why a similar way of proceeding fails to generate support for a cosmopolitan account pursued in the mode of activist political theory.

One often-cited reason for adopting idealized assumptions in particular circumstances of justice is that these assumptions contribute to reduce the impact of contingent features and selfish moral motives in the articulation of principles of justice. The aim of the thought experiment is to introduce informational restrictions designed to avoid a biased interpretation of the function and purpose of political institutions, and to produce a more impartial analysis of relevant social practices. By assuming that agents in circumstances of justice are unaware of their class and social status, do not have access to knowledge about their particular natural talents or social skills, and ignore their life plans as well as their psychological disposition to specific opportunities, the conditions under which agents make decisions should improve the chances of the theory obtaining overall plausibility.

These are some of the reasons endorsed by Rawls in motivating the fiction of the veil of ignorance within his theory of justice.[27] My aim here is not to assess the chances of success of a similar strategy but simply to consider its adaptation in the context of the global justice debate, where citizenship is typically included among the features that we are required to ignore.[28] The point is important for examining at what level of the analysis we should embrace ideal premises, whether political membership is the kind of assumption with regard to which we can afford to idealize in this way, and the implications of both points for a dialectical interpretation of the relation between principles and agency.

To explore these issues, two versions of the cosmopolitan thought experiment need to be carefully examined. The one that appears easier to dispense with features individual moral agents that abstract from the existence of any form of collective association and are asked to deliberate on whether the sphere of application of different principles of justice should coincide with a division of political boundaries following different territorial lines. Agents in a similar position are imagined to simply ignore the existence of states and reflect on whether some other form of collective organization, guided by alternative (as yet to be conceived) normative principles might more appropriately orient future political reform.[29]

This argument, however, would not take us very far. One obvious question, consistent with some of the objections against ideal approaches that we underlined in the previous chapter, is whether a similar idealization of agents in particular circumstances of justice also implies that the features of reality upon which we choose to theorize are arbitrarily selected. One might emphasize, for example, that, if pursued to its logical consequences, there is nothing to stop the cosmopolitan thought experiment from being extended as far as to bracket off every institution through which individuals organize collectively, not only states but also international organizations, civil associations, the market sphere, and even the family. As in some of the applications of ideal theory examined in the previous chapter, an unlimited endorsement of such informational restrictions would then raise the question of the relation between whatever elements concerning human agency are left, and the relevance of principles premised on their validity. What is there to prevent us from adding false assumptions to the thought experiment, and postulating agents who not only ignore their citizenship but also the generation to which they belong, the economic and political conditions in which their common problems might emerge, and even humanity's level of civilization? As one author puts it, 'if you do not know that a multinational cooperation exists, you will probably not imagine one as part of an ideal structure of global justice. . . . If you do not know about the Internet, it will not be easy to imagine it; but then you will not be able to address the inequalities created by differential access to it.'[30]

It is possible, however, to modify the application of ideal premises in a way that manages to circumscribe this objection. While the thought experiment requires agents to abstract from contingent personal features in particular circumstances of justice, it may not exclude knowledge of general facts about society and awareness of the basic principles of political organization. One important advantage of the hypothetical scenario depicted in this way would be that it would ask us to abstract as much as possible from specific individuals' preferences, talents, or social status but as little as possible from the general rules orienting our enquiry on relevant ideal principles of justice.[31]

Then the crucial question for cosmopolitans would not necessarily concern how far the thought experiment can proceed without becoming entirely irrelevant. It would rather be whether the agents' particular political membership is the kind of knowledge one can consistently afford to ignore.

This leads us to a second potential application of ideal assumptions to available information concerning political membership. One might postulate that whilst being aware of the existence of particular political boundaries, with all the political and social features that this implies, agents in circumstances of justice are deprived of knowledge as to how specifically they relate to each other. For example, individual agents might know that China, Zimbabwe, and the United States are part of the world's political map, and they might also have access to the general sociopolitical facts relevant to those countries. However, one might also assume that they ignore their particular political belonging, whether they are Chinese, Zimbabwean, or American. According to this second cosmopolitan interpretation, the only relevant feature to take into account while evaluating claims of justice would be whether individual agents have 'a capacity for an effective sense of justice and a capacity to form, revise, and pursue a conception of the good'.[32]

The appeal to agents' effective sense of justice is also crucial to the overall tenability of a theory of global justice pursued in activist political mode. However, it is worth analysing in more detail why this is the case, and to question whether it is possible to fully account for this feature given a conception of moral agency that tends to abstract from issues of political membership. In the absence of any explicit treatment of the problem in the cosmopolitan literature discussed here, it might be worth analysing the relevance of this assumption within a constructivist account of justification similar to the one many cosmopolitans tend to endorse. In the most sophisticated versions of the argument (e.g. that elaborated by Rawls), the sense of justice is typically understood to motivate agents to act by the relevant normative principles. This in turn serves to illustrate how a particular understanding of justice (e.g. justice as fairness) emerges as the most stable conception in the presence of a plurality of alternatives. As Rawls puts it, 'a system in which each person has, and is known by everyone to have, a sense of justice is inherently stable. Other things being equal the forces making for its stability increase as time passes.'[33]

This emphasis on time is crucial to understanding how the sense of justice develops and strengthens among agents placed in relevant practical circumstances. The argument rests on a conception of moral psychology emphasizing the importance of shared processes of moral and political socialization, and their role in informing the reasons agents might have for endorsing particular normative principles. One might try to make the point sharper by observing (as Rawls does) that when issues of agency come to the fore, appealing to the moral force of the 'purely conscientious act', 'the desire to do what is right and just simply because it is right and just' is clearly not enough.[34] This does not seem to be a controversial statement. Rousseau was among the first to raise the question of moral motivation when he noticed that 'luxury does not get rooted out with sumptuary laws. It has to be extirpated from the depth of men's hearts by impressing healthier and nobler tastes on them'.[35] Here the willingness to act depends not merely on coercive subjection to a shared political order but upon the development of concrete practices of social and political emancipation. It relates to specific learning processes, and is influenced by a history of the way in which agents come to form their beliefs, rely upon particular interpretations of the function and purpose of shared institutions, refine the values to which they are committed, and jointly invest in the transformation of given material and social conditions. In order for any particular conception of justice to emerge as the most stable interpretation of certain concerns and commitments, agents' sense of justice must reflect public norms of communication invoked in political emancipatory processes.[36]

A more nuanced analysis of these features against the background of particular circumstances of injustice will be crucial when examining the issue of conceptual innovation – a point to which I shall return in the following chapters. For now, it is important to see how the cosmopolitan reconstruction of particular circumstances of justice modifies these assumptions so as to unnecessarily weaken its own normative potential. The cosmopolitan application of ideal premises to the analysis of political agency requires that the history, traditions, and civic life informing the social expectations and motivation of different individual agents are considered arbitrary features. But assuming that such features play no essential role in the development of an effective sense of justice leads one to imprudently ignore issues of political and motivational sustainability. By bracketing off the background assumptions one needs to take into account when weighing up alternative views, and by ambiguously returning to an ideal doctrine of the purely conscientious act, the cosmopolitan account ends up with very few normative resources to analyse the social and political context where transformative political agency is required to intervene.

The influence of idealized premises on the cosmopolitan analysis of individual agency, and the tendency to abstract from agents' particular relation to collective political institutions, leaves us with a rather obscure understanding of individuals' effective sense of justice and a potentially weak account of how to motivate them to act in accordance with specific principles. Except for a few moral heroes, an effective sense of justice does not mature exclusively by virtue of agents' commitment to first-order moral principles but is socially and politically constructed, and appears specific to each form of collective political association. To claim that an innate, universal sense of justice, understood as unconditional commitment to rationally justified principles, might be quite rare or that one needs to take into account the way particular societies inform their members' justice-based aspirations does not imply ruling out specific distributive principles on a global scale. But idealizing agency may not be the most effective way to ensure that required principles of justice carry political appeal and motivational sustainability. The sort of premises that one would be brought to ignore in this case might affect what remains of the agents' sense of justice, thus undermining resources essential to developing the required activist account of global justice.

One might of course object here that the sense of justice amounts to nothing more than a motivation to comply internalized by virtue of living under just institutions. If this were indeed the case, idealizing individual agency would not conceal any important information. One might emphasize, instead, that all agents are characterized by a minimal motivation to obey the law so that whatever sense of justice we assume they possess by virtue of shared political membership, we can rely upon it even if political boundaries ceased to exist in their current form. It is certainly undeniable that, with regard to some issues at least, people's sense of justice overlaps worldwide, regardless of political membership. Perhaps one does not need to know where someone comes from to consider torturing babies wrong and certainly the sense of justice relevant to this case suffices to support institutions prohibiting such a practice. Whether this kind of thin, reactive motivation is also enough to support more demanding principles for global political reform required by activist political theory remains an open question.

In the case of shared political membership, the sense of justice does not develop simply due to citizens' endorsement of a coercive system of rules. Of course, political compliance plays an essential role in establishing institutions that reflect certain justice-based principles. But agents in charge of political transformation also tend to seek support for these institutions by taking advantage of other pro-attitudes developed in the course of specific historical processes, including being educated as a member of a particular political association and participating in practices that seek to interpret and revise a familiar public culture. Cosmopolitans need not consider these features arbitrary or detrimental to their own cause. The question of global political transformation can be answered by paying attention to the modes of internal transformation of political communities compatible with cosmopolitan goals.[37] Abstracting from political membership does very little to consolidate people's motivation to comply with cosmopolitan principles. It merely succeeds in undermining the sense of justice upon which relevant political agents might rely when seeking to promote global political transformation.

Viewed thus, rather than assuming fully developed moral dispositions compatible with cosmopolitan morality, we consider the state a cultivating ground conducive to the requirements of global justice. Taking part in collective processes of decision-making compels individuals to politically confront each other, teaches them to invoke past experiences of adaptation of particular normative principles, and educates them to a sense of the collective. These are crucial resources for normatively inspired political agents seeking to revise particular interpretations of the function and purpose of political institutions compatibly with cosmopolitan commitments. They should not be undermined when working out a plausible and coherent cosmopolitan account in the mode of activist political theory.

Assessing existent defences of global justice with a particular emphasis on the arbitrariness premise is important to obtain a fundamentally appropriate account of the relation between principles and agency in the global sphere. The cosmopolitan attempt to abstract from political membership is both unnecessary and unwarranted. It is unnecessary because it moralizes agents in particular circumstances of justice to the point of obscuring relevant instances of conflict and rendering justice superfluous. It is unwarranted because a similar idealization limits agents' sense of justice, and undermines potential efforts to render the principles of global justice politically effective and motivationally sustainable in the presence of particular associative relations. Rejecting the normative standing of political communities hardly supports the defence of global distributive principles; it merely draws attention away from some relevant conceptual tools necessary to analyse global political transformation.

## 3.5 CONCLUSION

Existing defences of the normative relevance of the state are usually coupled with a critique of all cosmopolitan arguments in favour of global egalitarian justice. Here, I tried to separate the two questions, and while forcefully rejecting several cosmopolitan attempts to idealize moral agency, I also criticized the opposite argument, that is, idealizing associative political relations to the point of neglecting relevant circumstances of injustice. The following chapter illustrates in greater detail how it is possible to reflect on circumstances of injustice in a way that neither idealizes individual agency nor limits normatively relevant relations to shared political membership. It argues that it is necessary to provide a diagnostic analysis of global distributive conflicts and, to do so, places their analysis within an appropriately fundamental interpretive framework sensitive not only to the facts of global poverty but also to the processes and agents that bring it about. Before going into the details of those issues however, let me restate briefly again where recent approaches to global justice seem to go wrong.

Having introduced a distinction between issues of principle and issues of agency, it is not difficult to see the problems determined by the lack of a systematic analysis of how ideal and nonideal premises should be reconciled. When the nature of states is approached by cosmopolitans from a merely ideal perspective, the analysis of agency in transforming social and political institutions tends to be undermined. Issues of political feasibility and motivational sustainability are, to be sure, occasionally raised. But even when they are, it is difficult to know precisely how political agents are supposed to proceed in reforming particular institutions, what kind of interaction of theory and practice is needed to generate transformative normative principles, and how arrangements reflecting these principles are supposed to emerge given cosmopolitanism's scepticism towards state-based agency.[38] Hence, even those authors underlining the need to take seriously empirical circumstances and institutional transformation end up emphasizing how although it is 'unlikely that the ideal would be fully realized it is implausible to insist that no necessary steps towards that ideal should be taken'.[39] This answer, besides providing a weak response to the motivational critiques that cosmopolitanism usually attracts, fails to produce a sufficiently sophisticated understanding of the relationship between principles and agency.[40] Taking seriously the issue of how political agency expresses itself in the real world (e.g. the role of state-based coercive power and the associative conditions under which principles of justice become politically effective and motivationally sustainable) is of significant benefit to an account of global justice interested not merely in interpreting the world but also in changing it.

On the other hand, when statists approach the nature of political associations from what they claim to be an ideal perspective, nonideal considerations of agency interfere with an appropriate analysis of principles. These accounts typically fail to distinguish between the relevance of specific associative relations in bringing about political change and the need to focus on other relevant circumstances when exploring issues of principle from a fundamentally appropriate normative perspective. They limit egalitarian concerns to particular political boundaries yet lack a normative account of how one ought to deal with cases in which agents placed in circumstances of justice relevant from a distributive perspective may or may not include those who share the same territorial jurisdiction. This is particularly evident if we consider the issue of global poverty – one important source of controversy between statists and cosmopolitans where the confusion between ideal and nonideal emerges clearly again. Analysing the terms of this controversy is the task of the following chapter.

# 4

## Global Egalitarianism

### 4.1 HOW TO DEFEND GLOBAL EGALITARIANISM

The previous chapter underlined the confusion between ideal and nonideal categories in recent debates on global justice with a particular focus on the agents that might give rise to egalitarian claims. It emphasized how all arguments either for or against the relevance of states invoked abstract or counterfactual assumptions to defend an idealized account of human agency, when they should have addressed the issue of political feasibility and motivational sustainability from a more nonideal perspective. A plausible alternative, we emphasized, should seek to place ideal and nonideal considerations at the appropriately fundamental level of analysis. It should reflect on existent circumstances of injustice and their relation to first-order normative principles with more attention to diagnostic capacity, innovation, and heuristic potential, and it should integrate its commitments with an agency-oriented analysis of particular relational practices.

When these tasks are combined, essential features of both statist and cosmopolitan accounts may be preserved. Endorsing a dialectical method that incorporates assumptions from ideal and nonideal approaches (provided that we are clear about the place and role of each) implies situating at the heart of normative theory an enquiry of fundamentally appropriate justice-based constraints, and an analysis of the ways in which political agents invoke these constraints to orient political practice. But how can we construct a global theory of justice which is sensitive to the distinction between principles and agency, and able to accommodate statist and cosmopolitan concerns at the appropriate level of the analysis? Taking up this challenge requires first clarifying the role of ideal and nonideal considerations with regard to the principles of global justice.

The aim of this chapter is therefore both critical and constructive. From a critical perspective, it explores the cosmopolitan–statist controversy to show that, contrary to the discussion on states, which was driven by ideal premises when it should have examined issues of political agency from a nonideal perspective, the opposite occurs with the analysis of principles. Here, both statists and cosmopolitans subject to critical scrutiny the consequences of global poverty without placing the analysis of its causes in an appropriately fundamental framework of enquiry. Taking the facts of global poverty as their starting point, statists only allow for sufficientarian principles of assistance to burdened societies, whereas cosmopolitans defend global distributive justice.[1] Yet in both cases it remains unclear why one should endorse either view without subjecting the causes of poverty to prior normative critique and without considering whether they warrant any link (be it domestic or global) between poverty and justice and then justice and inequality. An approach that fails to ask why the facts of poverty are what they are, and why they pose a problem of *distributive* justice (rather than, say, *remedial* justice or mere humanitarian assistance), runs the risk of conveying nothing distinctive about the agenda of each contending theory.

From a constructive perspective, the chapter seeks to illustrate in what ways first-order normative commitments and causally fundamental relations should be analysed so as to identify the principles of global justice from a fundamentally appropriate perspective. The thought here is that one should not be limited to noticing the 'facts' of global poverty and propose remedial principles that fail to address the issue of why poverty occurs in the first place. This argument is analogous to Marx's critique of those socialists who emphasized the need to improve the conditions of workers without engaging with the forces and relations of production that led to such miserable living conditions. As Marx emphasized, 'any distribution whatever of the means of consumption is only a consequence of the distribution of the conditions of production themselves'.[2] This point is not merely one of efficiency; Marx did not simply claim that policies addressing the problem of misdistribution at the level of production would be more successful than those tackling it at the level of consumption. Rather, as G. A. Cohen puts it, the critique plays at a more fundamental level: 'it is a confusion to direct censure against the predictable and regular consequences of a cause which is not itself subjected to criticism'.[3] The nature of the mistake made here is not just technical, it is normative.

Applied to the global justice debate, this argument illustrates that we would not be analysing relations of severe material deprivation from a fundamentally appropriate perspective if we based our critique on certain empirical facts without subjecting to scrutiny the reasons why such facts have emerged in the current form. I shall cover this issue in greater detail in the third part of the book. Before that, however, it is important to see why the misplacement of ideal and nonideal considerations in the global justice debate renders statist and cosmopolitan theories ill-suited to develop these points further.

Both the statist discussion on principles and the cosmopolitan objections advanced to it focus on the mere condemnation of a particular social condition (e.g. global poverty) instead of providing a fundamentally appropriate account of the injustice of its causes. As I try to show below, one of the limits of nonideal approaches to the issue of global poverty is that they only tell us that poverty is bad (or harmful), not that it involves a specific kind of distributive injustice. Condemning poverty as not merely bad but also unjust with respect to a relevant distributive dimension (e.g. equality) requires analysing at the fundamentally appropriate level the features and normative acceptability of the process that brings it about. To take another Marxist example, objecting to certain empirical facts without basing that objection on a normative critique of the process that brought them about equals the slogan of a slave leading a rebellion on the basis of the motto 'Slavery must be abolished because the feeding of slaves in the system of slavery cannot exceed a certain low maximum.'[4] The critique of the causes takes priority over the condemnation of specific empirical facts not merely for reasons of efficiency but, most importantly, because it reveals at a fundamentally appropriate level what the grounds are for a specific injustice.[5]

Understanding this point has important implications for the selection of relevant normative principles able to guide action by placing factual concerns and commitments at a fundamentally appropriate level of analysis. It also reveals the failure of existent cosmopolitan counterarguments to address these concerns in a manner that would have served the debate in much more productive ways. Instead of criticizing their rivals for confusing the role of ideal and nonideal assumptions, cosmopolitans have endorsed their methodological premises and entered potentially endless substantive controversies on the nature of associative duties and the corresponding principles of distributive justice. That, as we shall see in what follows, is problematic on various counts.

Defending relevant principles of global justice requires engaging with the causes of global injustice at the appropriately fundamental level of analysis. The need for specific principles of justice arises in particular circumstances of injustice, and such principles may have global scope if those circumstances are considered globally extended. This is the first point worth noting when examining the controversy between statists and cosmopolitans. The second point has to do with the extent to which such principles ought to target the reduction of inequalities worldwide. As we saw in the previous chapter, statists deny that this should be the case, limiting the scope of egalitarian principles to particular conditions in which associative obligations obtain. Cosmopolitans, on the other hand, defend the need to reduce inequalities between individuals on a global scale. However, failure to question their rivals' methodological premises when presenting arguments in favour of global egalitarian principles leads to confusion with regard to the kind of issues that really need to be raised in order to strengthen their commitments. Defending principles of justice at a global level and in a form that triggers the reduction of global inequalities requires an element that so far appears absent from either the statist or the cosmopolitan account of global poverty; it requires a fundamentally appropriate analysis of the injustice of its causes. To understand these points, it is important to begin by assessing how both rival theories proceed in the diagnostic task necessary to examine the circumstances of global injustice, and in what way this diagnosis is affected by approaching the question from a nonideal perspective.

## 4.2 POVERTY IN A NONIDEAL PERSPECTIVE: THE STATIST DIAGNOSIS

Statists tend to emphasize how the question of extreme poverty and the analysis of principles arising from claims related to absolute deprivation should be considered from a nonideal perspective. They argue that unequal access to particular goods in severely deprived regions of the world need not preoccupy global justice theorists as such, and fails to warrant principles of an egalitarian kind. Indeed, as one of the pioneering (and widely cited) authors examining this particular issue has underlined, remedial principles for global poverty only entail sufficiency-based obligations to *assist* 'burdened' societies facing unfavourable domestic conditions. Such conditions, so the argument goes, limit their participation as members in a good standing to the global society of states and are incompatible with our currently accepted interpretation of the function and purpose of allegedly just international institutions. The difference between a sufficientarian principle of assistance and one involving a proportionally equal distribution is that while the latter has no target and cut-off point, sufficientarian principles only apply until burdened societies have enough as is necessary to establish just political arrangements of their own.[6]

A step back to clarify some implicit premises of the argument might be required at this point. According to statists, the unequal development of political communities arises from features for which their citizens bear collective responsibility: a specific public political culture and societal traditions that support certain background political institutions. Principles aiming to reduce global inequalities are thought to represent an inappropriate alternative since the question of global poverty is not resolved by distributing resources from rich to poor countries without a clear target but involves improving the socio-political conditions that would allow deprived societies to stand up on their own.[7] Once that goal is achieved, these societies are deemed responsible for whatever level of welfare follows. To require an ongoing distribution would mean to unfairly interfere with the justified entitlements of other states, depriving their members of wealth and other benefits they might have deservingly created.[8]

Cosmopolitans tend to react to these claims by pursuing various argumentative strategies, each deserving of equal consideration. One is to force a choice between endorsing and rejecting piecemeal principles of distributive equality. If one accepts a responsibility-based argument similar to the one advanced by statists in the global sphere, cosmopolitans argue, its approval would weaken not only *global* egalitarian principles but also *domestic* ones. In fact, these critics object, an appeal to collective responsibility and respect for the autonomy of specific associative forms might also apply to families or other groups within the boundaries of particular states. A similar observation, if valid, seems to undermine any reasons for endorsing principles of distributive equality in the domestic sphere at least as much as it does when global interactions are analysed.[9]

However, instead of being embarrassed by the analogous application of the autonomy and responsibility constraints to domestic forms of political association, statists respond by emphasizing the different application of egalitarian requirements in different kinds of relational circumstances (e.g. domestic and global).[10] They typically argue that in the presence of particular political boundaries, the demands of equality might result from a specific interpretation of the function and purpose of shared political relations. Take, for example, an interpretation emphasizing how political institutions should guarantee citizens a fair treatment and equal access to public goods as required by the criterion of political reciprocity.[11] A statist theory of global justice may not be interested in an all-purpose comparison of the position of individuals across the world. It might limit itself to the pursuit of only those normative questions that arise from distinctive interactions determined by currently accepted forms of institutional practice.

This line of argument is very clearly linked to the nonideal perspective emphasized in the first part of our work. That perspective can easily explain why the target of global sufficientarian principles is determined by our interpretation of concerns and commitments embedded in existing institutional practices, and how the main focus rests on societies' ability to sustain decent political institutions. The statist interpretation builds on consent regarding the function and purpose of both international and domestic practices, and identifies sufficiency-based principles of justice as the best way to interpret and reform these practices. It then proceeds to argue that once the target of sufficiency is reached, egalitarian principles of global justice are no longer required.[12] But is the interpretation plausible? And are the principles it generates valid?

To answer this question, it is important to explain the difference between cosmopolitan and statist theories of justice with regard to their distinctive analysis of global political and economic practices. What facts the theorist chooses to focus upon, and how they are combined with specific first-order normative commitments are particularly relevant here. Cosmopolitans are interested in the relative comparison of the position of individuals across boundaries; their critics believe that the entitlements of individuals and the obligations owed to them are filtered by the political institutions through which they are represented.[13] For cosmopolitans, the existence of relative inequalities among individuals represents a *global* problem; for statists, the extent of inequalities across borders is irrelevant insofar as people are able to frame and preserve decent domestic institutions. Justice, the latter argue, prescribes different things at different levels, according to the features of the practice to which its principles are intended to apply. In domestic societies, egalitarian principles are justified given a particular background interpretation of the circumstances in which individual agents share the benefits and burdens of social cooperation. At the global level, those individuals are collectively represented by the states to which they belong.

It is worth considering in greater detail the different analysis of circumstances from which specific demands of justice are supposed to arise. The statist argument is based on a particular interpretation of the function and purpose of particular institutions, one that confers significant normative relevance on specific associative facts (e.g. cooperation, reciprocity, and subjection to a shared coercive order) and neglects others (e.g. practices of competitive interaction across boundaries). A particular interpretation of these facts is what seems to trigger certain (in this case: egalitarian) principles in domestic circumstances of justice but rules them out in a different context and practice. But what renders the selection of the unit of concern an authoritative one? And how do we justify the validity of this particular interpretation of the function and purpose of specific relational practices compared to an alternative, less-restricted one?

The response one is likely to obtain at this point seems to reproduce the same confusion between issues of principle and issues of agency observed in the previous chapter. The statist interpretation is grounded on an assessment of the cultural and institutional features that render certain political obligations feasible and stable in the domestic sphere and on the absence of such circumstances in the global case. However, as we already emphasized in the previous chapter, issues of political feasibility and motivational sustainability cannot limit the assessment of relevant principles of justice if there is an alternative (fundamentally appropriate) analysis of global political and economic relations. The different way in which nonideal agents operate in the domestic and in the global sphere could support an argument for diversifying the political interpretation of the reasons provided when endorsing certain principles of justice. If we ask ourselves how particular normative commitments could obtain political agency, issues of political feasibility and motivational sustainability become extremely relevant. Yet claims about principle are different from claims about how agents should act; they belong to distinct (though related) stages of activist political theory. The political practice of nonideal agents is a separate question from the attempt to reconcile first-order normative commitments with a fundamentally appropriate interpretation of certain circumstances of injustice. One does not change the value of equality by arguing for a difference in the political practice that seeks to promote it in particular political circumstances. Different circumstances will lead to different ways of endorsing specific principles of justice but they do not necessarily rule out that such principles may be the same.

The statist argument introduced above represents a typical instance of problematic, nonideal reasoning with regard to the principles required to articulate the function and purpose of particular institutions. Whilst placing exclusive weight on the state-based associative relations by virtue of which specific principles of justice become politically effective and motivationally sustainable, the account excludes other (potentially relevant) interpretations from which the necessity for alternative (and possibly more progressive) principles might emerge. At this stage of the theory, the principles of justice seem grounded on a partial account of relevant relational facts: facts concerning the circumstances in which justice is realized rather than facts concerning the circumstances in which the need for its principles might arise. For the statist argument to succeed from a fundamentally appropriate perspective, the relevance of its interpretation of particular institutional relations should be proved not only from the point of view of the circumstances in which egalitarian justice is realized but also from the point of view of the circumstances in which the need for its principles might arise. The theory should, in other words, establish that there are no circumstances of injustice at the global level such that the need for egalitarian principles might apply. Or, to put it in different words, it should illustrate (at a diagnostic level) that no global political relations could warrant a theory of global egalitarian justice. This is what the statist objections examined in the next section seek to provide.

## 4.3 CONFLICT AND THE CIRCUMSTANCES OF GLOBAL INJUSTICE

To undermine a rival interpretation of existing institutional practices that would trigger egalitarian principles with a global scope, statists might offer various arguments. One might be to deny that there may be globally relevant relations that constitute a fundamentally appropriate object of normative enquiry. Another might be to emphasize that globally relevant relations are not subject to claims of justice or, to put it slightly differently, that they do not embody 'circumstances of injustice'. Yet another objection might go even deeper and, whilst conceding that there are relevant circumstances of injustice, insist that these are not of a kind that triggers egalitarian principles. Let us examine them in turn.

The first kind of claim is perhaps the hardest to sustain. One problem that the argument poses is that it seems to defeat the purpose of discussing *global* problems altogether, be it from a statist or from a cosmopolitan perspective. Questions concerning global institutional arrangements make sense only if we accept the factual presence of these arrangements, and then go on to query their function and purpose and to defend or reject particular interpretations related to them. It is for this reason that, whilst articulating very different and competing normative principles, neither statists nor cosmopolitans deny the presence of global relations. They also agree that these relations constitute a significant object of normative enquiry.

The next question then is about our specific interpretations of these relations, what kind of agents they involve, and what kind of concerns and commitments they reflect. And here the statist objection starts becoming more sophisticated. Whilst conceding the normatively significant nature of relations between various agents in the global sphere, it is possible for a defender of the view to insist that these relations are not problematic from the point of view of *justice*. So, for example, one might agree that unregulated market interactions present a clear example of normatively relevant global relations but also emphasize how such relations are far from affecting *negatively* specific agents. In this sense, such relations do not constitute relevant circumstances of injustice. One might even side with libertarians and argue that the global extension of similar institutional (e.g. market-based) relations is far from being negatively involved in the production of global injustice and might instead be beneficial to the global poor: it contributes to the liberalization of specific forms of life, promotes a certain wealthy individualism in hierarchical societies, and enhances the values of toleration by bringing non-liberal states culturally closer to liberal ones.[14]

Finally, consider a further development of this argument. A statist might concede that there are normatively significant global relations, and he might even concede that these normatively significant global relations present a problem of justice. He might however insist that the most appropriate interpretation of this problem is simply not one that seeks to arrive at principles of an egalitarian kind. One might instead come up with alternative (e.g. sufficientarian) principles of assistance to burdened societies, and insist that those principles are better able to reflect the function and purpose of current international practices.

This last and more sophisticated version of the argument is also the one most commonly found in the literature. Yet it appears to have been inadequately opposed. Part of the explanation for such inadequacy seems methodological. Cosmopolitans have largely failed to place their counterarguments at a fundamentally appropriate methodological level: they have been unable to reconcile their commitment to certain first-order normative principles (e.g. the moral equality of all human beings) with an adequate interpretation of the causal and normative claims relevant to justify global egalitarian principles. On the one hand, as we saw in the previous chapter, they have placed too much weight on the persuasive force of such first-order normative commitments, hoping that they would suffice to convince the sceptic about the need to remedy global relative inequality. But moral equality, these sceptics argue, is not sufficient to generate equality of relative shares between individuals; alternative interpretations reflecting those values can still be plausibly advanced. So when cosmopolitan approaches rely too much on ideal assumptions similar to the ones we examined in the first part of this work, they end up appearing to their objectors either incomplete (at best) or irrelevant (at worst).

On the other hand, when the statist objections are addressed at a more specific level, trying to link first-order normative commitments (e.g. a commitment to the moral equality of all human beings) to a cosmopolitan interpretation of global relations of injustice, far too much is conceded to the statist, nonideal approach. The reason is that existing cosmopolitan accounts, like their statist adversaries, remain too focused on the consequences of global poverty rather than addressing the injustice of its causes, as well as the causal links between absolute deprivation and relative deprivation. The evidence provided on the existence and pervasiveness of global relations of injustice often relies on a series of empirical facts concerning how many children starve every hour around the globe, how little effort it would take to cure devastating diseases in the Third World, the catastrophic impact of environmental destruction, and so on.[15] But shocking as they may be, these facts will hardly move the entrenched statist. Simply registering the moral abomination of severe material poverty around the world and the contribution of affluent citizens to global relations of absolute deprivation does not prove that the state-centred justification of *egalitarian* principles and the theory of justice constructed around it are wrong. What it proves is that every individual in the world has certain important obligations to avoid contributing to absolute poverty as far as is in his power, yet such obligations need not be of a kind that requires more than sufficientarian principles of assistance to burdened societies. Even though a cosmopolitan account focusing, for example, on the contribution of citizens in affluent countries to perpetuating an unjust global order relies on some causal and normative claims necessary to an appropriately fundamental account of global justice, its exclusive focus on absolute deprivation leads to a very minimal set of commitments. The kinds of sufficientarian principles of global justice that a similar account seeks to justify are often identical (and sometimes even less demanding) when compared to those advocated by statists.[16]

To justify egalitarian principles committed to the reduction of relative (in addition to absolute) deprivation, our account of the circumstances of injustice needs to rely on a different combination of causal claims and first-order normative commitments. The set of objections we considered at the end of the previous section denied that egalitarian principles apply at the global level. And this, we observed, is not because we lack institutions capable of enforcing the claims of justice at the level of agency, but because there are no *global* circumstances of injustice warranting principles of an *egalitarian* kind. To argue the case, statists need not deny the presence of a global order, including political agents and institutions that go beyond domestic ones. They might limit themselves to showing that the kind of conflict relevant to trigger a demand for global egalitarian principles is absent from the analysis of global institutions, that insofar as the current global order may be ascribed any impact on the emergence of global relative deprivation, it will be that of historically contributing to its improvement, not deterioration.[17] Thus, statists might insist that the reduction of inequalities around the world is not subject to claims of egalitarian justice (at the global level) because of the absence of relevant relational circumstances of injustice which are both globally extended and irreducible to domestic factors. A fundamentally appropriate account of global justice should be able to answer this objection.

## 4.4 A FUNDAMENTALLY APPROPRIATE ANALYSIS

What do we need to reject the statist objections mentioned above? To prove that there are relevant relational claims of justice – and not simply humanity – we must show that there are relevant circumstances of *injustice*. Call this 'the test of circumstances'. To prove that the kind of principles to which the claims of justice lead are principles of an *egalitarian* kind, we need to show that what makes those circumstances unjust is the way in which goods are produced and distributed under conditions of scarcity and competitive interaction. Call this 'the test of principles'. To prove that this unjust pattern of production and distribution is globally extended, we must be able to show that the kind of injustice we observe is irreducible to the contribution of single agents (be they individuals, associations, or states), and results from their complex interaction in a *global* environment. Call this 'the test of global pervasiveness'.

In the next chapter, I will consider these issues together. I will try to show how in order to respond to the statist challenge we must establish a normatively fundamental link between agents' absolute deprivation and their relative position, globally considered. It is possible to illustrate the globally pervasive and equality-triggering nature of this link by analysing how in specific circumstances of injustice access to certain kinds of goods by a particular agent or plurality of agents modifies the relative standing of others. Cosmopolitans will be able to construct a strong case in favour of global egalitarian principles if they manage to offer diagnostic accounts of absolute and relative deprivation as causally related by virtue of the nature of global interactions. This relationship can in turn be illustrated by insisting on the relevance of a particular category of global goods (positional goods), the absolute value of which depends on the relative standing of their possessors compared to each other.[18] If we can identify relevant *global* positional goods, access to which cannot be guaranteed by sufficientarian principles of assistance but requires a kind of distribution that aims to reduce inequalities between agents worldwide, we will have responded to the statist objection considered above. Emphasizing the unequal distribution of positional goods at the global level and its implications for absolute deprivation will strengthen the justification of egalitarian requirements.

This is all very rough and will be outlined in more detail in the next chapter. But consider how an approach similar to the one just sketched might be able to pass the three tests mentioned above: circumstances, principles, and global pervasiveness. Firstly, the circumstances of injustice would be defined as the conditions under which certain processes of production and distribution determine unequal access to specific (and globally relevant) positional goods. Secondly, the principles required to resolve this conflict would need to be principles of an egalitarian kind since an agent could only be made better off by reducing inequalities of access to positional goods in comparison with others. Thirdly, access to *global* positional goods does not depend merely on internal domestic factors: however much a globally situated agent does to advance its domestic prospects, it remains vulnerable to improvement in the relative position of others. This means that any attempt to introduce regulations and enforce the territorial control of single political agents is insufficient to subvert a process that is structurally dependent on the activity of others.

What cosmopolitanism needs to reject the statist objections examined above is to establish a normatively fundamental link between absolute deprivation and relative deprivation supported by an appropriate diagnostic account that emphasizes the causal nature of their link. A similar analysis of the background circumstances under which global political interactions occur would lead to an improved way of justifying the global scope of egalitarian principles. Statist theories consider the issue of absolute material deprivation and extreme poverty simply as an unfortunate exception in the otherwise well-ordered global society of states, not as the product of a systematic failure to assess from the point of view of justice the conditions of production and distribution of specific goods, and their impact on the relative position of individuals across the world. In response to their arguments, cosmopolitans have failed to place their analysis of global poverty in an appropriately fundamental framework of enquiry, a framework which does not merely condemn the facts of global poverty but gets to the heart of its causes from a perspective relevant to the justification of global equality. Their present line of argument, as I tried to show, is not enough to counter the statist objections examined, and to produce a sufficiently distinctive alternative proposal.

Analysing the issue of the principles of global justice from a fundamentally appropriate point of view requires focusing on global circumstances of injustice and explaining how they generate *egalitarian* claims. An interpretation of the function and purpose of existent institutions which does not merely rely on the facts of poverty but is also able to investigate the moral and empirical nature of its causes offers the sort of relational analysis of global injustice upon which the cosmopolitan demand of a *particular* kind of global justice principle (e.g. egalitarian) can be grounded. In other words, the sort of justification outlined above provides a plausible account of the relevant circumstances in which egalitarian requirements might apply and of the reasons supporting the emergence of such requirements.

## 4.5 ON NORMATIVELY FUNDAMENTAL AND CAUSALLY FUNDAMENTAL PRINCIPLES

One might object at this point that the mere fact that the alternative account of global justice I have introduced above is sensitive to the causal link between absolute deprivation and relative deprivation (and between poverty and inequality) does not suffice to also illustrate the normatively fundamental relevance of its principles. A principle that appears to be causally fundamental, one might argue, is not necessarily also normatively fundamental. Simply because a particular diagnosis of specific problematic facts (e.g. the cosmopolitan analysis of global circumstances of injustice) has causal and explanatory priority with respect to its effects does not by itself illustrate that the principles derived from this factual diagnosis should also have normative priority. So even if a cosmopolitan interpretation of global relational circumstances similar to the one outlined above is able to show that relative deprivation is causally responsible for the emergence of absolute deprivation, this does not prove that principles seeking to reduce relative deprivation (e.g. principles of an egalitarian kind) are normatively fundamental. Their weight and plausibility still rely (from a normative perspective) on the weight and plausibility of alternative normative considerations, for example, considerations related to the morally problematic nature of absolute deprivation and the importance for individuals of avoiding falling below a threshold of sufficiency.

Hence, continues the objector, even if the cosmopolitan account introduced here is able to illustrate the causal relevance of its premises, its principles may not be normatively fundamental. For such cosmopolitan principles to also emerge as normatively fundamental, the critique of absolute deprivation should inherit its force from the critique of relative deprivation. Our concern for equality should ground our concern for poverty rather than the other way round. Simply put, the causal priority of an egalitarian interpretation of the circumstances of justice may not necessarily prove the normative priority of global egalitarian principles.

To see the force of this objection, consider the example that one prominent author provides to illustrate the relevance of the distinction between causal and normative fundamentals: the case of highway robbery.[19] Suppose, this author argues, that whoever is in a position to do so distributes guns to some people but not to others, and that possession of guns enables those who have them to engage in highway robbery. Suppose also that due to mutual deterrence, an equal distribution of guns would have produced no highway robbery, and suppose further that the only relevant use of guns is to commit or deter highway robbery.[20] Even though both the unequal distribution of guns and the existence of highway robbery seem to be unjust, they are unjust in different ways and for different reasons. The unequal distribution of guns is unjust because it tends to produce highway robbery. Highway robbery is unjust because it constitutes a transfer of money for the *wrong* reason (e.g. for fear that the victim will be killed unless such transfer takes place).[21]

Notice the difference to which the example points. Whilst being *causally fundamental* in explaining the occurrence and frequency of a particular unjust transfer, the unequal distribution of guns is not *normatively fundamental*. Its injustice is inherited from the *causal* contribution it makes to the proliferation of highway robbery, and resides in its impact upon the establishment of an intrinsically unjust state of affairs. The existence of highway robbery is causally secondary: it owes its existence to the effects of something else, namely the unequal distribution of guns across the relevant population. However, it seems to be normatively fundamental: highway robbery is unjust for what it is, not because it inherits its injustice from a different state of affairs. It is therefore easy to see that a principle might be causally fundamental without thereby having normative priority and also (vice versa) that a principle might be normatively fundamental even if it does not have causal priority.

There might seem to be an analogy between this example and my reflections on the relevance of the causal link between absolute and relative deprivation for a fundamentally appropriate theory of global justice. One might argue, for example, that even though the absence of egalitarian requirements is causally fundamental for the emergence of absolute deprivation, egalitarian principles might still remain normatively secondary. In other words, one might object that the circumstances in which egalitarian principles of justice are required are far from being normatively fundamental; their injustice is not intrinsic but seems inherited from a normatively fundamental assessment of the injustice inherent in the prevalence of absolute deprivation.

This objection has important consequences for the kind of argument I have presented in this chapter. At a first level, it seems that even though the egalitarian principles to which cosmopolitans aspire might be justified by virtue of their causal contribution to the satisfaction of sufficientarian requirements, the normatively fundamental assessment remains focused on absolute deprivation. This, one might argue, is precisely where statists ordinarily start. Moreover, it might seem that the attempt to provide a theory of global justice by placing its principles at the fundamentally appropriate level of analysis can only be considered successful if one remains undecided between the two meanings of 'fundamental' illustrated above. Once we clarify that causal fundamentals may not necessarily display intrinsic validity but inherit this validity from normative fundamentals, there might be no clear advantage to a theory that places so much emphasis on establishing causal priorities.

It is important to clear away these objections before proceeding to present, with the next chapter, a more detailed account of the causal relation between absolute and relative deprivation and its implications for the defence of global egalitarianism offered in the rest of this work. First of all, notice that these objections apply to an attempt to isolate one normatively fundamental *principle* of justice amongst various candidates but not to the attempt to identify a fundamentally appropriate *account* of global justice pursued in an activist mode. A fundamentally appropriate account, recall, is one that generates principles seeking to combine (in a way that is superior to its adversaries) first-order normative commitments and relevant causal claims in the light of a particular diagnostic analysis of the circumstances of injustice. Causal claims are particularly important in the context of activist political theory, that is, a theory that is interested not merely in identifying normatively fundamental principles but also in combining them with an interpretation of the function and purpose of existent institutions able to guide political transformation in the real world. Without any awareness of causally fundamental principles, a similar attempt to guide action in the normatively relevant ways would simply be condemned to fail.

If we are interested not merely in identifying the normatively fundamental injustice that has occurred (e.g. a wrongful transfer of resources) but also in changing the world in a way that removes this injustice, we will need a theory that is able to incorporate both normative and causal fundamental claims at the right level of analysis. Each of these claims will generate related remedial principles, principles that may be normatively relevant or causally relevant, depending on the particular set of background assumptions upon which they rely. But it is important to insist that an action-guiding theory of justice, as a whole, will need both kinds of principles and in equal measure. Knowledge of where the fundamental injustice resides, and of related normative principles, would not be sufficient to generate guidelines for action able to remove that injustice. Without a critique of the causes and an analysis of causally relevant remedial principles, the critique of consequences would fail to be sufficiently informative and sufficiently determinate to orient an effective change. To take a slightly different example, this time from the sphere of health, a doctor who is interested not merely in research into the symptoms of a particular disease but also in curing that disease will need to both investigate its symptoms *and* produce an analysis of its causes. Without the former one would not know what the disease consists of, and without the latter one would not know how to go about trying to treat it.

In this sense, there is a clear difference between the statist approach and the cosmopolitan one I have tried to justify. Whilst a statist might well pay attention to the importance of principles relieving absolute deprivation, he seems to ignore the causal link between absolute and relative deprivation. This in turn leads to an impoverished account of the circumstances of injustice, where the role of relevant political relations going beyond domestic ones is typically ignored and where remedial action trying to put an end to this unjust state of affairs ends up being misguided. On the other hand, a cosmopolitan theory developed according to premises similar to the ones I have outlined above avoids some of these pitfalls. Moreover, it does so in a framework that appears superior to the statist alternative in all three dimensions necessary to consider a theory more progressive than its rivals: in its diagnostic capacity, innovation potential, and heuristic role.[22]

Firstly, by combining causal and normative fundamentals at the appropriate level of analysis, it provides a diagnosis of particular circumstances of injustice which takes into account distributive conflicts typically ignored by the statist approach. Secondly, in trying to interpret such conflicts, the cosmopolitan account contains innovating potential: it promises to deliver principles that preserve all the normative benefits of statist rivals (e.g. commitment to absolute deprivation) whilst avoiding their failures (neglect of relative deprivation at a global level). Finally (and this is something on which more will be said in the last two chapters), it is able to combine these first-order principles with conceptual categories already available, displaying predictive capacity and paving the way for new reforms of existing institutions.

One final clarification follows. In the previous pages, I have conceded to statist accounts the claim that absolute deprivation is what matters at a normatively fundamental level, and that relative deprivation matters at the causally fundamental level. It is important to emphasize that I have done so *for the sake of the argument*. Endorsing what a rival theory already takes for granted in order to consider its implications for an alternative (more progressive) interpretation of its normative aspirations is compatible with the dialectical method outlined in the previous chapter. However, this does not necessarily commit us to the claim that absolute deprivation really *is* what matters intrinsically and that all other distributive principles are valuable insofar as they contribute to a sufficientarian theory of justice. We can afford to remain neutral with respect to this question. It may well be that we only care about relative deprivation because we are interested in absolute deprivation. But it may be that we discover that absolute deprivation is also not intrinsically important, that some other value, say the capacity for moral agency, or the value of humanity as an end in itself, is even more fundamental. Insisting that in particular circumstances of justice egalitarian principles are causally relevant to a full endorsement of sufficientarian ones does not imply granting that sufficiency is what matters intrinsically and equality is not. All that is required for purposes of my argument is to ascertain that, given certain global circumstances of injustice, those who are committed to global sufficientarian principles are also committed to global egalitarian principles, and that an account that succeeds in justifying the links between the two is more fundamentally appropriate than one that ignores the nature of these links.

This also does not imply that we have shown that equality *is* the more fundamental value, although, again, this cannot be ruled out. The argument I have presented does not assert that equality *is* what matters in itself; it simply says that given certain first-order commitments in the two rival approaches relevant to this work, and given a particular interpretation of the circumstances of injustice, a theory establishing the causal links between egalitarian requirements and sufficientarian ones has more chances of providing a progressive interpretation of the function and purpose of existing institutions compared to its rival accounts. This seems all the more important when the nature of the normative enterprise is such that it is directed not merely to the identification of certain true and intrinsically relevant normative commitments but also to an interpretation of these commitments that can hope to change, rather than simply interpret, the world.

## 4.6 CONCLUSION

Ideal and nonideal each have their place in political theory. A dialectical approach that illustrates the way in which insights from both can be combined is crucial when pursuing political theory in an activist mode. When investigating the role of states, we are more oriented towards nonideal assumptions (raising the question of what kind of agents and political arrangements are necessary and available to render politically effective the claims of justice) rather than towards ideal assumptions (asking whether states are necessary at all or whether they limit the scope of justice). On the other hand, when we investigate the nature of the principles necessary to guide political reform we ought not to be limited by nonideal considerations. Criticizing the process leading to the emergence of global poverty rather than simply reflecting on its outcomes is helpful to introduce an alternative interpretation of the function and purpose of existing institutions where both the circumstances of particular global injustices and the claims they generate are duly taken into account.

Clarifying the way in which ideal and nonideal considerations affect some controversial issues at the heart of the global justice debate is very important for constructing an account of global justice that places all its features at the fundamentally appropriate level of analysis. Both this chapter and the previous one tried to show that the main contending theories of global justice (statism and cosmopolitanism) have so far been ideal and nonideal in the wrong places, failing to suitably integrate both stages in a coherent theory of global justice. As I have tried to show, a fundamentally appropriate assessment of global circumstances of justice should be able to identify the reasons why we are interested in global distributive equality, and to construct relevant links between the facts of global poverty and the normative implications of the analysis of its causes. On the other hand, insisting on the special relevance of state-based associative relations is essential for making collective agency politically effective and motivationally sustainable in the real world.

Once this much is clarified, the controversy between statists and cosmopolitans is dissolved in the dialectical construction of a global theory of justice accommodating concerns from both: the defence of egalitarianism as a matter of principle and the role of existing political relations as a matter of agency. My discussion of how global egalitarian principles are related to the analysis of absolute deprivation and of how nonideal agents should operate to make those principles politically effective and motivationally stable might have appeared very succinct. The aim of this second part of the book has been to illustrate the use of ideal and nonideal assumptions in several discussions on global justice, and to prepare the ground for an alternative interpretation, to which I shall now turn.

# Part III

# Statist Cosmopolitanism

# 5

## On Principles

### 5.1 AN ALTERNATIVE ANALYSIS

This part of the book develops a dialectical approach to the analysis of global justice. It illustrates in what way it is possible to combine the principles of global justice identified at the fundamentally appropriate level with an account of political agency able to guide political transformation in the real world. More specifically, the present chapter takes one step forward the discussion initiated in the last one, and examines in greater detail the nature of the link between absolute and relative deprivation in global circumstances of injustice. It then invokes this link to justify global egalitarian principles, and to illustrate how an account of global justice incorporating similar principles provides a more plausible interpretation of the function and purpose of global institutional practices compared to statist rivals. The task of explaining how this interpretation both responds to already existing concerns of particular political agents *and* orients current expressions of political agency to initiate political transformation belongs to the remaining chapters.

To understand the distinction between egalitarian and sufficientarian principles and the implications of its use in the global justice debate, let us start with a real-world example. On Friday, 2 November 2007, Adonis Musati, a former police officer from the region of Chimanimani in eastern Zimbabwe, starved to death in Cape Town while queuing at the offices of South Africa's home affairs refugee centre.[1] Fellow Zimbabweans told the BBC news service that Adonis had crossed into South Africa to escape the economic crisis in Zimbabwe and was trying to obtain a temporary work permit in Cape Town. He was reported to have spent two weeks sleeping in a cardboard box, with nothing to eat, while repeatedly enquiring at the refugee centre about the fate of his work permit. Adonis' death was discovered by his twin brother Adbell by reading news on the internet. Neither the Zimbabwean consulate nor the South African government appears to have informed the family about the event.

Pretty much everyone agrees that letting people starve to death is bad. The controversy arises on how to make sure that similar events do not reoccur. Adonis' case is striking in many ways but this chapter explores only two crucial issues it raises. The first involves the distinction between absolute and relative deprivation and the conceptions of justice related to each of them. In the example above, absolute deprivation ultimately leads to starvation. Remedying it requires giving agents *enough* to have basic subsistence claims satisfied. We have called this the sufficientarian conception of justice.

The above case also presents an instance of relative deprivation. Adonis has been denied a relative share in the distribution of social goods enjoyed by citizens of South Africa; he has been denied an equal opportunity to work in Cape Town. Remedying relative deprivation requires distributing to agents in the relevant position a relatively equal share compared to that presently enjoyed by others. We have called this the egalitarian conception of justice.

The second issue this chapter raises is how to understand these distinctions within an appropriately fundamental normative analysis. The question concerns the relative merits of incorporating each (if either) of those conceptions of justice in an attempt to plausibly interpret the function and purpose of global institutional practices. On many cosmopolitan accounts, Adonis may legitimately claim equal access to a relative share of the social opportunities provided to the citizens or legal residents of Cape Town. On the statist interpretation, Adonis may be legitimately denied a relatively equal share of them. For many cosmopolitans, the relevant conception of justice to adopt when interpreting the function and purpose of global institutional relations is egalitarian. For most statists, the relevant conception of justice to adopt when reflecting on that very same issue is sufficientarian.

As we have seen in previous chapters, both the cosmopolitan and the statist interpretations have been subjected to significant criticism. At the level of principle, cosmopolitans are often criticized for failing to explain why citizens ought to give strangers more than enough. Statists are criticized for failing to explain why (all other things being equal) strangers ought to receive from citizens less than relatively equal shares. Having examined their controversy with a view to methodological concerns, this chapter advances some more substantive considerations supporting the justification of global egalitarianism. It does so by analysing global circumstances of injustice from a perspective that avoids the confusion between ideal and nonideal which we have seen affecting many versions of both statism and cosmopolitanism. Indeed, the alternative analysis offered here does not start with arguments on the moral arbitrariness of one's place of birth. At this point, it also avoids queries into how the world's political institutions would look if they were redesigned from scratch. Its defence of global egalitarianism is advanced from a position which takes for granted what rival theories are already committed to: the moral equality of all human beings and the defence of sufficientarian principles with global scope.

Compatibly with the dialectical methodology examined in previous chapters, our interpretation of global circumstances of injustice starts with an analysis of global conflicts, and examines the normative resources available to statist accounts when producing a diagnostic analysis of these conflicts. The study of normative and causal claims within a framework interested in the relationship between absolute and relative deprivation serves to ascertain the limits of statism in this respect. Once these limits are established, we are able to provide further support for a view which seems to avoid the normative shortcomings of its rivals but integrates their plausible first-order commitments in an alternative and more progressive framework. To further specify, by showing how, in current circumstances of injustice, the relief of absolute deprivation is causally linked to the relief of relative deprivation, an egalitarian interpretation of the function and purpose of global institutional practices emerges as the most appropriate account for guiding political transformation.

## 5.2 PRELIMINARY CLARIFICATIONS

What equality substantively requires at the global level depends on the aspects of relative deprivation that matter globally. The kinds of conflicts that are considered particularly relevant for purposes of this enquiry are conflicts concerning access to global positional goods. Positional goods have often been defined as goods the absolute value of which is determined by their relative possession.[2] They are comparative-relational. How much of a positional good an agent absolutely enjoys depends on how one fares compared to others. In the case of competition for access to positional goods, absolute and relative deprivation appear causally related. It is precisely that relation which opens up the space for our global egalitarian interpretation.

There are many kinds of positional goods with regard to which global conflicts arise, demanding an investigation of the causal relations between absolute deprivation and relative deprivation (globally speaking). Obvious examples are the impact of inequalities in access to the means of production and exchange in the international labour market, inequalities of purchasing power, inequalities of access to education, or inequalities of access to legal resources in the case of international litigation. There are also instances of other goods typically considered to have non-competitive value but which may, upon more careful scrutiny, show some latent positional aspect.[3] However, I shall not focus on these cases here. Instead, I shall draw attention to only one kind of positional good, reflection on which suffices to challenge even those who are willing to see global institutional relations from a strictly statist (rather than individual) perspective. The positional good I am mostly going to focus upon is the distribution of power between states.

In global circumstances of justice, power represents a positional good. One of the features of current global institutional relations, as we know them, is that agents compete in market structures in the absence of a hegemonic centre. As we shall see below, states can interact fairly and avoid being manipulated or made worse-off by others if these market interactions are unaffected by inequalities of access to power. When power plays the role of a positional good, it can be considered sufficient only when opportunities to access it do not favour some agents at the expense of others. The power of an agent may increase or decrease according to the relative position of others. In similar instances, principles of an egalitarian, rather than of a sufficientarian, kind are required.

The relevance of egalitarian principles tackling power inequalities between agents placed in the relevant position can be seen with reference to an analogy between positional goods that individuals in specific circumstances of justice need in relatively equal amounts, and the kind of positional goods states might need in global circumstances of justice. The argument of this chapter is that just as reducing inequalities of access to certain positional goods is necessary for individuals to prevent severe deprivation, a similar reduction in inequalities of power is needed in the international sphere.

Notice that claiming that the unequal distribution of power between states is responsible for important aspects of relative and absolute deprivation (both at the level of individuals and at the level of states representing them) is not the same as saying that the distribution of power is the *only* aspect of deprivation that globally matters. Convincing the sceptic about the existence of global goods with positional aspect, and offering an analysis of state power as a relevant case in point, are not intended to exhaust the causal analysis of the link between absolute and relative deprivation from a global perspective. Instead, the hope is that once that sceptic has conceded the coherence of the premises and the credibility of the conclusion that follows from them, it might be easier to extend our analysis to other empirically plausible and causally relevant cases. We might then be able to show that there are more goods with a global positional aspect than one might have initially imagined and that paying attention to the relative inequalities reflected in their access and their impact on absolute deprivation strengthens the global egalitarian case.

The converse point also applies. Some cosmopolitans might not be persuaded by the focus on state power and by the causal analysis deployed to show how state-based power inequalities are linked to the absolute deprivation of many individuals around the world. They might dispute the empirical evidence. Or they might have an alternative story to tell about the emergence of global poverty and its relationship to global inequality. They might focus, for example, on market, rather than state-mediated, interactions, and point to the relevance of unequal access to the means of production and exchange for the emergence of absolute deprivation.[4] So long as they can construct a plausible account of the causal links between absolute and relative deprivation (and my focus on positional goods is only one way of illustrating those links), their justification of global egalitarianism will be equally successful (and equally progressive). My claims about the need to reduce inequalities of power between states provide a complement rather than direct challenge to these alternative cosmopolitan approaches. They are offered as the simplest and most direct way of challenging the global justice sceptic. Even if we start with a state-focused interpretation of the function and purpose of global institutional practices, and even if we take sufficientarian principles as central to the normative critique of these particular practices, the case *against* a global egalitarian theory will remain without strong justification.[5]

The central argument made in the following pages is that in specific circumstances of injustice, the claim for sufficiency at the level of individuals triggers a claim for distributive equality (at least) at the level of states. This conclusion is reached, firstly, by emphasizing how there is a special category of goods, positional goods, with regard to which equality and sufficiency cannot be kept apart. Secondly, it is reached by showing how in global circumstances of justice, state power represents one example of a relevant positional good, access to which is in need of being proportionally equalized. But notice that neither of these claims necessarily commits us to endorsing *strict* equality as the *only* ideal of justice. One may claim that the possession of certain goods by relevant agents should be rendered as equal as possible along some dimension specified. This is a strong equalisandum claim, with regard to which I argue that in circumstances of global injustice one example of relevant agents is states and one kind of positional good in need of being proportionally distributed is power. But where to draw the line on how much inequality to reduce so as to guarantee fair access to global positional goods is a question that might need to be weighed against other competing considerations. In this sense, the demand for reducing inequalities of power between states can be defended compatibly with limitations imposed by other important values. In the case of global justice, one such limitation may arise from the requirement that the exercise of power be legitimate, by which I mean not simply that the state is formally authorized to act in the name of its citizens but that it also stands up to critical scrutiny in fulfilling this task. This is a weak equalisandum claim that I also endorse in the chapter.[6]

Notice also two further issues. Within egalitarianism, it is common to draw a distinction between intrinsic and instrumental versions of the account. An intrinsic egalitarian believes that inequality is bad in itself. An instrumental egalitarian believes that inequality is bad when it produces detrimental consequences. I concluded the previous chapter by commenting on the relevance of a similar distinction for an account of global justice pursued in activist mode. In what follows, I shall therefore not dwell on that distinction. Suffice it to underline that statists who are usually keen to emphasize that sufficien-tarianism alone has global scope should also embrace at least an instrumen-tal version of global egalitarianism. Insofar as very few statist interpretations currently available are prepared to incorporate this claim into their norma-tive critique of current global institutional practices, this is not a trivial claim.[7]

Within sufficientarian views, it is possible to distinguish between pure and mixed sufficientarianism. A pure sufficientarian thinks that only sufficiency matters and that equality does not. A mixed sufficientarian thinks that equality also matters when it improves the conditions of the absolutely worse-off. Mixed sufficientarianism is not so far away from instrumental egalitarianism. However, most statists have endorsed mixed sufficientarianism at home and pure sufficientarianism abroad. More specifically, they have argued that equality of relative shares matters in domestic societies but not in the global sphere. As Michael Blake puts it, '*only* the relationship of common citizenship is a relationship potentially justifiable through a concern for equality in distributive shares'.[8] Or as Thomas Nagel emphasizes, 'egalitarian justice is a requirement on the internal political, economic, and social structure of nation-states and cannot be extrapolated to different contexts, which require different standards. [W]hatever standards of equal rights or equal opportunity apply domestically, the question is whether consistency requires that they also apply globally.'[9]

Statists deny that this is the case. Cosmopolitans insist that where domestic and global circumstances of injustice are similar, egalitarian principles ought to apply consistently to both. This has led to a number of controversies on the domestic–international analogy that it is possible to avoid by simply asking a different question, a question that does not involve taking a stand on the inference from domestic equality to global equality. This chapter proceeds in a different way. Instead of defending the argument that if equality is justified domestically, it should also be justified globally, it shows that if sufficiency is justified globally, equality cannot be domestically restricted. To put it in different words, the kind of pure sufficientarianism endorsed by statists in the global sphere is indefensible. Statists can hardly deny that at least one variation of egalitarianism (instrumental egalitarianism) has global scope.

## 5.3 ABSOLUTE AND RELATIVE DEPRIVATION

Let us consider first the definitions of absolute and relative deprivation and the differences between them. One way to clarify such differences is by reference to those basic material goods that allow agents to pursue a functioning moral life wherever they are. An instance of absolute deprivation is nicely summarized by Pirate Jenny in Bertold Brecht's second finale to *The Threepenny Opera* when she claims: 'Now all you gentlemen who wish to lead us / Who teach us to desist from mortal sin / Your prior obligation is to feed us / When we've had lunch your preaching can begin.'[10] Jenny's comment that 'Erst kommt das Fressen, dann kommt die Moral'[11] suggests that in order to be able to exercise moral agency, people must, at least, be given a chance to survive. Absolute deprivation usually refers to an impediment in the satisfaction of certain basic claims – such as meeting nutritional requirements, sleeping, or being in minimally good health – without providing for which an agent could not function.

Claims for the relief of absolute deprivation arise from natural vulnerabilities that may be easily distinguished from subjective preferences, social requirements, and arbitrary desires to any good whatsoever. For example, the demands for calories, shelter, and minimal healthcare constitute claims to the fulfilment of basic requirements upon which every individual has a legitimate claim in order to lead a minimally adequate life.[12] As such, claims for the relief of absolute deprivation are non-comparative. A claim is non-comparative when it suffices to determine what is due to the claimant without concern for any other relational fact. By relational facts I mean facts regarding the position of other agents vis-à-vis the claimant.[13] To know whether someone has been absolutely deprived of access to basic necessities we do not need to consider whether others have also been deprived of the same. We assess the situation on its own merit according to an objectively valid criterion of well-being that we employ in order to make moral judgements.[14]

The non-comparative nature of basic subsistence claims introduces us to the differences between absolute and relative deprivation. Like absolute deprivation, relative deprivation arises from a failure to access certain goods. In the case of relative deprivation, the goods in question are comparative and relational. One's reasons for advancing a claim to them are linked to the way in which other agents presently enjoy such goods. They may, for example, depend on the existence of particular political and economic institutions, on what other agents possess, and on how they interact in these institutional circumstances. But what exactly do we mean by 'relative' deprivation?

'Relative' deprivation may have two different meanings. In the first one, 'relative' indicates the relativity of a desired specific good. One example of a relative desired good might be what Adam Smith defined as commodities that 'the custom of the country renders it indecent for creditable people, even in the lowest order, to be without'. One of Smith's examples clearly introduces the difference between relative and absolute deprivation as far as specific goods are concerned. A linen shirt, he argues, is, 'strictly speaking', 'not a necessary of life'. In ancient Greece or Rome (and perhaps still in certain tribal societies), people used no linen shirts, and the lack of one would not have constituted an instance of deprivation at all. Yet he emphasizes, 'in the present times, through the greater part of Europe, a creditable day-labourer would be ashamed to appear in public without a linen shirt'.[15] Here, being deprived of those goods would place one in a disadvantageous position vis-à-vis the rest of society. One's relative deprivation is determined by the lack of access to a share of specific social goods enjoyed by the rest of the group. But one's being deprived of those goods is relative: certainly it would be absurd to assume that one cannot survive without linen shirts or that everyone in the world is entitled to an equal share of them independently of where they live.

The second, more important, way of understanding 'relative' in 'relative deprivation' may indicate the relativity of the means through which a desired good is acquired. In competitive environments, political power, trade opportunities, educational resources, employment availability, returns for exchanging what one owns, and access to legal opportunities are means that determine an agent's ability to access specific goods. An agent's need for such means arises not simply because of what he does taken individually but also because of how other agents relate to one another given particular institutional circumstances. In a market economy, for example, where the improved conditions of life of one group of people determine an increased demand for some particular good and a consequent rise in its price, access to such good will be precluded to those whose wages are not regulated to match market fluctuations.[16] The agent suffering from a reduction of his purchasing power will therefore be deprived of the means through which this particular good could be acquired. Yet this deprivation is only relative. It would not arise in a planned economy where, say, prices are determined by the state or in a subsistence economy where people consume what they find in nature. Nor would it arise independently of how other agents act within a particular institutional framework. I will return to this point when assessing what kind of means allows us to conceptualize relative deprivation in a global world.

In the most general terms, relative deprivation has been defined as a condition determined by the lack of access by some to a relative share enjoyed by others. The satisfaction of claims for the relief of relative deprivation depends on the relation that the claimant entertains with other agents and on the circumstances in which they interact. If everyone else in a particular society enjoys certain benefits, the claimant would be disadvantaged by being arbitrarily deprived of a relative share of such benefits. Contrary to the non-comparative claims corresponding to absolute deprivation, claims arising from relative deprivation are comparative. Such claims refer to an impediment of a member of a certain group to access goods and opportunities shared by the rest of it.

## 5.4 EGALITARIAN AND SUFFICIENTARIAN JUSTICE

Absolute and relative deprivation are often thought to involve two different conceptions of justice, conducive to different kinds of principles. Remedying absolute deprivation leads to a conception of justice that we have called sufficientarian. Sufficientarian justice requires guaranteeing the satisfaction of justified claims for the relief of absolute deprivation. Its principles seem non-comparative in form: in order to decide how much is enough to save a hungry man from starvation we do not need to consider the position of other agents, for example, how much food other people consume in the same time. The alleviation of absolute deprivation requires providing agents with 'enough' as is necessary for them to function. However, it does not require comparing their claims with those of others.

On the other hand, remedial principles for relative deprivation lead to a more complex conception of justice: egalitarian justice. Plato defined it as that 'which distributes to each what is proper according to this principle of [rational] proportions' and called it 'political justice'.[17] In Aristotle, egalitarian justice is 'that which is shown in the distribution of honour and money or such other assets as they are divisible among members of a community'.[18] The idea of agents related to each other in the modes of accessing or enjoying certain goods is analytically contained in the claim for a proportional distribution of relative shares. In order to know *how much* to distribute of *what*, we must have some idea of *who* are the relevant parties concerned as well as *where* a specific distribution ought to occur. I shall return to this issue when examining what egalitarian justice requires in a global world. For now, notice the different form that claims for the relief of relative deprivation take. If agent A lacks O, and A's modes of accession or enjoyment of O partly depend on another agent's (call it B) modes of accession or enjoyment of O, then we will need to settle a way for regulating access to O. We shall do so by having recourse to some criteria for the distribution of benefits and burdens between A and B, and taking into account the claims of each. Thus, egalitarian justice is comparative in form.

How do egalitarian justice and sufficientarian justice relate to each other? Sufficientarian justice is a matter of having 'enough', whereas egalitarian justice is a matter of having 'as much as'.[19] Being absolutely deprived is a matter of poverty. Being relatively deprived is a matter of inequality. Sufficientarian justice and egalitarian justice may therefore be analysed independently from each other. They generate different kinds of principles: non-comparative principles in the first case and comparative principles in the second one. The logical independence of these principles has induced some to think that they must also be independent in scope: sufficientarian justice is global, whereas egalitarian justice is not.[20] It is precisely this view that I now wish to challenge.

Let us examine first the reciprocal relations between sufficientarian justice and egalitarian justice. Consider the following. One typical case of absolute deprivation is the lack of food leading to starvation. One typical case of relative deprivation is the absence of a relatively equal share in accessing specific goods: say an equal opportunity to work, equal enjoyment of certain social benefits, or an equal chance to access the means through which this good is obtained more generally speaking. Statists usually emphasize that absolute deprivation requires sufficientarian principles securing access to 'enough' basic subsistence goods, and that such principles have global scope. Yet they also emphasize that this does not imply satisfying relative claims to social shares since distributive equality is only justified in domestic circumstances.

Such a distinction in scope that statists introduce is hard to justify. Consider again the case of starvation with which we started. Starvation occurs when people do not have enough to eat. But what causes starvation is not always a shortage in food supply. There may be plenty of food available but particular groups in society may not have access to the means necessary to acquire food: be those means employment, educational opportunities required to access certain market benefits, or simply purchasing power. Even more interesting is that the worsening in the social position of such groups may relate to the advancement of others. Absolute dispossession is linked to relative depriva- tion, and poverty may result from larger social inequalities. What is required in those cases is reducing inequalities in the means through which a sufficient amount of end-use goods (i.e. food) could be obtained. This requirement can of course be independently defended. But in the cases we are examining, it arises from the necessity to satisfy the global scope of sufficiency. If we recognize the global validity of sufficientarian claims, and if we agree that, under certain circumstances, such claims can only be satisfied through com- parative principles of an egalitarian kind, introducing a priori distinctions in the scope of each seems like an unwarranted move.

That absolute deprivation and relative deprivation are causally linked to each other is confirmed by the analysis of some of the greatest famines of the past century.[21] In all those cases, what led particular groups of people to starvation was not a shortage in food availability but rather their being left behind while other groups advanced economically in new political circum- stances. In the case of the 1943 Bengal famine, for example, difficulties arose not as a result of shortage in rice (harvest was relatively similar to that of previous years) but due to modifications in exchange entitlements and the emergence of groups relatively deprived of the means through which food was acquired. More particularly, general inflationary pressure and a shortfall in the food release due to war panic combined with an unequal increase in incomes and purchasing power of people engaged in war-related activities. Those employed in the military and civil defence sector could earn more, exerting strong demands on food and leading to an increase in its price which others employed in less-profitable activities were unable to match.[22] People starved because they were absolutely poor, yet they became absolutely poor due to the emergence of relative inequalities.

The Bengal famine case is by no means an unfortunate exception. Furthermore, the conclusions drawn from it do not lend themselves to easy generalizations on the domestic nature of the link between absolute and relative deprivation – as those defending a purely sufficientarian approach to global justice often maintain.[23] In April 2008, the United Nations Food and Agricultural Organization reported a 70 per cent increase in world food prices within only one year. It also lamented its detrimental contribution to growing political instability, constant impoverishment of vulnerable sectors of society, and violent hunger riots all over the world: from South Asia (Bangladesh or the Philippines) to West Africa (Ivory Coast, Cameroon, Senegal); from Eastern Europe (Ukraine and Russia) to South America (Haiti, Argentina, Mexico).[24] Here, just as in the famine case mentioned above, the increase in prices was not determined by a shortage in food availability. On the contrary, the total cereal crop in 2007 had been 1.66 billion tonnes, the largest ever witnessed, and some 89 million tonnes bigger than the harvest of the previous year, which already had been a record.[25] As one of the World Food Programme's executive directors declared to the press: 'we are seeing more urban hunger than ever before [...] we are seeing food on the shelves but people being unable to afford it'.[26]

Here, again, the problem at the root is not absolute lack of access to basic necessities but growing relative inequalities. Take the following example. One of the reasons why people in poor countries cannot afford bread is that people in richer countries are consuming more meat. Indeed, one of the major causes of the recent increase in global food prices is reported to be the dietary shift that has recently occurred among growing urban middle classes in the largest rice- and wheat-exporting countries such as China and India.[27] The fact that people in these countries can now afford to buy meat and other dairy products means that farmers keep more animals than they previously did and feed larger amounts of cereals to them, significantly contributing to an increase in the demand for cereals and therefore to a consequent increase in price. This affects not just the domestic poor who, one might plausibly argue, can always be assisted through domestic distributive schemes and other public policies. It affects also the poor in other parts of the world, where food accounts for at least half of the consumer price index and whose states rely on trade with the major exporting powers to obtain necessities such as rice, grain, and wheat. In a global market economy, the relative improvement in material conditions for some has significant consequences not only for vulnerable members of a domestic society but also for the citizens of some of the poorest states. States such as Bangladesh (reportedly facing its worst food crisis since the 1974 famine), Nepal, Benin, or Niger, which depend on India or China for their food supply, are the first to suffer the consequences of fluctuations in the domestic markets of those countries.

Consider another frequently cited reason for the increase in food prices: ethanol consumption. It is often remarked how the use of ethanol to produce biofuel diverts farmer investments from basic agricultural products to maize (used to produce ethanol), rendering those products scarcer and more expensive resources.[28] Here again the modification of relative life standards in one part of the world has significant consequences for the poor in other parts. The increase in demand for ethanol as fuel for cars in places like the United States modifies the patterns of agricultural production and trade. Thus, relatively affluent countries where cars constitute the favourite means of transport may condition the levels of food consumption and threaten the subsistence threshold of poor citizens in the poorest states.

Empirically, it is clear that the effects of such modifications in societal style and environmental standards cannot be tackled through domestic measures, which are unable to prevent globally determined inequalities. But the issue at root is deeper. These examples show that claims for the relief of absolute deprivation are causally related to the non-fulfilment of claims for the relief of relative deprivation. Poverty and inequality appear closely intertwined. The distinction between the scope of sufficientarianism and the scope of egalitarianism that statists introduce does not capture those cases. Pure sufficientarianism requires only that we make sure that people have 'enough'; it does not tell us anything about the need for some to obtain 'as much as' others: in fact it explicitly rules this out by saying that distributive equality is *only* justified within the state. It also does not consider that some may not be able to obtain 'enough' precisely because they have not had 'as much as' others. Yet, as the cases above show, sufficientarian principles trigger egalitarian ones. In global circumstances of justice, a number of claims for the relief of absolute deprivation would not arise if claims for the relief of relative deprivation were satisfied. Where causal links are established, the weight of, scope of, and relation between different candidate principles ought to be rethought. This, as we emphasized in the previous chapter, has important implications for an account that seeks to place its grounding principles at the appropriately fundamental level of analysis.

A similar reflection sheds a different light on the distinction between principles responding to absolute deprivation and principles responding to relative deprivation with regard to the scope of justice. It shows that one cannot restrict egalitarian principles to domestic circumstances and advocate pure sufficientarian principles for the global sphere. It also invites a different type of account of the links between sufficientarianism and egalitarianism. On this alternative account, claims for the relief of absolute deprivation are closely related to claims for the relief of relative deprivation. There may still be a conceptual difference between them. But this difference does not map onto the distinction in scope that statists trace. If we consider the relationship between 'absolute' and 'relative' deprivation, 'comparative' and 'non-comparative' principles from the point of view of what generates absolute destitution in global circumstances of justice, restricting egalitarian principles to domestic societies appears difficult to justify.

Let me clarify here what is at stake in the critique of the pure sufficientarian approach that statists advocate. If absolute poverty is linked to the emergence of relative inequalities it would of course not be very efficient to try and address the former yet leave the latter unchallenged. Some sufficientarians recognize this point when they claim that equality might prove to be 'the most feasible approach to the achievement of sufficiency'.[29] But the main point is not one of efficiency or feasibility. The main point concerns the question of what kind of global justice theory contains a more fundamentally appropriate interpretation of the circumstances of injustice: one that acknowledges the role of causally fundamental principles, or one that ignores it. We would not be taking really seriously claims for the relief of absolute deprivation if we ignored the kind of relative social inequalities that might in turn produce them. The greatest failure of pure sufficientarianism advocated at the global level is that it places exclusive moral weight on non-comparative principles of justice. Statists restrict the scope of comparative principles to domestic circumstances of justice and advocate non-comparative ones on the global scale. This restriction, as I tried to show, is unjustified. Non-comparative principles do not allow taking into account the links between absolute and relative deprivation and issues such as the relative advancement of certain agents in society vis-à-vis others.

I shall return to this point in the next section. For now let me stress again that by maintaining a strong distinction in scope between sufficientarian and egalitarian justice we would not simply be acting in the least efficient way possible. We would also be acting in a methodologically deficient way. We would worry about the morally objectionable nature of absolute deprivation and the consequences of global poverty but fail to consider the morally objectionable nature of the social, political, and distributional mechanisms that trigger it. What is problematic here is not the feasibility or efficiency of pure sufficientarianism. What is problematic is that its lack of theoretical sophistication promotes a significantly weaker articulation of demands emerging in global circumstances of justice compared to rival views.

Sufficientarian principles cannot be considered to have an entirely different domain of application from egalitarian ones. An alternative assessment is required. One ought to engage more seriously with the structural roots of absolute deprivation and address the impact of economic and political mechanisms through which subsistence claims arise, the way they relate to each other and relate to relative social inequality and political injustice, both domestic and global. Highlighting the ways in which egalitarianism should integrate sufficientarianism requires making a choice between two different ways of conceptualizing the links between absolute and relative deprivation, poverty, and inequality.

The first one considers absolute deprivation and the principles generated by sufficientarian justice as non-comparative principles of assistance to people in extreme need. It confers global scope on sufficientarianism, yet insists on the domestic scope of egalitarianism. The second one, which I am trying to suggest, considers claims for the relief of absolute deprivation causally linked to claims for the relief of relative deprivation. In the first case, the analysis of poverty neglects the background structure in which global inequalities arise. In the second case, remedying absolute deprivation requires tackling relative deprivation and reducing social inequalities: inequalities in income and means of accessing basic material resources but also inequalities of power and opportunities for political participation more broadly conceived. From the perspective of the former, absolute and relative deprivation, sufficientarian-ism, and egalitarianism have different domains of application. From the perspective of the latter, they may be conceptually different but they ought to generate a theory with related remedial principles. According to a similar theory, when poverty and inequality are related, and sufficientarianism has global scope, egalitarianism ought to have global scope too. A theory of justice which acknowledges this point provides a more plausible (and progressive) normative articulation of global circumstances of justice, compared to one that does not.

## 5.5 ILLUSTRATING THE ARGUMENT: INEQUALITIES OF POWER

In circumstances where claims to access the means for obtaining certain goods are in conflict with each other, sufficientarian justice requires principles of an egalitarian kind. The case of people living in different states, who – through their states – interact with one another in a global competitive market, provides one possible example of such circumstances. Arguing that in this case global sufficientarianism requires global egalitarianism supports an alternative de-fence of cosmopolitanism, which need not rely on assumptions about the moral arbitrariness of one's place of birth or on an attempt to imagine how the world's political institutions would look if they were redesigned from scratch. But how is the reduction of global inequalities justified in a similar case?

Our attempt to link sufficientarian justice to egalitarian requirements relies on the assertion of a causal relationship between absolute and relative deprivation. As we emphasized, the claims of absolute deprivation generate non-comparative principles, whereas those of relative deprivation generate comparative principles. Linking non-comparative principles of sufficiency to comparative principles of equality raises a number of questions regarding the environment in which comparative principles operate, *what* they distribute or fail to distribute, and among *whom*. Since egalitarian principles are grounded on a comparative conception of justice and require an equal distribution of relative shares, they can only be further articulated by specifying the exact nature of the relation between egalitarian and sufficientarian claims.

On closer inspection, it may seem that the relationships of individuals across the world are simply not such that they allow us to specify what concretely each of them is relatively deprived of, how well they fare compared to one another, and especially how to account for what kind of global inequalities should be reduced or neutralized.[30] Several critics point out that once we go beyond the most obvious instances of absolute deprivation, identifying what exactly remedying relative deprivation requires in a culturally and politically plural world becomes problematic. Indeed, what counts as relative deprivation for individuals in one place may not be that relevant in another. Relative deprivation, remember, triggers distributive obligations when some members of a group are unable to access benefits enjoyed by the rest of them, thus ending up in a disadvantaged position in society. But how do we make sense of this claim in the global sphere, where what counts as relative – as opposed to absolute – deprivation of individuals across countries is much more difficult (if not impossible) to specify?[31]

One way to answer this objection might be to emphasize that, instead of attempting to equalize specific goods that all individuals in the world should enjoy, we ought to focus instead on their ability to make use of whatever goods allow them to be functioning moral agents, wherever they are. As one advocate of cosmopolitanism puts it, 'global equality of opportunity requires that persons (of equal ability and motivation) have equal opportunities to attain an equal number of positions of a commensurate standard of living'.[32] One might still complain here that the expression 'of a commensurate standard of living' is too vague to respond to the global metric of equality objection.[33] But that is not the basic problem. The basic problem, more constructively, is that if we bracket the argument on the arbitrariness of political membership, the question of why a globally egalitarian rather than a globally sufficientarian type of principle is required remains unanswered. We have failed to explain why it is always important for people in one place not merely to have 'enough' for themselves but also 'as much as' people in another. In other words, the risk with such an answer is that it fails to articulate in sufficient detail the egalitarian agenda. It also neglects to explain the nature of the link between absolute and relative deprivation that we are trying to justify.

There is an answer to these concerns. It can be provided by focusing on a particular kind of goods, global goods with positional aspect, and on the impact for absolute deprivation of one's relative place with regard to their distribution. Of course, a complete articulation of that answer should be informed by a more detailed empirical (as well as normative) exploration of the quantity and kinds of such goods with positional aspect in *global* circumstances of injustice. In the absence of that more informed empirical account, a theoretical piece of work can only begin to sketch the argument. However, to facilitate the task, it might be helpful to focus on one example of a global positional good that is appealing even for statists: the case of state power. One virtue of the example is that it allows us (for the sake of argument) to bracket the more familiar cosmopolitan attempt to substantively equalize the position of individuals across the world and concentrate on the relations between the states representing them.[34] The way to compare the position of individual agents is to see them as citizens of specific states, then in turn compare the position of those states to one another, and raise the question of what inequalities in access to positional goods can and should be reduced or neutralized. If and when more relevant empirical information becomes available, extending that line of argument to other agents and goods with positional aspect should facilitate the cosmopolitan enterprise.

It is important to clarify here that even though the argument presented in this section makes use of some empirical evidence, it does not rely exclusively on that empirical evidence to assert its conclusion. I am far from claiming that power is the only positional good that globally matters, or even that the evidence in favour of considering power as a positional good is uncontroversial. So long as one accepts that, given existent circumstances of injustice and the constitution of international markets, there are *some* global goods with positional aspect, the core of the argument remains unaffected and the empirical example is open to revision.

Now, to return to our case study, consider the argument against global egalitarianism that I have summarized above. The first premise in the objection – as it stands – notes that distributive equality requires comparing relative shares of individuals across the world. The second premise denies that such comparison is ever possible given the influence of domestic political institutions and particular cultures on how individuals value goods across boundaries or on the use that is made of them. Hence, one might quickly conclude, distributive justice can only have domestic scope. Equality only makes sense when it is possible to identify a way of distributing goods that are equally valued, equally desirable for all affected parties in the world, and equally in need of being shared.

But if in the dispute above we consider the impact of global positional goods, the argument in favour of global egalitarian justice begins to become more plausible. In the case of global goods with positional aspect, relative inequalities with regard to their distribution affect the absolute value for their possessors. One paradigmatic instance of a similar good in the international sphere is that of state power. Just as inequalities of access to positional goods in the domestic sphere affect their absolute value for their possessors, an analogous point applies to state power. In global circumstances of justice, power represents a positional good. Inequalities of access to it ought to be reduced in order to improve the conditions of the absolutely deprived.

Before we consider the details of this argument, it is important to clarify that we are discussing the distribution of power in global circumstances of injustice. It is possible that in other kinds of environment, hierarchies of power would be justified. In certain contexts (e.g. universities or other professional environments), we would not consider an unequal distribution of power between professors and students or between managers and secretaries to be problematic. In those latter examples there would be a clear hierarchy serving the purpose of a specific collective activity for which an unequal distribution of power is required. Interactions between states in the global sphere are different. An unequal or hierarchical distribution of power would be responsible for rendering some agents absolutely worse off and undermine the value of fair competition. Let us now examine why.

Let us start with some general observations on power. First, power is a dispositional concept; it refers to a capacity to yield certain outcomes. Locke's early definition of power conveys this idea: to have 'power', he writes, 'is to be able to make, or receive' (and one could add 'resist') 'any changes'.[35] Power therefore consists in the ability to do certain things, independently of whether the agent chooses to actually exercise it or not.[36] Second, power is a relational concept. An agent's successful capacity to exercise power depends on there being other agents upon which such power is exercised. An agent's ability to exercise power is impeded if there is some other agent able to resist the change. In a widely accepted definition, power refers to 'subsets of relations among social units such that the behaviour of one or more units (the response units, R) depend in some circumstances on the behaviour of other units (the controlling units, C)'.[37] Finally, power is a comparative ability: an agent is powerful or powerless according to how he fares compared to others (with more or fewer abilities). Lemuel Gulliver, for example, is powerful in the island of Lilliput, yet powerless in that of Brobdingnag. This is not because anything in him has changed but because of how he fares compared to the natives of those countries.

This last point is perhaps the most important for purposes of our discussion. Hobbes makes it very clear in *Leviathan* when he emphasizes that what motivates the struggle to obtain more power in the international sphere is not 'that a man hopes for a more intensive delight than he has already attained to, or that he cannot be content with a moderate power'.[38] Rather, he argues, it is because 'he cannot assure the power and means to live well, which he hath present, without the acquisition of more'.[39]

In global circumstances of injustice, states compete with each other in a global market. In similar conflicting circumstances, power represents a positional good. The most plausible way to enjoy sufficient power is to possess it in relatively equal amounts. In circumstances where power is presented as a positional good, levelling down might be required to improve the position of the absolutely worse off. Sufficiency and equality cannot be kept apart. 'Enough' can only be secured by enabling all agents to have 'as much as' others.

To understand what it means for power to be a positional good in a competitive environment, consider the following example. In Sicily, both the state and the Mafia exercise power over people's lives. Clearly, there is a sense in which the state exercises some power: the police are able to impose fines on drivers if they fail to respect traffic laws, people can take each other to court, and so on. Yet the state is not 'as powerful as' the Mafia; indeed the existence of a police apparatus does not prevent the owners of shops from paying part of their monthly returns to the Mafia simply because they have been asked to do so. For the state, having a 'sufficient' amount of power, when it comes to how that sufficient amount is comparatively enjoyed, does not matter that much. Only the way in which the power of the state and that of the Mafia fare in relation to one another determines the absolute value of each. In the case of a positional good such as power, enough is not enough without it being relatively equal.

## 5.6 POWER AS A GLOBAL POSITIONAL GOOD

Why is it plausible to consider state power as one example of a global positional good? Let us press further the analogy with other cases. In competitive environments between individuals, positional goods represent means, the possession of which enables an agent to access other desired things. Moreover, what determines the absolute value of similar goods is how many of them one has access to, compared to others. So for example, in the case of a typical positional good such as education, the value of, say, a master's degree in the job market depends on whether other people have PhDs. In the case of resources for legal representation in court, the value of one's defence depends on the assets of the counterpart.[40] In the case of positional goods, equalizing the position of parties (even by levelling down) appears unobjectionable because it is designed to ensure that agents are not absolutely deprived. Reducing inequalities of access to positional goods is necessary to ensure that the rich and privileged do not accumulate benefits at the expense of the poor, and that trade-offs do not occur at the expense of vulnerable agents. Reducing inequalities of access is necessary to avoid being absolutely dispossessed. And, in the case of positional goods, the only way to have 'enough' is to obtain access to 'as much as' others.

Notice that power in the international sphere represents a kind of positional good where all these criteria apply. Just as in the individual case, equal access to positional goods such as education is necessary to improve one's absolute position in a competitive environment, in the case of states equal power plays an analogous role. Power represents a means through which other end goods are obtained. It gives states the ability to interact with one another in global circumstances of justice. But when this interaction takes place, the relative distribution of power (like that of other positional goods) affects the absolute position of all states.

To appreciate this point, consider one dimension along which state power has often been articulated: military power. The absolute value of possessing a great number of guns, for example, cannot be determined independently of what kind of weapons are available to other agents. It requires enquiring into the relative status of the agent who possesses guns vis-à-vis all others with an alternative system of defence. If all other states dispose of a much more advanced military arsenal (say nuclear weapons), the absolute value of guns for the defence of that particular state is consequently affected.

Of course one might not want to measure power in terms of military power. But this issue is of little relevance, and one could easily think about the role of 'money' rather than 'weapons', as we did in the case of the food crises examined above. The overall point would not change. If we focus on the particular nature of certain means for accessing particular end goods, and on a mode of accessing these goods which cannot be determined without reference to relative distribution, the empirical examples might differ, but the normative analysis would remain the same.[41]

There is another normative dimension with reference to which it is possible to establish important links between absolute deprivation and the relative distribution of positional goods (in this case: state power). Most of the arguments presented above could be independently endorsed by those who emphasize the value of fair competition.[42] In global market circumstances where political decision-making is essentially based on states competing and bargaining with each other, reducing inequalities in the distribution of power is necessary in order to improve the absolute position of weaker agents. The establishment of terms of trade benefiting not just safely rich countries but also more poor and vulnerable ones, the ability to coordinate in the exercise of the state's coercive capacity, or the potential to sign effective international conventions crucially depend on the absence of power inequalities which would otherwise corrupt fairness in international rounds of negotiation. Again in this case, ensuring fair competition might require levelling down with regard to power. As some authors put it, 'in competitive contexts it seems plausible both that only a fair chance is enough of a chance, and that only an equal chance is a fair chance. In that case, the (good-specific) sufficientarian and egalitarian cases will coincide and there will be reason to completely level down.'[43]

All this implies that we would be wrong to understand the claim for reducing inequalities of state power in a merely formal guise. Clearly, formal guarantees – principles such as 'pacta sunt servanda' as well as other founding principles of international law – matter enormously. But consider again the analogy with domestic litigation and the positional goods (i.e. legal representation) involved in that case. In the domestic case it is important that individuals do not merely enjoy certain formal legal opportunities but have access to an equal share of resources (e.g. equally good lawyers) in order to be able to take advantage of such opportunities and interact on fair terms with each other. So too in the international case, the formal guarantees of international law (non-intervention, respect of state sovereignty, recognition of international treaties, conventions, and agreements) would be meaningless unless they were backed up by a proportionally equal empowerment of states, allowing them to make effective use of such guarantees.

Consider, for example, the impact of power inequalities in the establishment of agricultural trade agreements and tariff barriers on poor countries. Agriculture in developing countries counts for 40 per cent of the GDP, 35 per cent of exports, and 70 per cent of employment and, as we have seen, is one of the sectors that renders them most vulnerable to trade liberalization.[44] However, evidence from all the recent GATT/WTO negotiation rounds shows that powerful states have been able to shape the agricultural trade agenda in ways that increased subsidies and protective barriers when this served the interests of domestic farmers and agricultural industries, while ignoring persistent requests from developing countries to reduce tariffs for products in which they had a comparative advantage.

Powerful countries deploy various strategies to shape the WTO trade agenda to their own advantage. They play developing states off against each other by promising some bilateral or regional negotiations and benefits that they deny to others. They combine material resources and informational advantage in negotiation and litigation meetings that only a few representatives from developing countries can afford to attend. They bribe or threaten vulnerable states to obtain their support when challenged on specific issue areas. They take advantage of diplomatic networks or expensive legal resources to bring poor states into court. They form partnerships with large multinational corporations to prevail in settlement negotiations over trade disputes. They use financial coercion and liberalization discourses to elide development-related issues; or they deploy extra-legal tools that developing countries do not have at their disposal in order to find convenient ways of interpreting WTO rules and exemptions.[45]

Without reducing inequalities in the distribution of power between all states, the asymmetries generated by relative distribution will always condemn their citizens to a position of subordination threatening absolute deprivation.[46] They will always be constrained to endorse whatever more powerful actors determine on their behalf, even if they continue to receive, say, foreign aid in sufficient amounts. Instead of empowering in equal measure all affected parties, instead of requiring that every agent in the democratic society of states have access to as much of the means required to equally perform their role vis-à-vis their citizens and vis-à-vis each other, a pure sufficientarian approach here creates dependence and cultivates deference. It preserves a hierarchy of donors and recipients and it does very little to narrow the gap between powerful states and powerless ones. The first progress in relative terms, dictate the rules of the game, and make decisions on how much ought to be given to everyone else; the latter keep at a respectful distance and should gratefully look forward to whatever goods they will be supplied with, *if* they have been compliant.

Earlier we saw that a pure sufficientarian approach to global justice displays a lack of methodological sophistication when it undertakes to eradicate absolute dispossession yet refuses to consider its link to relative inequalities. Whilst avoiding looking beyond non-comparative principles, that lack of sophistication leads to fundamentally inappropriate normative principles. But as we can now see, that lack of sophistication also threatens to legitimize an international order in which the relatively weak are taken advantage of by the safely rich. It runs the risk of having nothing distinctive to say against global conflicting circumstances where coercive offers, selfish promises, and implicit threats are the norm rather than the exception. Ultimately, that lack of sophistication threatens to absolve the subtlest forms of international oppression.

## 5.7 OBJECTIONS

In circumstances where agents compete for access to positional goods, a fundamentally appropriate account of global justice should combine causally fundamental and normatively fundamental principles, a commitment to sufficiency with principles for reducing inequalities. Since power constitutes one example of a positional good at the global level, reducing power inequalities appears necessary even if we take for granted a normative commitment to sufficientarian justice.[47] Here, a number of objections may be raised. The first is almost certainly bound to remind us that states might abuse their power. By asking to distribute a proportionally equal amount of power to each of them, we might end up strengthening all sorts of dictatorial regimes, contributing to human rights violations, and ultimately harming the population of these states. Remember, however, that at the beginning of this chapter I endorsed a weak equalisandum claim. I argued that equality is one value among many and that it should be promoted compatibly with those others. Reducing power inequalities is necessary in order to integrate rather than replace other important principles of international law (non-proliferation, respect for international treaties and conventions, compliance with international conventions). Egalitarian justice does not conflict with these principles; if anything it guarantees that they are applied fairly and not just when this serves the interests of powerful states, as now occurs all too often. To reject egalitarian principles in the global sphere because there is a chance that some states misbehave is analogous to arguing against domestic distribution on the grounds that some citizens might end up being criminals. Surely, the answer to that threat in domestic environments is not to dismantle the welfare state but rather that those are different issues and should be addressed following different kinds of principles. Statist cosmopolitanism does not object to that; neither does it require equality to be the only principle one ought to promote when discussing the problem of global justice.

Another objection might be the argument that the position of weak states in the international arena is not constrained by the relative power of others. One could plausibly maintain that domestic features such as population growth, social employment policies, and cultural and religious values seriously affect the way in which different countries develop and the relative wealth they accumulate. Critics of global egalitarianism who defend global sufficientarian principles tend to stress those domestic features when emphasizing the 'non-ideal' nature of their approach to extreme poverty in burdened states. Examples of isolated societies living in autarchy and reaching specific societal standards due to their autonomously developed political culture are deployed either to undermine claims for an egalitarian distribution of relative shares across borders or to emphasize how all countries deserve their respective relative wealth.[48]

But one must be aware that autarchic-society examples lead to an unwarranted partition of the world which says that one ought to recognize the global scope of sufficientarian principles but is unwilling to grant how egalitarian ones might follow from that acknowledgement. Here, I do not mean to deny the relevance of domestic factors or arguments on national responsibility and collective desert. The point I am making is different and could be independently raised. Where groups of people are related to one another through patterns of exchange and trade, where the advancement of some societies modifies the relative ability of others to access certain goods, there seem to be plausible, independent reasons for wanting to establish a system of political cooperation placing distributive constraints on relatively advantaged agents, even when their position of advantage is well deserved. If Rich prevents Poor from being able to access bread at prices Poor could previously afford, it seems that Poor can press a claim for an equal share of the means through which bread is accessed without further need to enquire about whether Rich deserves to be Rich and whether he acquired his wealth through inheritance, theft, winning the lottery, or honest work. Likewise, it seems that Rich is under an obligation to share such means equally with Poor without the need for Poor to explain to him which gods he worships, what he does in his leisure time, and whether he is thinking of having another child rather than placing his savings in an investment bank. (Of course, Poor has all the more reason to demand equal means of accessing bread if Rich has promised that under no circumstance would he let Poor starve, but I will not press that point again.)[49] The important issue to bear in mind is that when the equal distribution of access to certain positional goods (e.g. power, in the case of states) is required to ensure agents' absolute status is not affected, a number of additional discussions on desert, responsibility, choice, and luck could be reserved for another time.

## 5.8 CONCLUSION

In this chapter, I investigated the nature of the link between absolute and relative deprivation with regard to the issue of global justice. I argued that in circumstances where positional goods are at stake, an appropriately fundamental account of global justice should include a clear commitment to both sufficientarian and egalitarian principles. One example of a similar global positional good, which might find a sympathetic audience even among statists, is that of state power. There may be other examples too, and other kinds of goods with global positional aspect, which would warrant much the same conclusions. Even though some critics might find the empirical evidence deployed in this chapter selective and occasionally even controversial, it is worth emphasizing that the descriptive part of global political circumstances adds nothing distinctive to what both cosmopolitans and statists often already acknowledge. What is distinctive about the argument is its insistence that a progressive interpretation of the function and purpose of existing institutional practices should integrate both normatively fundamental and causally fundamental principles and combine global sufficientarian and global egalitarian requirements.

Of course, a defence of global egalitarian justice like the one proposed above does not exhaust the range of topics one is confronted with when examining other kinds of conflicts between agents in the international sphere. This chapter did not attempt to settle questions related to the legitimacy of external interference in the case of domestic political injustice. It also did not address issues related to compensation for past violations of human rights, decolonization, or some such. Important as these concerns are, our interpretation of the function and purpose of particular institutional practices focuses on how best to articulate conflicts occurring in the present and involving interactions irreducible to domestic factors. It is for this reason that the account I have presented is limited to reflecting on the impact of the relative distribution of global positional goods on the absolute status of those competing for their access. These issues can be raised in their own right, and the problematic aspects of the distribution of state power present a relevant case in point. A society where agents interact on the basis of exploitative offers, implicit threats, and false promises, and which endorses an overarching account of justice likely to cultivate (rather than abolish) absolute deprivation, is not a comparatively just society. The validity of that judgement clearly does not depend on where the boundaries of such a society lie. An interpretation focusing on conflicts concerning the distributive effects of access to relevant positional goods in the global sphere appears more progressive (both with regard to its capacity for diagnosis and to its innovative and heuristic potential) than one which ignores the problem altogether.

# 6

## On Agency

### 6.1 STATIST COSMOPOLITANISM

We seem to have established the plausibility of global egalitarian principles at the appropriately fundamental level of analysis. Whether and in what form such principles can be reflected in existing expressions of political agency remain to be seen. As already emphasized, activist political theory is not limited to the identification of particular normative constraints; it also requires the transformation of political institutions compatibly with them. The present chapter focuses on agency and defends the normative relevance of state-based associative conditions for the cosmopolitan development of political institutions. It tries to show how states provide a unique associative sphere in which the cosmopolitan principles such as the ones justified in the previous chapter become politically effective and can be motivationally sustained.

Broadly speaking, political agency obtains when it is both feasible, that is, relevant political, legal, and social mechanisms are in place to operate the necessary changes in the system, and when the outcome of political action is sustainable, that is, it has a chance to survive without disrupting existing social ties, and it generates a sense of the collective that is likely to endure throughout time. Politics is an essential element for both requirements. In the first case politics should be understood in a more institutional sense, as the sum of processes and agents through which specific goals affecting citizens' public interactions are achieved. In the second case, politics should be understood in a more civic sense: sustainability may be secured only if the relationship between citizens on matters of common concern is one of ongoing participation rather than mutual exclusion and if the development of collective institutions accomplishes individual emancipation.

The following pages explore the background circumstances under which political agency with a cosmopolitan scope could be considered successful. By background circumstances, I understand those societal (both cultural and political/legal) conditions under which political agency is feasible, and the outcome of political action is sustainable. There are three ways of conceptualizing the background associative circumstances in which political agency is typically expressed. The first account, which I shall call the 'civil society model of the political community,' is characterized by both normative and political universalism. It claims that there are universal normative constraints bearing equally on individuals worldwide (normative universalism) and that all sets of institutions are equivalent in their desirability (political universalism).[1] No special relevance is attached to particular associative schemes either from a normative perspective, regarding how individuals ought to interact with each other, or from a political one, determining what kinds of agents are most suited to render politically effective the universal claims of justice. The civil society model understands the polity as a set of collective institutions and practices instrumentally relevant for regulating conflicting interests in accordance with certain first-order normative commitments considered valid for everyone. If those institutions failed to perform their designated social role, they could easily be replaced by alternative sets, enabling new ways of rendering the principles of justice politically effective.

By contrast, the second account, which I will call 'the political community as a large family,' is characterized by both normative and political particularism. It emphasizes that shared institutional practices, a common language, history, and a particular political culture confer unique values upon particular associative relations and ground among members special obligations that do not exist between them and outsiders.[2] Its normative particularism resides in the claim that fundamental moral commitments do not derive from abstract first-order considerations but are constrained by particular relational facts characterizing social life. Different types of human relations trigger different types of obligations so that the principles according to which we relate to, say, members of our family, colleagues, or fellow citizens, may be different, at the basic level, from those according to which we relate to outsiders. Similarly, the political particularism of the family model resides in the claim that the value of institutions embodying particular relations cannot be reduced to what instrumentally serves the aggregative interests of individual members. Rather, by taking part in the establishment and historical development of specific social institutions, members create collective goods rendering those institutions unique and worthy of preservation.

As we saw in the second part of the book, both models of the polity are familiarly flawed. The civil society model is generally derided for its political universalism, ignoring the peculiarity of different forms of political association, failing to cultivate an adequate sense of justice or to engage its members' disinterested concern for the collective, and, ultimately, giving rise to social instability and 'political disaffection'.[3] The family model is derided for its normative particularism, insufficiently sensitive to relevant interactions with outsiders which might demand political transformation, and leading to potentially exclusionary practices. Building on the strengths of the two models whilst avoiding those familiar weaknesses in them, I shall here argue for a third, dialectical conceptualization of the circumstances of political association.

The dialectical model will be characterized by normative universalism and political particularism. After distinguishing between first-order reasons and particular motivational sets, I shall explore the role of state-based expressions of political agency in rendering the cosmopolitan interpretation advanced so far politically effective and motivationally sustainable. Two features of political cooperation appear very relevant in this respect: mechanisms that allow the imposition of mutual political constraints upon members, and the existence of particular political agents (i.e. avant-garde agents) shaping the basis with reference to which cosmopolitan principles can be politically developed. By focusing on the relevance of the political for the associative conditions in which cosmopolitan principles obtain agency, we can see how each of the previous accounts neglects relevant components of the other – the relevance of pre-existing collective commitments in the civil society model, and dynamics of political conflict and social transformation in the family one. Thus, the conditions in which political agency may be considered politically effective and motivationally sustainable are lacking in both of them. Instead they are substituted by two kinds of orthodoxy: the orthodoxy of law in the civil society model, and the orthodoxy of cultural identity in the family one.

The dialectical way of conceptualizing associative political relations combines features of the civil society and family models and clarifies the conditions under which political agency would be effective, and the outcome of political actions would be motivationally sustainable. These features emphasize key requirements of the democratic tradition in political theory: popular sovereignty and civic education. As I try to show, in the absence of the first one – politically legitimate decision-making mechanisms – any transformative initiative would be unfeasible. Yet, in the absence of the second – sensitivity to pre-existing schemes of understanding and a willingness to put these in the service of conceptual innovation – any outcome achieved would be unsustainable. Popular sovereignty, on the one hand, allows cosmopolitan interpretations to enter a deliberative political process, enabling the transformation of political institutions in accordance with their normative requirements. Civic education, on the other hand, complements this process by progressively inserting new normative commitments in pre-existing cultural, political, and historical practices. Both, I suggest, are indispensable conditions if we want global justice to be more than a cosmopolitan manifesto: popular sovereignty for global egalitarian principles to become politically effective in the first place and civic education for them to be motivationally sustained. These ideas are explored in the following sections.

## 6.2 CIVIL SOCIETY OR LARGE FAMILY?

The civil society and family models of political community seem to rest normatively on mutually exclusive premises. The civil society model is often understood as an atomistic one. Its subjects are mutually indifferent and self-contained units, each with a multiplicity of needs and wants and an independent plan on the best way to promote their satisfaction. Interactions are based on enlightened self-interest; the mode of cooperation relies on calculations of mutual benefit; and membership in the association is partly, or entirely, voluntarily based. The worth of the association can be instrumentally reduced to the sum of the advantages derived by its members. Collective institutions are supposed to exercise their functions within the limits of the technical purpose they serve, letting citizens promote their own good in their own way.

The large family model adopts a holistic approach in order to clarify the background associative circumstances in which a genuine concern for the common good – missing in the civil society model – is thought to be present. A family is a self-contained unit, whose members identify with it not for instrumental reasons, such as taking advantages from the benefits it provides, but because participating in its organic life is a part of who they are; it cultivates their sense of justice. Where membership in the civil society model is a quasi-arbitrary feature, sharing a set of collective cultural and historical practices is in the family account a source of internal gratification, something through which individuals are fully realized.[4] Members in the family model recognize each other as both the authoritative source and the subjects of collective institutions, consider the unique mode of their interactions to constitute a common good, and are jointly engaged in cooperative practices aiming to promote not only the welfare of existing members but also that of future generations.

Traditionally, the civil society model has been criticized for its atomistic features, failing to engage its members' disinterested concern for the collective and leaving the public sphere open to potential risks of corruption, accumulation of power, and the degeneration of political institutions in specific historical circumstances. Benjamin Constant was among the first to voice such a critique. The danger, he emphasized, is that 'absorbed in the enjoyment of our private independence and in the pursuit of our particular interests we shall surrender too easily our right of participation in political power'. For this reason, he claimed, 'the work of the legislator is not complete when he has simply brought peace to people. Even when people are content, there is still much to do. Institutions must achieve their moral education.'[5]

Many cosmopolitans implicitly adopt the civil society model of political association while insisting on a radical reform of existing political institutions to make them compatible with principles of global justice. Typically, they argue for the need to create supra-state or transnational bodies able to render politically effective a particular cosmopolitan account.[6] However, the issue of how such institutions could, once established by legislative means, be histori-cally maintained – that is, the question of what might motivate people to comply with the principles reflected in them – is seldom raised. But, as Rousseau once reminded his readers, 'no constitution will ever be good and solid unless the law rules the citizens' hearts. So long as the legislative force does not reach that deep, the laws will invariably be evaded.'[7]

But how can hearts be reached?[8] The civil society model of political associ-ation is able to engage their interests, their reciprocal respect – at best their moral imperatives. Institutions maintain strength and stability as long as they promote justice, and justice is promoted as long as everyone does his fair share in the political scheme. However, justice, 'even of the utmost integrity', is not enough to motivate everyone's disinterested concern for the collective, because 'justice, like health, is a good which one enjoys without feeling it, which inspires no enthusiasm, and the value of which one feels only once it has been lost'.[9] The real difficulty, Rousseau thought, is not limited to creating institutional responsibilities, but rather fixing them in a way that avoids defection and preserves whatever achievements emerge as a result of cultural and political practices that shape members' political socialization. Hence the importance attributed to civic education and to social participation, as well as the emphasis placed on citizens' mutual assumption of responsibility for their collective enterprise.

The family model of political association takes seriously these objections to the civil society model by combining them in an alternative account of the nature of political association. It starts with assuming a set of specific associa-tive circumstances in which members develop social habits that make them comply more willingly with communal obligations. By emphasizing the collective source of mutual constraints, the family model minimizes the possibility of defection not by threatening to punish, but by appealing to deeper feelings of associative loyalty, historical ties to a particular political sphere, and reciprocal solidarity. Loyalty is here understood as a widespread sense of commitment to the well-being of the entire political body. It is a commitment independent of the respective benefits to individual members in specific historical situations and does not merely arise out of concern for possible sanctions. The collective goods produced by community life, its traditions, culture, and distinctive political institutions provide a source for mutual recognition, significantly shape the identity of members, and consti-tute a stable basis for social cooperation that citizens would want to defend even in the presence of an external threat.

Consider the case of Poland which, as Rousseau reminds us, would have been assimilated by its Russian neighbours at various points in history if feelings of associative loyalty and the prevalence of collective attachments over individual interests had not led its citizens to rise, even to the point of sacrificing their lives, in defence of the distinctiveness of their communal form of life. As Rousseau puts it: 'it is national institutions which form the genius, the character, and the morals of a people, which make it be itself and not another, which inspire in it the ardent love of fatherland founded in habits impossible to uproot, which cause it to die of boredom among other people in the midst of delights of which it is deprived of its own'.[10]

One might of course object that the family model of political association overstates the extent to which people are, as a matter of fact, motivated by communal attachments of a Rousseauean kind. Yet, just from a casual inspection of newspapers, it seems that the number of people willing to make significant sacrifices to foster their community's emancipation is large enough to justify the claim that patriotism is not simply the product of an old-fashioned, nostalgic mind. But this attitude does not seem to prevail towards transnational institutions, however well designed or deeply integrated. As one author puts it, despite being subject to similar globalizing forces, 'citizens of Western democracies are able to respond to these forces in their own distinctive ways, reflective of their "domestic politics and cultures". And most citizens continue to cherish this ability to deliberate and act as a national collectivity, on the basis of their own national solidarities and priorities.'[11]

## 6.3 NORMATIVE REASON AND MOTIVATION

The family model of political association seems then to provide a thicker account of moral motivation than the civil society one. It speaks to the majority of people's hearts, as Rousseau would have put it, and appeals to the principles of moral psychology in explaining how specific associative circumstances develop the shared social meanings and ties of reciprocal solidarity that institutions need in order to obtain sustainability. However, the family model is also not without problems. Its shortcomings emerge more clearly if we consider the moral theory that it derives from a set of empirical observations on the circumstances of motivation – normative particularism.

Particularists insist that universalism relies on an inadequate account of moral motivation. By grounding obligations on a universal view that requires people to abstract from particular sentimental ties or special inclinations, a cosmopolitan, universalistic view of morality makes particularly demanding claims with which fallible individuals may not be able to cope. More specifically, particularists emphasize that most people find it difficult to abstract from their social relationships and comply with universal principles only because there is an obligation to do so. As one author puts it: 'it seems unlikely that rational conviction can carry the weight required of it, except perhaps in the case of a small number of heroic individuals . . . For the mass of mankind, ethical life must be a social institution whose principles must accommodate natural sentiments towards relatives, colleagues, and so forth, and which must rely on a complex set of motives to get people to comply with its requirements – motives such as love, pride, and shame as well as purely rational conviction.'[12]

Normative particularism thus emerges as an alternative view of morality which considers obligations embedded in particular political institutions, customs, and a given public culture. It claims to offer a more appropriate account of moral motivation and attempts to reconcile normative principles with community habits that members develop by taking part in specific associative practices. But one needs here to distinguish carefully between two systematically separate questions. The first is related to the justificatory source of obligations. The second goes back to the circumstances of their performance. The fact that in certain circumstances I am happier to comply with a particular duty than in others does not make those circumstances or my happiness a guiding principle for justifying my obligations, as a particularist would seem to claim. The reasons for which I ought to perform in a certain way are a wholly separate question from the way in which I happen to perform today. Put differently: how you do something is not the same as what you ought to do. One might well agree with particularists that, apart from a few moral heroes, it matters to a great number of people whether duties can be combined with pre-existing social commitments, and whether discharging obligations can be done in a way that also brings satisfaction. This does not mean, however, that satisfaction is the source of moral agency, just as it does not mean that feelings of love, mutual sympathy, or consideration for some particular agents are the only reasons why we act in a morally justified way. If we only focus on shared understandings and existing social dispositions that motivate imperfect moral agents, we might end up neglecting other significant sources of political conflict, marginalizing those with whom we do not share any strong associative bond, and running the risk of legitimizing deeply exclusionary practices.

The previous chapters have already commented on the dangers of a similar approach when applied to the analysis of circumstances of justice.[13] What matters at this point is to insist that, having traced a distinction between principles and agency, between the justification of specific normative commitments and the way of executing them, it seems perfectly possible both to accept that particular associative relations are essential for developing compliant attitudes in people and at the same time to reject the need for an alternative justificatory apparatus. It is possible, for example, to share the egalitarian account of global justice developed in the previous chapter but still insist that we need particular associative circumstances to get a motivational grip on people by activating their shared understandings so as to render

politically effective particular principles of justice. Similarly, one can concede to particularists that many people are more easily motivated in the
presence of familiar schemes of understanding or feelings of mutual trust
than by respect for rationally endorsed principles. However, this does not
imply conceding that similar shared practices are the only, or indeed the
most appropriate, foundation of appropriate normative principles. What it
does imply is that they constitute an important resource upon which to rely
in particular moments of contestation and challenge, when interpretations
claiming to develop these shared practices in a more progressive direction
are likely to emerge.

The fact that empirically, in given circumstances, people undertake certain
commitments more willingly than in others is extremely important. But the
fact that it is important does not mean that it is always right. Of course, it also
does not mean that those circumstances are arbitrary and one can change
them at will, as some cosmopolitans might emphasize. Instead, empirical
observation tells us that, if we are interested in the effective development of
transformative political agency, we should realize that imperfect moral agents
will discharge their obligations differently, in different associative circumstances. Hence, we end up with a view that is able to recognize the unique
relevance of specific political practices, and to articulate from a normative
perspective the transformative potential embedded in such practices. This is
also the view I advance in the next section while arguing for the conditions in
which political agency succeeds. For now, let me consider some objections to
the idea that I have just expressed, that is, that one can distinguish between
normative reason and motivational sets to overcome the flaws of the civil
society and family models of political association and still make sense of some
relevant intuitions underpinning each of them.

One possible objection to this idea is that distinguishing between normative
reason and motivation leads to a sort of 'moral schizophrenia' introducing
incoherence, fragmentation, and disharmony in the structure of our ethical
judgements.[14] Consider the following case. The universalist knows that the
worth of his actions is due to his adherence to specific normative principles.
Yet he realizes that pure commitment to virtuous action might not be
common or reliable enough in ordinary people and that pre-existing feelings
of trust, friendship, and mutual solidarity are more likely to motivate imperfect moral agents than the mere obligation to comply. Critics have pointed out
that the universalist is here likely to face the following dilemma. Either he
should recognize that his own normative outlook is distorted or incomplete
because it does not make room for pre-existing dispositions and social inclinations, which might contribute to increasing the value of his actions, or he
should allow such inclinations to enter the process of normative deliberation,
thus corrupting the universalist's pure initial motives.

Is there a way out of such a dilemma? Interestingly, Kant once emphasized the distinction between normative reason and motivation in response to Schiller's similar objection that his account of obligation involved a 'monastic frame of mind' which left out people's dispositions and natural tempers entirely. Writing during the Terror of the French Revolution, Schiller had argued in several papers that moral imperatives needed to be reconciled with observed inclinations and existing social practices if normative principles were to realize themselves in the empirical world. This would help humans avoid being either 'savages', with feelings ruling over principles, or 'barbarians', with principles destroying feelings.[15] With these ideas, he intended to criticize Kant's account of morality, which seemed to exclude the possibility of socially cultivating inclinations because of the risk of corrupting the purity of moral imperatives. Kant's surprising answer was that there was no principled disagreement between him and Schiller on this point. Indeed, he denied the possibility of an irremediable conflict between duty and motivation by tracing an implicit distinction between the source of normative commitments and the manner of their execution. As Kant put it, 'I am unable to associate gracefulness with the concept of duty, by reason of its very dignity.' However, when it comes to the duty's 'temperament' and the way in which a moral subject develops his resolve, 'a slavish frame of mind can never occur without a hidden hatred for the law', whereas only in the presence of a 'joyous frame of mind' one can also gain a love for virtue and definitely acquire it.[16]

Thus, it seems perfectly possible to defend rationally justified principles without conceding that a rightful action, if complemented by a positive motivation other than that of acting from duty, would lead to a moral failure. After all, insisting that an action has moral worth when it is performed from the motive of duty alone is not the same as saying that such an action suddenly becomes worthless if it is also supported by other positive motives. Therefore, a universalist can still maintain that an action holds moral worth when determined by the intrinsic validity of normative commitments. This does not necessarily identify him with the claim that a similar state of affairs is preferable to another where other cooperative inclinations are present too.[17] But if, as particularists suggest, we ground all our principled commitments on feelings of trust, friendship, and solidarity, how could we cope with states of affairs marked by the absence of such inclinations yet in need of moral rectification? The burden of proof in this case is with the normative particularist. While the presence of an additional positive motive to that of acting from the intrinsic validity of norms does not badly affect a given state of affairs, the same could not be said about the absence of the motive of duty in the presence of contrary inclinations. The universalist may thus agree that endorsing an interpretation of the function and purpose of particular practices which takes into account shared cultural or institutional features positively complements our justified normative commitment. He can also admit that relying on pre-existing social inclinations increases an agent's disposition to act in accordance with the principles embedded in a similar interpretation. Yet he can also consistently doubt the particularist's claim that all this is sufficient to justify his own alternative interpretation, developed exclusively on the basis of such features and with almost no concern for intrinsic normative considerations.

This leads to a second objection which questions the legitimacy of institutions and practices brought about to develop virtue in a particular direction and to promote acting in conformity with cosmopolitan principles of justice. On the one hand, educating fellow citizens to adopt similar attitudes, inculcating them with a cosmopolitan sense of the collective, and helping them surpass particularist limitations seem necessary in order to overcome the shortcomings of the civil society model of political association. Indeed, a society in which individuals fail to spontaneously do their share and simply comply with the laws out of fear of being punished is likely to face the sustainability problems discussed above. On the other hand, one might argue that encouraging universal normative commitments and promoting cosmopolitan virtues among imperfect moral agents run the risk of corrupting their own capacity for goodwill. Is it really possible to continue emphasizing the value of independent judgement and yet advocate the necessity of moral education to cultivate people's disposition for certain types of decision-making?

The dialectical account of political association introduced in the following sections attempts to tackle this objection by placing emphasis on the political process through which a collective association emancipates throughout time, and can cultivate particular learning processes. It presents an analysis of shared political activity which, far from constituting a limit to individuals' capacities to endorse certain normative commitments, acts as a condition for their further development. It focuses on a particular mode of political agency through which two central features of democratic theory (popular sovereignty and civic education) are placed in the service of a progressive interpretation of the function and purpose of political institutions. The former guarantees the legitimate allocation of political obligations and thus makes cosmopolitan agency politically effective; the latter motivates citizens to a voluntary concern for cosmopolitan goals and consequently makes the political association sustainable.

## 6.4 A DIALECTICAL ACCOUNT OF THE POLITICAL COMMUNITY

The two models of the associative relations underpinning a political community sketched in the previous sections seem to rest normatively on mutually exclusive premises. Each account lacks some essential features found in the other and fails to satisfy the requirements of feasibility and sustainability that are necessary in order for cosmopolitan principles to obtain political agency. Thus, the civil society model accounts for how to create political institutions but not for how to render them motivationally sustainable. On the other hand, the family model accounts for how to support these political relations throughout time but not for how to integrate innovative political interpretations. The former can thus provide feasibility but not stability in the political association; the latter provides stability but with no margins for transformation. In both cases, politics as a specific process in which the role and composition of the collective body is historically and progressively shaped, criticized, and renegotiated appears neglected.

An alternative way of considering the background associative circumstances in which political agency with a cosmopolitan scope can succeed is by starting with a historically sensitive analysis of the political community. This account, rather than providing a fixed set of ontological attributes that inhere in the substance of a political community, aims to capture the relevant relational properties that qualify it as a unique social entity in dynamic development. What drives this evolution is politics, broadly understood in terms of a distinctive set of practices and institutions through which agents interact with each other as joint authors of the same system of rules and are entitled to place legal and institutional constraints on each other. But it is also politics understood in a more civic sense, as a learning process through which citizens develop particular interpretations of the function and purpose of their joint institutions, question them in times of crisis and political tension, emancipate themselves from morally problematic views, and eventually substitute them for more progressive understandings of the basic terms of political association.

Being concerned with the historical conditions in which political agency is effective and the outcome of political action sustainable, such an account of the political community reflects the dialectical method emphasized in earlier chapters. A similar account is sensitive to historical development but also alert to the emergence of new interpretations of the purpose and function of collective institutions. It captures relevant features of political reality but is not entirely reducible to them. Of course, a critic may still object that the practices of many existing political communities are not entirely compatible with the description presented in the following pages. Yet my hope is that the basic contours of such a description are familiar enough to sound plausible, and plausible enough to claim persuasion.

Indeed, forms of collective political organization similar to the ones described here exist everywhere in the world. Their concrete historical development seems to have played a major role in the way specific normative principles have been interpreted and given life to different (more or less progressive) political, legal, and even cultural institutions. The history of modern ideologies with a universal inspiration such as liberalism and social-ism cannot be traced without understanding the different, more or less peaceful, interpretation of their principles in the context of specific political and cultural practices, following different patterns of social change and in response to different conflicting circumstances.[18] Hence, the important point to bear in mind while assessing the dialectical account is that I analyse the political community as it is and its practices as they have historically devel-oped through long-term learning processes based on collective economic, social, and cultural transformation.

Some might consider this development a great fortune, others a regrettable obstacle. I try not to start with an abstract definition of society or with an ideal of human interactions – either atomistic as in the civil society case or holistic as in the family one – but rather consider the way in which state-based political relations have embodied the joint existence, conflict, and often revision of both models throughout history. It is precisely this historical non-arbitrariness of the political sphere, I suggest, that makes the background associative circumstances of the political community distinctive and the patterns of interaction among its members unique. And it is precisely because of this distinctiveness and uniqueness that the state emerges as the most relevant context for the political development of cosmopolitan projects.

But what is the political community? In one of its most widely accepted definitions, it is described as a collective, historically situated, and non-voluntary association of people that occupy a defined territory and stand in particular economic, institutional and cultural relations with each other.[19] As in the civil society model, such relations exemplify a complex system of interdependent needs and interests, which require – in order to be satisfied – collective interactions, including the division of labour among community members and the acknowledgement of certain collective institutions assigning specific duties and responsibilities. As in the family model, its members recognize each other as both the authoritative source and the subjects of these institutions, consider associative ties to constitute a common source of emancipation, and are collectively engaged in developing their human capa-cities to promote not only the welfare of existing members but also that of future generations.

The fact that members are engaged in mutual practices of constructing collective institutions with a long-term perspective does not necessarily qualify their interactions as cooperative. The interdependence of needs and interests does not imply that they also constitute a homogeneous whole where each member, by furthering his own good, promotes that of his fellow citizens. Nor does the mutual recognition of a shared public good mean that this is a substantive good shared by everyone at the same time. Specific mechanisms of production or the popular impact of certain ideologies could be such that, in particular historical circumstances, the political community appears profoundly divided and new institutional and legislative measures have to be enacted in order to preserve its unity. But one could assume that in trying to address these conflicts, invoking a shared history and conceptual categories present in the public culture supports even radical political changes. It is precisely on these elements that avant-garde political agents rely in introducing innovative interpretations.

I shall return to this point in the following pages. For now it is important to remember that, on the one hand, we do not have to agree on the possibility of harmonizing different needs and interests by simply engaging in cooperative activities; nor do we have to rely too much on the organic unity among members of the same community and no one else. We only have to acknowledge that interdependent needs and interests require reciprocity in various social activities, and that different political agents confront each other in the public sphere with different interpretations of the function and purpose of shared institutions. Convergence on very basic principles of coordination and methods of enforcement allows society to avoid a condition of perpetual anarchy and violence, and to establish minimal rules for channelling political transformation. We also have to acknowledge that, by participating in the political life of the community and being involved in matters of public concern, citizens might develop an interest in the collective good which is irreducible to its identification with a particular normative body of thought. On the contrary, clashes between various interpretations and the learning processes enacted by these allow the progressive elimination of morally problematic interpretations and their replacement with more and more progressive ones. Of course there is no guarantee that such progress will continue forever. However, it is reasonable to assume that, to the extent that political transformation is guided by normative principles (or by interests that coincide with these principles), a political community will, over time, come to refine both the instrumental mechanisms for accommodating conflicting concerns and the civic practices that act as unique communal bases of political emancipation.

Another feature of our definition of political community bears clarification: its non-voluntary aspect. Insisting that interactions among members are not voluntary does not imply denying citizens any possibility of exit and of being accepted in a new political community, should they wish to migrate. What it means is that exit and entry are not arbitrary; they are neither a priori denied nor a priori accepted but rather organized in a way that is compatible with and accountable to the collective political body.[20] This requires that issues regarding the administration of emigration and/or the treatment of newcomers be considered political ones, subject to public deliberative (and potentially adversarial) processes in which members are ready to acknowledge the existence of conflicting views on the institutional interpretations of existing concerns and commitments. Thus, membership being a non-arbitrary feature does not exclude the possibility of its constant renegotiation, provided that the reasons for such renegotiation can be made intelligible to all citizens.

Hence, unlike the civil society model, specific normative views may not be endorsed simply because they constitute the outcome of a rational agreement of all relevant subjects. This is because, although members may agree on the general desirability of certain principles, they may conflict on the understanding of how specific institutions should reflect these principles; or they may have differing motivations to comply with what those institutional arrangements prescribe. This division does not arise for trivial reasons; it may reflect profound convictions rooted in different conceptualizations of what counts as political conflict, the agents affected by it, or the causes of its emergence. All of that should necessarily emerge and be confronted. It is only in the political processes of public deliberation, negotiation, and protest that this confrontation takes place and different political agents create public constituencies, shape their alliances, and try to influence each others' actions.

Now, as we have observed, conflicts of interpretation can be more or less severe and more or less latent according to the different historical stage in which a political community finds itself. There is no need to suppose that institutional cooperation always prevails on insurrection and one can only assume that an established system of legal rules, a specific political tradition, and the existence of a public culture will play an important role in facilitating political transformation over time. But it is only in the light of the historical development of collective social practices and by relying on specific background understandings that members can meaningfully confront their views and advance their own interpretations of the function and purpose of shared political institutions.

This is where the dialectical account of the political community gets closer to the family model. It relies on the general principles of moral psychology to explain how people prefer complex to more simple forms of goal fulfilment and develop associative loyalties which need not always be based on the satisfaction of personal preferences but on a development of particular attachments to the public good.[21] It emphasizes how, over time, individuals internalize social norms and interact with each other on a more clearly defined basis. In this way, practices of civic commonality, mutual trust, or solidarity are created and feelings of guilt or shame tend to emerge when members of a joined associative scheme fail to do their part. As generations replace one another, a shared system of meanings and different ways of knowing and behaving provide the basis for social emancipation. In the presence of a normatively appropriate system of rules, members' political participation educates their defective inclinations, moderates their passions, tempers their interests, and contributes to developing their moral powers. If and when the emergence of different sets of problems and new expressions of political agency challenges particular practices and institutions, this shared background provides the basis against which the dialectic between preservation and innovation unfolds. On the one hand, citizens have come to value particular cultural practices, and take pride in past scientific, artistic, or political achievements and have developed associative loyalties partly dependent on these. On the other hand, this shared background is invoked precisely when emergent interpretations need to question existent political arrangements, focusing on the relevance of historical episodes that contribute to positively develop their views or criticizing those that serve to further illustrate the genealogy of particular conflicts. In this way, shared understandings are placed at the service of moral learning and collective institutions that have survived unchallenged for a significant amount of time act as symbols of joint historical progress in social emancipation. These elements contribute to the maintenance of a dynamic system of rules, and ground what is often referred to as the public sense of justice. But clearly, however strong, the existence of a public sense of justice, as well as its foundation on existent background understandings, does not guarantee that interactions among members will always be peaceful. What this particular analysis of conceptual innovation and social change does provide is a basis for the integration of new interpretations with reference to a common good that, although political and not moral, members might consider worthy of preservation.

## 6.5 POPULAR SOVEREIGNTY AND CIVIC EDUCATION

In conceptualizing how political transformation takes place in similar associative circumstances, democratic theorists have traditionally drawn attention to two important features of modern societies: popular sovereignty and civic education. Popular sovereignty provides an account of the criteria that a political decision must meet in order to be considered legitimate. It explains under what conditions citizens are entitled to place coercive constraints on each other's actions and distribute political obligations. According to this view, the only political decisions that citizens may be coerced to comply with are those that they have freely and collectively consented to.

'Freely consented to' may be subject to two interpretations. First, one may understand that what a collective 'freely consents to' is the content of specific decisions. A decision is then freely consented to by members of the collective when it is unanimously endorsed, that is, every single member of the collective agrees with the content of every single decision. But there might be difficulties in securing this type of agreement: the size of the collective, the number of options on the table, and the disparity of views are likely to render it a remote prospect. An alternative understanding of 'freely consented to' might therefore be developed in response. In the context of a plurality of conflicting inter-pretations, what a collective 'freely consents to' is a procedure for selecting decisions. Here, 'freely consents to' implies that if one endorses the procedure of selection of a certain decision, then they also commit to accepting its outcome whatever this might turn out to be. In this case, unanimity is only required once, namely in establishing the procedure of decision-selection; it is not required for any subsequent, specific sets of deliberations.[22]

Following this second interpretation, popular sovereignty lays out the external conditions for a meaningful exercise of one's normative powers within a plurality of interpretations of the function and purpose of political institutions.[23] In the absence of freely agreed-upon procedures of decision-selection and the collective recognition of what Rousseau and Kant called 'the general will', there would be no possible mechanism for coordinating a multiplicity of ends and means. Popular sovereignty constitutes the collective political expression of the individual concept of moral autonomy. To be morally autonomous means to obey the moral laws that you have given to yourself. To be politically autonomous means to obey the political laws that you have contributed to establishing as a member of the collective. Political autonomy constitutes the external condition of possibility under which moral autonomy can develop. Popular sovereignty grounds political autonomy by establishing that the authors of laws ought also to be subject to them and contains the criterion by which political obligations can be legitimately en-dorsed. Yet, whilst contributing to making specific normative views politically effective, popular sovereignty does not guarantee, by itself, that people will also find them motivationally sustainable. Once a decision is adopted following a method to which people have freely consented, what is to stop them furthering their own (incompatible) interests by some other means?

This is where the second feature of democratic theory – civic education – acquires a primary role. Civic education is the process by which citizens progressively learn the virtues of political participation, the centrality of engaging in public deliberation, and the relevance of voicing critiques. If citizens' particular interpretations of the public good must be confronted every time specific institutions are challenged, then their critical capacities need to be cultivated, their sensitivity to the nuances of different political positions ought to be sharpened, and the discursive resources ensuring their meaningful political participation must be provided.[24]

Civic education consists in the collective activity of distributing the abilities required for an effective exercise of popular sovereignty. Typically, it takes place in schools, but schools need not be the only public spaces in which civic education occurs. Civil associations, political parties, the media, and the workplace, for instance, might be just as plausible candidates. Schools, however, seem to have a primary role to play. This is not simply because of the compulsory nature of the service they offer or because of the educative function they are institutionally designed to perform. Schools, together with families, are arguably the most important associative environments for the development of one's character. Schools familiarize children with the notion of authority, help them improve social skills, cultivate civic virtues, and introduce children to past and present features of the political association.[25]

This process is particularist at the start. It would be absurd to try and implant in children a comprehensive sense of justice by lecturing them on abstract principles, explaining the relevance of individual autonomy or the role of the concepts of freedom and equality, or training them to make moral decisions by calculating moral harms and benefits. One usually starts with concrete examples, familiar episodes, and stories of emotional identification with those closest to children's understanding, for example, members of the family, those who interact with them, those who speak the same language, or share the same environment. Then progressively one builds towards more abstract narratives, refining children's critical capacities. Educational curricula fulfil precisely this role: they expose future citizens to a pool of knowledge on their communal history, literature, cultural practices, and political institutions, and thus establish a basis for meaningful social communication. It is often said that this process is likely to be effective only if it espouses a type of patriotism that emphasizes glorious achievements in the interactions among community members and marginalizes episodes of oppression, exclusion, or intolerance towards others.[26] But this need not be the case. Indeed, if civic education promoted patriotic dogmas rather than self-critical historical reflection, it would only encourage social hypocrisy and create citizens unwilling to engage critically with shared political institutions. This would hardly contribute to rendering the allocation of particular political obligations motivationally sustainable.[27]

## 6.6 COSMOPOLITAN AGENCY

Having examined the extent to which conflict and a basis for mutual agreement are present in most political communities, we are better able to see how particular expressions of political agency interact with their environment. Citizens struggle together to realize political projects compatible with certain normative conceptions – being divided in the specific understandings of how collective institutions ought to promote first-order values but united in the recognition of their relevance and in the necessity of transforming their shared institutions. Yet, in the absence of a learning process relying on shared understandings, political alternatives can hardly be evaluated, and innovative shifts in courses of action could only seldom occur. A similar process reveals a backward-looking and a forward-looking nature.

Interpretations of the function and purpose of particular institutions are both rooted in existent concerns and commitments and subject to continuous revision and expansion in the light of emerging political projects and ideals of social transformation.

The particular defence of global egalitarianism presented in the previous chapter could itself be considered an emerging political project. That interpretation questions the moral status of existing national and transnational arrangements when they fail to cope with conflicts over the distribution of relevant global goods, and when they are responsible for the emergence of both absolute and relative deprivation. However, whether existent institutions live up to their normative commitments or whether they are more or less able to cope with the negative effects of, say, a global market economy is not a natural fact, it is a question of political will. Political will requires revising these normative commitments in the light of more fundamentally appropriate interpretations, able to articulate emerging political claims, and to trigger political transformations. Yet these transformations can only produce lasting effects if the kind of agency expressive of their reasons is both politically effective and motivationally sustainable.

State-based associative relations play an extremely important role in this respect. This is not because each political community exhibits an exclusive understanding of a substantive collective good, impossible as such to be shared with strangers, much less negotiated. Instead, they constitute spheres of interaction and dependence in which the problems of living in common can be institutionally addressed, in which members recognize each other as mutually responsible for the outcomes of their collective enterprises, and in which conflicting claims may enter the public arena with a clear reference to what values are called into question. Background historical institutions and a public sense of justice are in this case important not for some kind of intrinsic capacity to accommodate all possible controversies, but for offering the associative frame within which innovating political agents can intervene in circumstances of conflict by referring to shared reasons and transforming existing political loyalties. Far from excluding the possibility that states evolve, enlarge, or even fundamentally transform their character (including in a cosmopolitan sense), it is important to emphasize that such changes would still have to occur from within a set of common practices referring to historical institutions, legal texts, and a public political culture that members regard as meaningful and worthy of preservation.[28]

We are now in a position to link more straightforwardly the requirements of political effectiveness and motivational sustainability for cosmopolitan political agency to the features of political communities emphasized above, namely popular sovereignty and civic education. Popular sovereignty is a condition of possibility for the political allocation of responsibilities determined by cosmopolitan principles. It allows enforcing a specific interpretation of the function and purpose of political institutions that is better able to articulate existing concerns and commitments compared to its normative rivals. Civic education guarantees, in the long run, the possibility that everyone, even those particular agents that initially oppose or find it difficult to comply with a similar interpretation as a matter of external coercion, progressively internalize their requirements.

Let us examine both features in more depth. If we agree that conflict with respect to particular interpretations of the function and purpose of shared institutions is an irreducible feature of modern societies, we would have a hard time trying to have all citizens endorse the same view roughly at the same time. Take an interpretation similar to the one advanced in the previous chapter, which emphasizes the necessity to reduce global inequalities of access to positional goods. Typically, such an interpretation will require a transformation of domestic institutions and systems of production and distribution coercively imposed on all members of the political association in a way that also benefits non-members. Although one might sympathize with the first-order commitments that contribute to ground these requirements, a libertarian will perhaps object that the distribution of material resources should be a private matter, a nationalist will argue that levelling down on access to specific positional goods might undermine self-determination, a statist will defend the priority of distribution to non-citizens, and so on.

The point of the institution of popular sovereignty is, however, that the authority of political communities is due to legal and political arrangements guaranteeing the compliance – although perhaps not through unanimous agreement – of all subjects with political decisions that may not correspond to everyone's interpretation at a particular historical stage. Political membership is not an arbitrary feature. Recognition of the basic principles that regulate life in common authorizes fellow citizens to place constraints on each other's actions following political decisions that have been collectively endorsed through public processes of decision-making. Thus, reluctant citizens may object to certain interpretations or refuse to participate in their adaptation (e.g. by not voting), but they cannot avoid complying with the principles prescribed by them once they have been collectively enforced.

One might of course object here that, even if members value non-instrumentally their membership of a political community, they will not necessarily also endorse whatever decision happens to emerge from its internal political processes. On the contrary, precisely because, say, libertarians or nationalists might care for the well-being of fellow citizens, they are more likely to engage in actions of civil disobedience, trying to resist what they consider as objectionable normative conceptions. But notice that acts of civil disobedience are usually justified when the state ceases to be representative of all its citizens, when there are no further grounds for believing that it reflects even minimal norms of equality in its distribution of social roles, and when

popular sovereignty is thought to have failed at guaranteeing legitimate conditions for public deliberation. The kind of injustices that justify civil disobedience are usually deep-going, severe, and determined by the exclusion of
particular political or ethnic groups from the public sphere or by profound
violations of human rights within or outside the state's borders.[29] This would
not seem to be the case with the kind of cosmopolitan interpretation we have
tried to defend in the previous pages. Its justification was developed from
principles that rival accounts were already committed to, by emphasizing the
nature of the link between normatively fundamental and causally fundamental
claims, and by illustrating how a similar conception both preserves the most
persuasive elements typically found in rival views and contributes new categories to the articulation of conflicts that they seem unable to capture. Most
people would not consider the justification of egalitarian principles that
follows from the acknowledgement of sufficientarian requirements an insult
to human dignity. The problem, as pointed out by critics, is one of motivating
people to endorse a similar interpretation, or indeed even to recognize obligations flowing from it as something that domestic institutions ought to impose.
Such motivational weakness might have different sources: people might think
that it is not their job to take initiatives to support citizens in other states, they
might prefer to devote their energies to family and friends, or they might judge
it a useless activity unless everyone did the same everywhere in the world.
These are precisely the concerns that the emphasis on the legitimate exercise
of popular sovereignty attempts to address.

Popular sovereignty allows the legitimate enforcement of certain principles,
rendering commitments derived from a particular normative interpretation
politically effective. But popular sovereignty only explains how it is possible to
reach and exercise power legitimately and compatibly with a specific interpretation of the function and purpose of political institutions, not how to preserve
its concerns. If citizens do not progressively identify with the laws, if cosmopolitanism as a political project fails to foster certain forms of identification
with cross-border concerns and get a motivational grip on people (besides
requiring them to comply), it is not likely to have a very long life. Transformative political agency needs civic education in order to be effective, but civic
education does not develop in a vacuum. Nor can it be implemented purely
legislatively. This would mean recreating the problem it is trying to resolve.
Political obligations are likely to be effective only if they are preceded, and
followed, by an attempt to establish a cultural as well as a political hegemony.
However, this attempt to hegemonize the public sphere is necessarily linked to
a historical sense of the collective, to the self-understanding of citizens as
participants in shared practices, to familiar ways of reasoning and debating, to
particular forms of artistic expression, to dominant religious doctrines and
legal texts, and to critical reflection on the legacy of particular historical
institutions. Civic education encourages citizens to engage with all these

features every time a new interpretation of the function and purpose of shared institutions is proposed by particular political agents. A similar political project can hope to be continuously endorsed only if these features are part of ongoing public confrontation.

Various authors have explored ways of realizing a cosmopolitan civic education within particular political communities. We need not go into the details of their proposals here.[30] It is enough to mention some of the institutions through which cosmopolitan civic education processes could take place: the role of schools in offering educational curricula where a plurality of cultural and political perspectives emerge and are confronted, the role of the media in documenting pressing economic and social questions even outside one country's borders, and the role of local civil and political movements in directing their efforts to issues of global social justice. One might object that a similar cosmopolitan civic education diverts attention from community life and would 'rob' people from their 'concreteness' and 'immediacy'.[31] This need not be the case, especially if we emphasize (again) that even within particular political communities national culture, traditions, and patriotic allegiances are not the symbol of an eternally harmonious life in common, but of the politically mediated effort to create unity out of a variety of different, often incompatible, perspectives. The exposure of modern societies to the possibility of cross-cultural tensions, especially with regards to the integration of migrants, might motivate initiatives for a more cosmopolitan civic education, preparing citizens to reflect upon relations between countries and cultures from a critical global perspective. But if this is so, why not try 'any' political route to cosmopolitanism? Why insist on the relevance of state-based associative relations?

Machiavelli wrote that 'he who desires or wants to reform the State of a City, and wishes that it may be accepted and capable of maintaining itself to everyone's satisfaction should at least retain the shadow of ancient forms'. For, he added, often 'the general mass of men are satisfied with appearances, as if it exists, and many times are moved by the things which appear to be rather than by the things that are. This ought to be observed by all those who want to abolish an ancient (system of) living in a City and bring it to a new and more liberal one.' And, 'as new things disturb the minds of men, you ought to endeavour that these changes retain as much as possible of the ancient (forms) . . . [O]nly he who wants to establish an absolute power, which by authors is called a Tyranny, ought to change everything.'[32]

Cosmopolitan political agency can be politically effective only by taking seriously the background associative circumstances determined by shared membership in particular states. Cosmopolitanism becomes a transformative project by taking advantage of the legislative and political mechanisms that allow citizens to modify the shape of collective institutions by placing specific constraints on each other's actions. It may hope to be motivationally

endorsed only by appealing to familiar institutions, particular social allegiances, cultural frames of reference, and shared schemes of understanding
that motivate imperfect moral agents. Imperatives flowing from new interpretations of the point and purpose of shared institutions would in this case
not appear over-demanding and citizens would not comply simply out of fear
of coercive mechanisms. They would do so as part of their allegiance to
political institutions to whose development they have contributed.

Now, this analysis of cosmopolitan political agency from the internal
perspective of particular states might seem unable to address the question of
how political transformations with global inspiration could not only take place
in limited associative conditions but also involving citizens of different states.
Cosmopolitanism is ultimately a theory concerning the transcendence of
particular political boundaries. Even though it should rely on existing background associative circumstances to realize political obligations, one cannot be
content until that particular normative view has been globally endorsed. But
how can cosmopolitan political obligations be enforced in the first place? If it
is right to say that ordinary people are more likely to take seriously particular-
istic commitments than principles placing them in particular institutional
relations with other human beings, why hope that there will be enough of
them interested in issues of global justice and equal distribution to lead
cosmopolitan political campaigns? If certain political processes are successful
in one particular sphere, what guarantees that the same will occur in another?

Chapter 7 explores some of these issues in further detail. However, it might
be worth spending a few words on one general objection looming above all of
them. The objection runs as follows. Either it is reasonable to assume that
ordinary agents can be motivated by cosmopolitan principles or it is not. If the
answer is yes, the statist route to cosmopolitanism seems unnecessary since
even a purely instrumental account will suffice for the politically effective
allocation of cosmopolitan political obligations. If the answer is no, then the
statist route appears irrelevant since it ends up being as utopian on the
effective possibilities for transformative political agency as the alternatives it
tries to challenge.

This objection would be plausible if politics were a matter of 'either – or'. In
most cases, historically at least, the transformation of political institutions
seems to have been a question of how much, when, where, and how. Several
political projects may have sounded utopian in a certain place at a particular
time, and yet prove perfectly feasible in different associative circumstances at a
later point; that is, they may have been received with hostility in an initial phase
only to become a collective identity marker in a successive one. Two hundred
years after a progressive philosopher's invective against human rights, even the
most repressive government would be embarrassed to publicly declare those
rights 'nonsense upon stilts'.[33] The same might apply to cosmopolitan principles now. They motivate some agents, some they leave indifferent, and others

might object to them. The important issue to focus on is: in what associative circumstances is cosmopolitan political agency most likely to prove politically effective?

The previous pages have tried to answer this question by emphasizing two important features of state-based associative conditions as we know them: popular sovereignty and civic education. Popular sovereignty clarified how cosmopolitan agency might become a politically effective option. Civic education clarified how cosmopolitan projects within the polity could be motivationally sustained. In many countries, there might be sufficiently motivated political agents seeking to transform political institutions in their own states, but there are probably not enough capable of doing it on a global scale. Within particular states, once certain cosmopolitan goals are brought into particular public spheres, they can be made reciprocally acceptable to members by employing legitimate mechanisms of institutional transformation. And once the enforcement of political responsibilities compatible with them is achieved, newly shaped institutions operating within a shared public culture may develop practices of voluntary constraint among members. The statist route to cosmopolitanism seems far from superfluous.

## 6.7 CONCLUSION

This chapter tried to develop an account of the associative conditions under which transformative cosmopolitan agency might become politically effective and motivationally sustainable. It suggested that cosmopolitan interpretations of the function and purpose of particular institutions should be analysed by paying attention to the relationship between preservation and innovation in the development of political transformation. When enforcing political obligations, citizens can legitimately coerce fellow-members and act collectively to reform particular political institutions so as to align them with cosmopolitan commitments. Where this kind of political action has been successful, a polity can continuously support cosmopolitanism and preserve the terms of a political association by relying on historical and cultural practices developed among community members. There are no absolute guarantees that political agents will succeed in enforcing a cosmopolitan interpretation like the one discussed in previous chapters. But it is possible to try and sketch a model according to which a similar transformation might occur by placing emphasis on how particular political agents interact with these background circumstances and seek to renegotiate the terms of political association. Illustrating this model is the task of the following chapter.

# 7

---

# A Cosmopolitan Avant-Garde

## 7.1 POLITICS AS ART: THE IDEA OF A COSMOPOLITAN AVANT-GARDE

The previous chapter defended a dialectical account of the background associative conditions under which the practical realization of cosmopolitan principles could be considered both politically effective and motivationally sustainable. It tried to show, on the one hand, how cosmopolitan interpretations of the function and purpose of political institutions can be endorsed where the members of a specific associative scheme are able to use legitimate decision-making mechanisms to constrain reciprocal public interactions. On the other hand, it emphasized that where political institutions have historically acquired the collective support of the citizen body, progressive interpretations of collective institutional practices are more likely to be maintained throughout time.

The present chapter explores the link between principles and agency in relation to the role of agents in charge of cosmopolitan political transformations within particular associative circumstances. The point is crucial in order to understand how normative views are both inspired by existing political conflicts and support the efforts of relevant political agents by contributing to the coherence and plausibility of their emerging projects. Conceptualizing the relationship between normative principles and political agency in this regard is of the foremost importance when political theory is pursued in an activist mode.

To analyse these issues, the present chapter further explores a concept already introduced in the first part of this work, that of avant-garde political agency. As we have already seen, in addition to the normative critiques cosmopolitanism encounters at the level of principle, an important part of the challenge is mounted at the level of agency. Those who seek to undermine an egalitarian interpretation of cosmopolitan commitments tend to emphasize its weak motivational force in the absence of special associative relations and without a shared ethos of global solidarity. Now, the strength of analysing both issues of principle and issues of agency in the mode of activist political theory is that a similar perspective allows us to see the development of cosmopolitan principles as a political and not just moral task. Such an analysis does not need to make heroic assumptions about what ordinary citizens will or will not be motivated to do when it comes to specific initiatives promoting cosmopolitan justice. It is enough to focus on particular political agents that are already exposed to and affected (both morally and socially) by inequalities of access to relevant global goods (in the case of our analysis: positional goods) prompting the diagnosis of the circumstances of injustice that we obtained in previous chapters. Once a basic normative framework for analysing these concerns and commitments has been developed, theory joins the innovating efforts of these political agents and we are able to understand the dynamic of cosmopolitan political transformations within particular associative relations.

The concept of a 'cosmopolitan avant-garde' is therefore used here to refer to those citizens, civil associations, and political actors relevant to our dialectical understanding of the relationship between principles and agency in the context of global justice debates. The chapter starts by exploring how one should understand the idea of an 'avant-garde' movement, illustrating first the usage of the term in the context of artistic activity. The analogy between artistic and political innovation is emphasized to underline the creative element of avant-garde movements, their ability to both critically interrogate and deploy resources available in tradition to promote particular interpretations of existent relevant practices. In a second step, the chapter discusses some of the evidence concerning the role of avant-garde *cosmopolitan* agents and how their normatively inspired political initiatives might creatively intervene to transform the function and purpose of existing institutions compatibly with relevant principles of global justice. These agents, I shall argue, typically play a crucial role in sensitizing local publics to issues of transnational conflict and global inequality, and in enacting the learning process that gradually leads to challenging and replacing old categories and conceptual resources with new and more progressive ones.

The implicit assumption, here as elsewhere, is that political transformations, including those inspired by cosmopolitan objectives, are influenced by particular economic, social, and political factors and develop against the background of debates specific to unique learning processes and historical events shaping the way in which citizens mobilize. The attempt to promote cosmopolitan political agency should therefore be considered as a continuation of the democratic struggle for the expansion of progressive interpretations of the function and purpose of political institutions. A cosmopolitan avant-garde would transform society following a dynamic similar to those of previous artistic and political innovators in critical historical stages: inspiring the emergence of new normative interpretations; enriching, correcting and adapting those in particular associative circumstances; and taking the lead in persuading fellow citizens to endorse emancipatory political projects.

## 7.2 THE CONCEPT AND ITS DEVELOPMENT:
## ARTISTIC AVANT-GARDES

The notion of an 'avant-garde' movement is of course not new. According to the *Oxford Dictionary of Art* (1998), the term originally appeared in the fifteenth century to denote 'the foremost part of an army advancing into battle (also called the vanguard)'. Later on, it has been used both in art and in politics to emphasize the leading role of particular individuals or collective actors in transforming existing cultural and political practices in light of new projects for the emancipation of society. As I illustrate below, these cultural and political initiatives have historically played a crucial role in developing the learning process by virtue of which previously discredited or problematic interpretations of the function and purpose of shared institutions have been replaced by more and more (allegedly) progressive views. Exploring the role of these agents for a dialectical understanding of the relationship between principles and agency might help us clarify how a coherent egalitarian account of global justice is further developed and endorsed when pursuing political theory in an activist mode.

Apparently, the first use of the term avant-garde in its politically emancipatory connotation is owed to Claude Henri de Saint Simon's *Literary, Philosophical and Industrial Opinions*. Here, Saint Simon emphasizes the power of art in using imagination to appeal to people's feelings in order to facilitate society's transition towards a more progressive and civilized age.[1] His idea of artist-leaders placed them at the centre of a trial administrative elite composed of scientists and industrialists/artisans and assigned them a crucial role in communicating to the masses through didactic means whatever science achieved through solid demonstrations. In the course of a dialogue between the scientist and the artist on the role of each for the project of human emancipation, he has the latter declare in a somewhat superior tone:

> Let us unite. We, the artists, will serve as the avant-garde: for amongst all the arms at our disposal, the power of the Arts is the swiftest and most expeditious. When we wish to spread new ideas amongst men, we use in turn the lyre, ode or song, story or novel; we inscribe those ideas on marble or canvas [ . . . ] We aim for the heart and imagination, and hence our effect is the most vivid and the most decisive.[2]

And further:

> What a most beautiful destiny for the arts, that of exercising over society a positive power, a true priestly function, and of marching forcefully in the van of all the intellectual faculties, in the epoch of their greatest development![3]

By reserving to the artists a crucial role in promoting human emancipation, Saint Simon intended to confer a more straightforward political meaning on the Enlightenment ideal of art as a means for conveying socially useful projects. Already in the French *Encyclopédie* (1751) of Diderot and D'Alembert, the entry on 'Beaux Arts' (believed to have been written by Diderot himself) exhorted academics to visit the ateliers, and produce works that determined 'the artists to read, the philosophers to think usefully and the powerful to make a useful (*utile*) exercise of their authority and recompenses' – a call that would be literally taken up later by the avant-garde movement of the Bauhaus.[4]

In continuity with this project, early artistic avant-gardes were characterized by their political commitment to social justice and by the attempt to use aesthetic means to influence mass culture.[5] Inspired by the ideas of Saint Simon, Proudhon, Fourier, or Marx, and influenced by the events leading to the Paris Commune, avant-garde painters (from Courbet to Picasso), writers (from Zola to Brecht), and musicians (from Wagner to Schoenberg) perceived their work in society as a break with conventional aesthetic canons and tried to use existing artistic techniques to raise public awareness on burning social issues. The aim was appealing to familiar expressive means but in a way that conveyed a radically different message on the role of art and its relation to mass culture. Whether it was in music, literature, architecture, or visual arts, the link that avant-garde movements established between existing cultural practices, innovations in aesthetic canons, and political initiative acted both as a critique of present cultural and social institutions and as a concrete instance of their political emancipation.

The most interesting feature that the movement exhibited was that, in most cases, theory followed closely the creation of artistic products. As one critic has put it, the avant-garde could only make sense 'if it remained dialectically related to that for which it served as the vanguard – speaking narrowly to the older modes of artistic expression, speaking broadly to the life of the masses which Saint Simon's avant-garde scientists, engineers and artists were to lead'.[6]

Gustave Courbet, arguably one of the pioneers of the historical avant-garde movement and a committed social activist, explicitly adopted this point of view in works judged by critics as 'a pursuit of ugliness' because of their rebellious realism and poignant representation of the workers' conditions in industrial societies. When his now famous painting 'Burial at Ornans' (1849) was rejected by an official international jury in Paris because of its 'brutal' realism in representing manual labourers as heroic characters, Courbet reacted by opening his own exhibition space called 'Le Réalisme'. The event was relevant not simply because it created a precedent for the representation of works refused by official exhibitions, a habit that was to become later one of the identifying features of historical avant-gardes. Courbet conceived his work above all as a means to increase the public's awareness about social conditions in industrial societies, as well as a protest against the allegedly 'idealistic' and 'elitist' canons of official aesthetics. 'An object abstract, invisible, nonexistent,' he claimed, 'is not in the domain of painting.'[7]

It would be difficult to explain the origin and development of historical avant-gardes in art without considering how their aesthetic innovations were shaped by, and aimed to account for, the profound political transformations in which their protagonists took active part. The originality and interest of early avant-garde works lie precisely in their attempt to combine art criticism and social engagement in a way that both speaks to tradition and progressively abandons it by pointing to new routes of development. In the second generation of the movement, for example, this issue was explicitly theorized by impressionists with socialist and anarchist sympathies such as Camille Pissarro, Paul Signac, and later Pablo Picasso and affected not just the content of their works but also their painting techniques. So, for example, Paul Signac thought that the pointillist style of painting represented the artist's testimonial of 'the great social process which pits the workers against Capital' and that revolution 'will be found much stronger and more eloquent in pure aesthetics... applied to subjects like working-class housing'.[8]

The call for taking the lead in promoting human emancipation through artistic innovation became most inspiring for several avant-gardes in the decades going roughly from the October Revolution in Russia to the affirmation of Nazism in Germany and Stalinism in the Soviet Union. In literature, for example, the Surrealist movement supported by important intellectuals and activists such as André Breton, Louis Aragon, Paul Eluard, and Jacques Prévert theorized the 'mechanic style of writing' as a means of liberating thought from the commodified conventions of bourgeois society and establishing a new cultural hegemony. Its intentions were made clear in the early 1930s by changing the name of its official journal from *Révolution surréaliste* to *Le surréalisme au service de la révolution*.[9] The time had come for poets, Eluard declared, 'to affirm their right and duty to be deeply immersed in the life of other human beings, in ordinary life [ ... ] Real poetry is included in anything that does not conform to ordinary morality, a morality that can only preserve the constituted order by building banks, garrisons, prisons and churches.'[10]

Participating with enthusiasm in the affirmation of the October Revolution, Russian avant-gardes went even further in advocating the relevance of artists as 'social engineers' involved in the production of work which had to be both functional and accessible even to the uncultivated public. Ranging through a variety of styles and themes, from Malevich's and Lissitzky's suprematism to Rodchenko's constructivism, the goal of avant-garde movements was hermeneutical, critical, and didactic at the same time. It aimed, on the one hand, to put an end to the common-sense understanding of art as an activity that could interest only the cultural elite. On the other hand, and more didactically, it tried to familiarize the masses with abstract thinking and the use of creative associations. It is for this reason that, for example, Lissitzky's experimental art developed into work in typography, exhibition design, and architecture and that Malevich defended his abstract paintings as showing the progressive liberation of people from the domination of work and as constituting the true expression of their newly acquired freedom.[11]

The most persuasive avant-garde attempts to introduce innovations in art and society, however, were those which tried to subvert specific interpretive patterns from within, while continuing to act as their critical voice. The point becomes particularly clear if one contrasts the scarce success among the mass public of Futurist and Dadaist attempts, aiming to destroy centuries of historical accumulation, with the popularity of emergent forms of art such as cinema and later jazz, which combined traditional ways of enjoying aesthetic products with their extrapolation from the realm of high culture.[12] More generally, the most interesting and promising avant-garde productions seemed to be those that were perceived by their authors in continuity with the classic works that inspired them. Picasso, for example, spent several years analysing and absorbing the style of authors such as El Greco, Rubens, Velasquez, and Titian before advancing into new territory. Even then, some of the most brilliant paintings represented variations on classical work, as testified by the many reinterpretations of Velazquez's 'Las Meninas' or of Courbet's 'Demoiselles de la Seine'. In a similar way, Brecht's epic theatre, far from mounting a radical attack on art as such, tried to appropriate tradition in order to change its function and cultivate critical distancing in the public. Aristotle's *Poetics* and its focus on feelings remained a constant reference point for Brecht's articulation of the concept of 'estrangement' (*Verfremdung*), a concept denoting the attitude of a public which did not emotionally identify with the characters of a drama (as in the Aristotelian tradition) but rationally adopted a politically productive critical perspective.

The effort to act as 'the creative conscience of a usable tradition' constituted the main concern of several avant-garde movements and represented a much more arduous and subtle task than that of rejecting all existing institutions and tastes.[13] Indeed, as one critic puts it, 'tradition already had its official guardians, who, armed with an elaborate system of sanctions, were determined to resist any change that required them to reconsider the precious inheritance in their charge'. Instead, 'a constant reconsideration and revaluation of the past is precisely what the master artists of the avant-garde were forcing upon the official guardians of taste, and doing so not out of any conscious determination to "subvert" tradition but, on the contrary, to rescue it from moribund conventions and redefine it in the most vital terms – terms that spoke directly to the sensibility of the age'.[14]

Avant-garde art did not initially constitute simply one aesthetic fashion among others – as occurs all too often in our days – but represented the first major attempt to radically reinterpret the role of artists in society. By challenging the traditional division of labour between history, art, philosophy, and politics, it tried to construct a more transparent relation between socially engaged artists and the broader public to which their call for a different, more equal society was addressed. Whether it was in music, literature, architecture, or visual arts, the link that avant-garde movements established between existing cultural practices, innovations in aesthetic canons, and political initiative acted both as a critique of present cultural and social institutions and as a concrete instance of their social emancipation. The means through which historical avant-gardes pursued their goals might have been different, and more or less successful, but the attempt to appropriate centuries of artistic legacy, reinterpret it, and put it at the service of a larger social project was shared by many.

It was when such a fruitful relationship with tradition waned, or was deliberately rejected by its protagonists, that the historical avant-garde became most vulnerable to attack.[15] It was when references to tradition disappeared from the project altogether (both consciously and unconsciously) that the project of historical avant-gardes came to an end.[16] As we shall shortly see, similar risks threaten political avant-gardes and similar opportunities present themselves. As Brecht put it, 'a vanguard can lead the way along a retreat or into an abyss. It can march so far ahead that the main army cannot follow it, because it is lost from sight.'[17] Political avant-gardes, just like artistic avant-gardes, can avoid either leading backwards or losing their way only if they are able to adequately combine normative commitments with being rooted in particular political circumstances, and only if they are able to innovate in a way that also communicates with existing concerns and commitments.

## 7.3 CREATIVE INTERPRETATION IN ART AND POLITICS

The first explicit shift in the use of the term 'avant-garde' from the sphere of art to that of politics occurred when Lenin in his famous 1902 essay 'What is to be done?' referred to the Communist party as the 'vanguard of the revolutionary forces in our time'.[18] The transformative activity of particular political agents was here perceived in analogy with that of innovative artistic movements, invoking a new normative interpretation of shared political institutions and progressively removing obstacles to its realization.

The image of politics as a special kind of creative activity, as the art of governing the polity goes back at least to Aristotle. Rousseau, in *The Social Contract*, also emphasizes how 'the constitution of a man is the work of nature; that of the State is the work of art'.[19] The interesting addition coming from the notion of 'avant-garde' political agency is its focus on critical circumstances in which existing norms and discursive resources appear exhausted or insufficient to articulate pervasive conflicts in society. The activity of avant-garde movements is there to indicate that normative visions do not belong to an abstract realm of the hypothetically possible but may be promoted (and in fact are) in real-world circumstances.

In a way similar to artists, avant-garde political agents must use imagination and invest creative energies in giving concrete shape to abstract interpretations of the function and purpose of shared institutions. Both kinds of movements aim at transforming society by introducing new conceptual categories, leading a particular public to become aware of the limits of existent discourses and of the opportunities available for innovation in each particular sphere. Both constitute goal-oriented activities whose strategies of mobilization rely on the ability to link the past – what has already been achieved – with a vision of the future – what remains to be done – and of persuading the public that their project is a meaningful one. And in both cases, subjective participation plays a crucial role: the whole project may succeed or fail according to the ability of theorists and activists to subordinate tradition to the goals of a more progressive intellectual and political reform: a reform desperately needed, if not yet fully articulated.

This complex relationship between tradition and innovation with regard to avant-garde political agency is illuminatingly introduced by Antonio Gramsci with a metaphor emphasizing the analogies between art and politics. As Gramsci puts it:

> The active politician is a creator, an initiator; but he neither creates from nothing nor does he move in the turbid void of his own desires and dreams. He bases himself on effective reality, but what is this effective reality? Is it something static and immobile, or is it not rather a relation of forces in continuous motion and shift of equilibrium? If one applies one's will to the creation of a new equilibrium among the forces which really exist and are operative – basing oneself on the particular force which one believes to be progressive and strengthening it to help it to victory – one still moves on the terrain of effective reality, but does so in order to dominate and transcend it (or to contribute to this). What 'ought to be' is therefore concrete; indeed it is the only realistic and historicist interpretation of reality, it alone is history in the making and philosophy in the making, it alone is politics.[20]

As modern substitutes for the role played in history by reflective activists, in Gramsci's conception, avant-garde political agents are assigned the duty to awaken and develop a national collective will by introducing and adapting

progressive conceptions of justice to particular cultural and political circumstances.[21] This notion of the avant-garde agent as a 'modern prince' able to
understand the motion of progressive social forces, organize them, and invent
strategies of political mobilization could be better understood in light of the
analogy between artistic production and political activity and the emphasis
placed on the theoretical stage of the process.[22] The role of avant-garde agents
is not exhausted in the application of a political programme that promises to
fulfil the needs of particular strata of society in a given historical situation.
What is at stake is not merely providing a political platform that is supported
by the greatest number of people and can claim to operate the necessary
political changes. 'Numbers,' as Gramsci underlined, are 'simply an instrumental value, giving a measure and a relation and nothing more.' The difficult
task is intervening at the level of that which is measured: 'the effectiveness, and
the expansive and persuasive capacity, of the opinions of a few individuals, the
active minorities, the elites, the avant-gardes – i.e. their rationality, historicity
or concrete functionality'.[23]

The work of avant-garde political agents begins with the process of discov-
ering the ideational centre of production of specific discourses on political
agency, subjecting it to critical scrutiny, and interacting with theorists to
provide alternative interpretations on how existent institutions ought to be
transformed. Avant-garde movements challenge the common-sense view that
'all individual opinions have "exactly" equal weight' and argue that ideas and
theories do not spontaneously arise out of isolated cognitive processes but are
rooted in specific social practices, which determine their political shape and
must be subjected to critical investigation. The institutional operationalization
of ideas, 'the counting of votes' is only 'the final ceremony of a long process, in
which it is precisely those who devote their best energies to the State and the
nation who carry the greatest weight'.[24]

Considered from a broadly historical perspective, the relevance of avant-
garde political movements has consisted in their ability to elaborate concrete
projects for the emancipation of society by occupying the empty space
between the critique of existing institutional practices and normative interpretations in need of being contextually recognized. In a way similar to artistic
avant-gardes, political ones have both acted as the critical conscience of a
particular political tradition and made use of the cultural resources that it
provided in order to bring into the public sphere issues previously excluded or
at the root of particular conflicts in society. Their social conditions, political
initiatives, or discursive emphasis on the contrast between the plausibility of
particular principles of freedom and justice and the circumstances of oppression of given social groups could be considered among the main artifices of
expansion of the democratic public sphere. Due to the activity of avant-garde
agents, what initially appeared odd or unacceptable to consolidated elites
or was considered over-demanding by existent institutional standards

progressively matured into a persistent popular request for modifying the scope and franchise of democratic citizenship.

Consider, for example, the way in which the formal recognition of the universal dignity of all human beings in the 1789 Declaration of the Rights of Man could go hand in hand with the exclusion of women or workers from participating in political decision-making. Or how one of the most fundamental assumptions of natural rights theory, the idea that every human being is born free, coexisted for almost three centuries with the institution and practice of slavery. Few people today would question the right of women to vote or would defend the legitimacy of holding slaves; few would have doubts condemning apartheid or racial discrimination. There tends to be widespread endorsement of the validity of certain normative standards. Yet not so long ago, several of these issues were subject to heated debate even on the side of an educated public. Several ideas of justice, now standard reference in international human rights documents, were introduced and articulated further through difficult processes of domestic transformation. They only reached the global sphere in a second stage, once there were enough citizens in a sufficiently prominent number of states to have recognized and internalized these norms. The merit of political avant-gardes consisted in taking the lead to initiate a process of political confrontation which familiarized fellow citizens with the theories invoking similar principles and motivated them to undertake political initiatives compatible with them. Only in a successive moment did a similar dynamic start expanding in an international dimension.

Internal political structures have an essential role to play in the initial stages of this process, when citizens become familiar with new repertoires of collective action and conceptual innovation begins to take shape. Ordinary citizens must be able to understand conflicts requiring special attention, connect to them through local experiences, see how they relate to the concerns and commitments of other agents, and perceive the need for political transformation. They ought to have a clear awareness of the limits of existent political institutions in coping with these new challenges, and also be able to invoke particular learning processes to be eventually persuaded that alternative normative interpretations might be available.

Consider, for example, the way in which women's movements initiated with claims for domestic changes within a small number of countries before such claims entered the international domain. Despite the existence of several suffrage organizations in the nineteenth century, a real international campaign was initiated only in 1904, when the International Women's Suffrage Association (IWSA) was founded. Between 1890 and 1930, the struggle had been only domestic, with several groups fighting within various states and national governments making concessions only in the face of strong ideological and practical pressure. Nor did such pressure emerge by itself. Avant-garde movements led by characters such as Elizabeth Cady

Stanton and Susan B. Anthony in the United States or Millicent Garrett Fawcett and Emmeline Pankhurst in England constantly engaged in domestic campaigns of 'moral proselytism' trying to persuade other women about the importance of participating in public life and to shift opinion in favour of their own normative commitments.[25]

In addition to rendering more concrete these innovative interpretations of the function and purpose of shared institutions, and, in order to make their voice heard, suffragettes engaged in several acts of civil disobedience. They chained themselves to fences, they resorted to hunger strike, they damaged public buildings, or they refused to pay their taxes. Only after these political avant-gardes succeeded in having key states modify their electoral laws did the shift from the old conceptual framework to a new and allegedly more progressive one reach a threshold point. Then a 'cascade' effect would occur and allow for easier subsequent transformations in a greater number of states. In the case of women's suffrage, that threshold was reached in 1930 when twenty states (roughly one-third of the total states system) had endorsed the claims of the movement. Once a number of key actors accepted such normative shifts, it was easier for political actors in other places to exercise pressure on their respective states and seek to initiate similar transformations. It took eighty years for the first twenty states to adopt women's suffrage, yet in the twenty years that followed forty-eight countries had internalized the norm.[26]

A similar dynamic has been observed with regard to some of the greatest movements for social reform during the eighteenth century and nineteenth century (anti-slavery movement, workers' movements) as well as the twentieth century (anti-apartheid or anti-colonization movements). The history of the British abolitionists, for example, is often thought to have started with a meeting of only twelve ordinary citizens, who sat around a table in a London printing shop on 22 May 1787 to discuss the content and strategies of involvement for a campaign that, starting with widespread scepticism if not open hostility to the issue of slave trade, would soon occupy the centre of British political life.[27] At a time when ideas of justice and equality were the order of the day, yet over three-quarters of the human population lived in bondage of one kind or another, those anti-slavery activists were the first to draw the attention of fellow citizens to the hypocrisy and moral failures of those very institutions in which they had placed their hopes for thorough social reforms. The pamphlets they produced invoked familiar Enlightenment concepts of human dignity and universal community of humankind to remind people of the distance between their normative commitments and the illegitimacy of practices in which they and their states were involved. The consumption of goods such as sugar, tobacco, coffee, and rum, produced and exchanged through the deployment of slave labour, could not stand up to the test of public critique advertised in many Enlightenment texts celebrating the age of progressive liberation from the error and dogmas of the past.[28]

But the success of these campaigns was in great part due to the activists' ability to link between the local and the distant, to question the legitimacy and nature of national self-interest, and to mobilize citizens to sign petitions that baffled many a critic for 'stating no grievance or injury of any kind or sort affecting the petitioners themselves'.[29] As William Fox, one of the most influential campaigners against the British slave trade, put it in a pamphlet entitled 'Address to the people of Great Britain' and published in 1791, 'the offices of humanity and functions of justice' are not 'circumscribed by geographical boundaries'. If those who consume goods produced by slaves, Fox emphasized, think 'that our share in the transaction is so minute that it cannot perceptibly increase the injury; let us recollect that though numbers partaking in a crime may diminish the shame, they cannot diminish its turpitude. [...] For into how many parts soever the criminal action can be divided, the crime itself rests intire and compleat on every perpetrator.'[30]

In this case too, the leading role for both raising consciousness on the sources and effects of unjust social conditions and creating political occasions for criticizing and reforming existent institutional practices was played by 'avant-garde' domestic movements: groups of committed intellectuals, social activists, and enlightened political reformers without whom the transformations we are all familiar with would have hardly occurred. The means through which these groups tried to exercise influence in the public sphere, ranging from initiating debate to publishing newspapers, to spreading pamphlets, to protest or strike, and to exercising pressure on political institutions might have differed as much as in the case of artistic avant-gardes. Yet the goal pursued by all was a similar one: gradually shifting assumptions on the function and purpose of political institutions and replacing existing views with more progressive normative accounts.

Analogous processes may be observed in our day with regard to the interpretation and endorsement of particular human rights norms in several, initially hostile, states.[31] The most effective campaigns here have been those able to persuade the citizens and political representatives of these states of the moral relevance of civil and social rights in a way that both related to existing traditions and sought to correct their most problematic aspects. The process developed through various phases: in a first stage, both domestic and non-governmental actors, linked through transnational advocacy networks, tried to exercise pressure on governments despite their claims being endorsed by only a handful of citizens. This was also the stage in which the ability of avant-gardes to connect to a domestic public seems to have been most crucial. It was necessary to mobilize as many resources as possible in order to alert the representatives of these states of internal sources of conflict and dissatisfaction, and to the absence of appropriate normative standards reflected by existing institutions. However, in the absence of democratic mechanisms of representation, avant-garde actors could only achieve their goals by resorting to discursive argumentation, persuasion, and symbolic narratives linking their normative accounts to familiar historical episodes of social protest, able to invoke specific learning processes, and to deploy these as resources of political emancipation.

Where these campaigns were successful and obtained sufficient internal support by ordinary citizens, governments started making rhetorical concessions. This opened the discursive space for further challenge on the side of critics, thereby increasing the means available for applying more pressure. Questioned about their responsibility in rights' violations, governments responded by either denying their occurrence or by rejecting the charge that they represented a systematic phenomenon. At this point, however, the confrontation had become more detailed and parties recognized each other as valid interlocutors. This paved the way towards a more complete internalization of human rights norms. Once that process was over, initially reluctant states not only transformed their institutions to reflect human rights norms but even perceived themselves as pioneers in the region, trying to persuade other states to follow their example and construct new institutional imperatives in accordance with the claims of domestic activists. In all those cases the reform of existing institutions could not have been easily predicted at the outset without taking into account the way in which local avant-gardes intervened to modify their function and purpose.

## 7.4 THE COSMOPOLITAN AVANT-GARDE

The struggle for inclusion in the polity of a cosmopolitan account such as the one we have defended in earlier chapters should be considered in continuity with such historical efforts. One way to see this point is by interpreting the arguments presented so far as part of a political ideal seeking to transform domestic and global institutions compatibly with global egalitarian principles. Applied to the cosmopolitan discourse, the concept of an 'avant-garde movement' would capture all those political agents for whom the goal of state institutions should not be limited to the reduction of inequalities between those who happen to share particular political boundaries, but ought to include others placed in relevant circumstances of injustice.

Thus, the notion of avant-garde political agents embraces, at an immediate level, all those individuals and social groups who appear distributively affected by current globalization processes and whose experience of conflict in particular societies forces us to rethink understandings of the function and purpose of existing political arrangements. Once their concerns and commitments have been normatively articulated, theory becomes action-guiding and the practice of these agents assumes a political transformative function. This process of transformation includes both the discursive shift in available normative resources and more concrete political initiatives such as the reform of global processes of production and distribution of goods (e.g. the market), the modalities of knowledge sharing and transfer, and other relevant aspects global interaction.

There are several existing political agents to whom we might, in a broad sense, appropriately apply the label of a cosmopolitan avant-garde. These comprise many institutional and political actors, ordinary citizens (e.g. workers and migrants), as well as the countless number of social movements or civil associations that form part of what has often been called the sphere of global civil society.[32] Among institutional actors, it is possible to list public officials, government representatives, state agencies, and political parties sensitive to the negative effects of the interdependence of domestic and global institutions on both citizens and foreigners. Then there are the various associations and networks committed to civil or political campaigns fighting against global injustice, for example, campaigns for the reduction of inequalities worldwide, in favour of the protection of workers affected by unregulated globalization processes, campaigns defending the right of migrants, and movements calling for the relevant transformation of both domestic and global institutions. Through this broad characterization, we would capture both formal procedures of decision-making and decision-enforcing and the more spontaneous forms of action in the public sphere that try to influence or reshape state-agenda in a way that reflects new democratic global imperatives.

These cosmopolitan avant-gardes are committed to a comprehensive ideal of distributive equality, to promoting inclusion and solidarity with foreigners in the domestic sphere, and to establishing non-aggressive and non-exploitative global institutions based on ideas of cooperative sovereignty. They perceive domestic and global issues as interdependent on both normative and empirical grounds. They give voice to concerns about the presence and effects of global inequalities on the life of vulnerable citizens around the world, point to deficiencies in current institutional arrangements, and emphasize the need to transform domestic institutions compatibly with these arising demands. They also show that the modalities of global interaction, the policies particular governments promote or endorse at the international level, and the impact of liberal markets on global access to positional goods make a significant causal contribution to the ability of citizens in vulnerable states to cope with the effects of absolute deprivation. It is from the empirical observation of the concerns and commitments expressed by similar agents that a theory such as the one articulated in the previous pages could be further developed from a normative perspective.

Who is part of the cosmopolitan avant-garde? A growing number of authors in recent years have documented the emergence and consolidation of various political groups and social movements aiming to raise public awareness and build transnational networks of protest against the negative effects of neo-liberal globalization processes and in favour of more just and equitable global political institutions.[33] Typically, such networks include formal organizations (e.g. socialist, social-democratic and green political parties as well as trade unions), informal associations (groups campaigning on migration issues, indigenous movements, land-workers, and peasants' organizations), as well as various non-governmental associations with both a local and international dimension (e.g. different associations represented in the World Social Forum).[34] Some of these organizations are not new; they have emerged during previous mobilization campaigns (e.g. during the 1968 students' and workers' protests or in support of decolonization movements in the Third World) and survived their temporary decline only to re-emerge and adapt their agenda to new political circumstances.[35] Others constitute recently created groups targeting neo-liberal global economic institutions and advocating transnational control over markets and a fair global distribution of resources. It is, for one example, the case with the French association ATTAC, now present in several European countries as well as North Africa, Latin America, and Canada, founded in 1997 with the aim of promoting control over global economic transactions (ATTAC stands for Action for a Tobin Tax to Aid Citizens) and a more equitable distribution of global benefits and burdens.[36]

Within the model of political association outlined in the previous chapter, the role of the cosmopolitan avant-garde in transforming political institutions compatibly with egalitarian requirements would appear to be crucial. On the one hand, these agents play a vital role in directing the critics' attention to relevant practices of global interaction and the conflicts and commitments necessary to reinterpret the function and purpose of existing political institutions. On the other hand, their very existence responds to the critique that cosmopolitan imperatives are unable to mobilize the citizens of a particular society on issues that elude their direct interests and immediate spheres of concern. It reveals, for example, that the citizens of Italy, Germany, or the United States may, and in fact do, participate in mass mobilizations against neo-liberal and exploitative policies promoted by international financial institutions in Africa and Asia or against, say, an unequal treatment of migrants in their own political communities.

Moreover, by focusing on the role of the cosmopolitan avant-garde in taking the lead to challenge the establishment of unfair global rules, it is possible to respond to a second critique many cosmopolitans typically attract. This critique underlines its inadequate reliance on limited individual actions to bring about large-scale global political transformations and points to the weaknesses of this perspective in resolving consequent collective action problems. The emphasis on the cosmopolitan avant-garde shifts attention away from the charitable initiatives and personal motivation of individual citizens and focuses on the activity of collective political agents playing the role of intermediaries between ordinary citizens on the one hand and domestic and international structures on the other. As with historical avant-gardes mobilizing for inclusion in the democratic sphere, their purpose is twofold. On the one hand, these forms of political agency render ordinary citizens progressively more sensitive to alternative discourses on pressing global issues; on the other, they affect the development of institutions that produce a shift in standard ways of conceptualizing the relations between citizens and strangers.

Consider, for example, the recent call from activists in Europe and the United States to boycott the products of multinational companies which make profits by employing cheap labour force – in some cases child labour – in particular areas of the Third World. Several campaigns of mobilization have led to the organization of public debates and sit-ins, propaganda and information campaigns and activist demonstrations at the outlets of e.g. Nike, Levis, Gap, trying to raise public awareness concerning the labour policies of such multinational corporations abroad. In many US universities, student associations have organized rallies and educative events, occupied campus buildings, threatened hunger strikes, and tried to put pressure on their university administrations to end contracts with sportswear companies responsible for paying manufacturing workers abroad salaries which disadvantaged them compared to workers in wealthy states.[37] These activities urged fellow-citizens to think about the consequences of their preferences as consumers, to take their share of political responsibility for contributing to the increase in global inequalities, and to pay attention to the exploitative practices promoted by multinational corporations leading to the severe deprivation of others across the world.[38] Emphasizing the claims of those typically excluded from state-centred concerns has played a fundamental role in challenging consent about the function and purpose of existing political institutions and in drawing attention to the need for a new interpretation of their role.

Also consider, for example, the pro-migrant campaigns of international networks of associations active in countries with restrictive immigration and asylum policies, such as the members of the European Union, the United States, or Australia. Building alliances between unionized workers, immigrants, refugees, and militants, these associations have organized international border blockades, planned actions of civil disobedience at checkpoints, and coordinated information seminars on non-violent resistance. They have protested against the deportation of migrants, denounced the miserable conditions of detention camps, and promoted the extension of citizenship rights and a more equal distribution of access to relevant goods. The goal of such activist campaigns has not simply been to target the institutions responsible for the unequal treatment of migrants but also to raise public awareness among fellow citizens about the limits of globalization, which only applies to the free movement of capital and goods but increases barriers and inequalities among people. It is precisely on the basis of claims such as these that a theory like the one we have tried to defend in the previous pages could emerge and be further developed.

Clearly, once a more coherent normative account of these concerns and commitments is available, the issue of political transformation compatible with certain principled requirements takes a further direction. Avant-garde agents at this stage do not merely reflect the symptoms of a certain conflict and help provide the necessary material for the development of normative reflection; they join the theorists' efforts in seeking to promote politically effective and motivationally sustainable initiatives. Of course, it is possible to criticize the early stages of these initiatives for being merely facade activities, unable to modify the structural conditions on which unjust globalization processes depend. It is certainly true that without the kind of structural institutional adjustments requiring strong state intervention civil society actors would have limited options for change and perhaps would gain merely symbolic rewards. The practices of avant-garde cosmopolitan agents rely on institutional guarantees for security, the provision of public goods, and the creation of conditions under which oppositional groups may grow, develop, and exercise pressures on institutions. In several South American countries, for example, global justice activists risk their lives on a daily basis and alarming reports continue to arrive of trade union activists, peasants, or members of civic groups being killed or falling victim to paramilitary violence.[39] In all these situations, the political empowerment of oppositional groups and a share of institutional representation in state decision-making would appear to be crucial. Connecting local struggles to advocacy networks on global issues has proved to be one of the most successful strategies of mobilization in this regard.

The environmental movement, whose agenda in the 1950s was entirely unknown, offers one example of effective avant-garde work linking global issues to local activism. By the end of the 1990s, the movement had managed to establish itself as one of the most important transnational networks, placing environmental issues at the heart of most electoral agendas in democratic states. One of the main factors contributing to its growth was the capacity to connect successfully an issue with potentially global impact such as the environment to the local struggles of several indigenous communities and peasant unions in South America and Asia. For example, one of the turning points in its political campaign was reached when Washington activists made contact with rubber tapper organizers and indigenous communities from Acre (Brazil) who had been fighting since 1975 to ensure land use rights and improve living conditions in the Amazonian rainforest. The former helped indigenous communities gain visibility for their struggles in the international domain by supplying them with important information and access to international decision-making arenas, whereas the latter helped to show the Western public that tropical deforestation was more than a set of technical or biological issues and affected the living conditions of destitute peasants. Despite the subsequent assassination of Chico Mendes, the movement's leader, indigenous communities and international activists succeeded in exercising joint pressure on the Brazilian government and on World Bank representatives and obtained important results, later institutionalized through the newly created environmentalist Workers' Party Government of Acre.[40] A movement whose initial ambitions were rooted in conflicts of relevance to only a handful of local community members and conscientious activists had thus reached international prominence, providing both an example of how to develop effective political change and a source for future learning and support.

Another equally revealing example is provided by the establishment of initiatives from tradeunion organizations and activists operating across borders to strengthen joint pressure on local governments and transnational corporations and to ensure that saving workers from cuts in one area of the world does not come at a severe cost to those employed by the same company in a different region. Cases of international union collaboration and attempts to build networks of workers within particular transnational corporations are now starting to be observed in a range of sectors, from metalworking to transport to utilities, from telecommunication to the food industry. Other activities, emerging from bottom-up protest campaigns (see the well-known examples of the networks of unions challenging Rio Tinto or the protests surrounding responses to Coca-Cola's actions in Guatemala in the 1980s), illustrate that when local struggles are inspired by imperatives of global justice, new avenues of political transformation open up and political agency can become both politically effective and motivationally sustainable.[41] The converse point also holds: without maintaining awareness of the dynamic of development in a particular tradition of political mobilization, the principles and discourses promoted by relevant agents begin to lose both their ability to meaningfully communicate with the public and their capacity to resonate with local commitments and concerns.

From a normative perspective, the interest of avant-garde agency lies in the transformative capacity of concrete collective actors, the link they seek to establish between normative ideals and differing interpretations of existing political institutions, and the contribution they make to the process of moral learning that renders progressive theories politically effective and motivationally sustainable. Without a widespread public awareness of the relevance of alternative interpretations of the function and purpose of concrete political institutions, without significant assumption of political responsibility on the part of citizens in both affluent and poor states, the structural and institutional reforms required to fight global inequality would lack both intelligibility and the popular support needed to be established in the first place. It is the highly contentious question of political transformation and mass political motivation rather than that of making concrete policy proposals in defence of some rather than other cosmopolitan political structures (an issue which relies on political practice as much as on normative argument) that our analysis of the role of the cosmopolitan avant-garde has mainly tried to address.

## 7.5 CONCLUSION

This chapter explored the concept of avant-garde political agency in order to illustrate how existing political institutions and state-based associative relations might be transformed in a way that reflects global justice imperatives. The idea of relying on political agents who are already politically and/or morally sensitive to the cosmopolitan discourse provides an unambiguous response to critiques focusing on the weak motivational strength of cosmopolitanism and its inability to be politically effective. Within the model of political association that I have outlined in the previous chapter, the role of cosmopolitan avant-gardes both in educating ordinary citizens to alternative discourses of political agency and in taking the lead to collectively enforce cosmopolitan political transformations would appear to be crucial.

The cosmopolitan avant-garde is rooted in a particular public sphere but it is also outward looking. One of its major assets is the ability to address political concerns in a way that makes sense to every member of a shared associative practice and that can transform existing political structures compatibly with the requirements of global equality. Its efforts focus on both increasing citizens' sensitivity to global conflicts with a comparative, positional dimension, and contributing to the emergence of existing interpretations of the point and purpose of shared practices with more adequate, progressive alternatives. Of course, the modes of action as well as the degree and type of involvement of avant-garde political agents might vary from place to place, depending on the political circumstances in which such attempts are to be found. One could expect similar expressions of political agency in the United States to be quite different from those in India or Brazil, conditioned by the different nature of public political interactions in each of these countries, and by the different degree of citizen involvement and influence of their states in the international sphere. As a matter of political strategy, the cosmopolitan avant-garde has still a long way to go in homogenizing its objectives, building transparent international networks of activism, sorting out the degree of inclusion of different actors, and developing coherent proposals on what kind of political institutions should be reformed to satisfy the claims of egalitarian justice. However, the presence of collective political agents committed to the cosmopolitan project and seeking to place existing associative relations in the service of global justice is not just a pious wish; it is a reality in motion.

# Conclusion

Many cosmopolitans think that states, and the associative political relations underpinning them, hardly matter normatively. Many statists think that states matter so much that they override global distributive equality. Statist cosmopolitanism – the account of global justice this book tried to develop – argued that both the state and global distributive equality matter. States matter so much that without them global distributive equality would not be politically effective and motivationally sustainable. Global distributive equality matters so much that without it the partitioning of people into states would hardly be defensible.

We sought to explore these issues in the mode of activist political theory. Theorizing in that mode implies that we are interested not merely in criticizing the world but also in trying to change it. To understand how that can be achieved we had to distinguish between claims about principle and claims about agency. Claims about principle tell us what we should do. Claims about agency tell us how we do what we do. Most cosmopolitan accounts focus on principles and neglect agency. Most statist accounts focus on agency and derive principles from it. This book relied on a dialectical way of combining principles and agency. It argued that once the discussion of these categories is placed at the right level of analysis, both the global scope of equality and the normative relevance of the state promote an avant-garde account of global justice.

An important tradition in political theory starts by taking people as they are and the laws as they can be. Contrary to that tradition, most cosmopolitans start with an ideal of how laws can be and overlook the way people are. Most statists start with the reality of how people are and overlook how laws can be. Following that tradition, the version of global justice developed in this book pays attention to people as they are and to the laws as they can be. It defends a version of cosmopolitanism able to account both for the normative desirability of the cosmopolitan ideal *and* for its political feasibility and motivational sustainability.

But how should laws be? Laws, it is often said, should protect individuals' lives and guarantee the satisfaction of their basic needs. They should make sure that no one falls below a subsistence threshold and that every individual in the world has enough as is necessary for him to lead a minimally decent life.

Both cosmopolitans and statists agree upon as much. Yet once as much is agreed upon, then (at the level of principle) a great deal more follows than statists are usually prepared to grant. The combination of causally relevant claims with normatively fundamental commitments implies that a concern for the relief of absolute deprivation gives rise to a concern for the relief of relative deprivation. On matters of principle, even if we start as statists we might end up as cosmopolitans.

If we take seriously global equality at the level of principle, then (at the level of agency) much more follows than cosmopolitans have been prepared to discuss. We have to think about what sorts of obligations to place for relieving relative deprivation and about how such obligations could be effectively and sustainably allocated. This book argues that egalitarian obligations should be understood politically and not just morally. It further suggests that for political obligations to be effectively allocated, we must acknowledge the primary role of states. On matters of agency, even if we start as cosmopolitans, we might end up as statists. But what kind of statists?

To answer that question we developed the concept of a cosmopolitan 'avant-garde'. The cosmopolitan avant-garde is both rooted and outward looking. It acts within the state, yet thinks beyond it. It talks to people as they are about how the laws can be. It takes seriously existing concerns and commitments yet endorses egalitarian theory to transform institutions in a progressive political direction.

One way to criticize the argument outlined in the previous pages might be to point out that it relies on an over-optimistic account of the transformative potential of avant-garde political agency. It is undeniable that in many countries, especially Western democracies, avant-garde movements with a cosmopolitan orientation need more political cohesion, more clarity of purpose, transparent mechanisms of accountability, and greater normative awareness in order to be politically effective. The arguments presented in this book seek to make a contribution in more than one of these dimensions. Yet theory is only one component. It would hardly suffice by itself to trigger political transformation. It would be naive to assume that theorists need not rely on other kinds of resources, both political and cultural, in order to promote their emancipatory goals. In many European states, citizens who appear most affected by globalization processes are also those that tend to channel their reactions by either manifesting symptoms of political disaffection or seeking refuge in reactionary, populist and xenophobic policies. Admittedly, here the distance between political reality and our normative aspirations might appear very great indeed.

Even the most clear-thinking theorists would be powerless if they sought to proceed alone in changing these attitudes. Rescuing political agency where it appears weak or misguided requires active support by other actors (be they political, legal, or social) able to meaningfully communicate with the relevant fraction of the citizenry, and to channel their claims and concerns. Yet it would also be a mistake to perceive the task of reflecting on existing civic attitudes as purely a matter of political strategy, entirely separate from normative concerns. Political theory, provided it is pursued in an activist mode, has a vital role to play. It enables agents on the ground to take seriously existing concerns and commitments, but it also integrates their efforts with innovative interpretations of the function and purpose of shared political institutions. By linking older modes of political participation with fundamentally appropriate and coherent normative discourses, it is able to gradually shift the public culture in a way that contributes to the development of progressive projects. It is impossible to declare with certainty whether such projects will in the end succeed or fail. But objecting to them on grounds of optimism or pessimism, and on the basis of predictions concerning how things are more likely to go, seems much less productive than taking these projects seriously and trying to develop them further.

From a pragmatic perspective, clarifying exactly how local agents should interact with each other and within global advocacy networks, what degree of inclusion in the state cosmopolitan social movements should seek in order to make their claims more effective, and to what extent domestic political institutions should try to influence civil society actors or involve them in internal electoral processes are complex issues. An adequate answer to this puzzle would require a case-by-case analysis taking into account the specificities of each political community, its tradition of social mobilization, its institutional past and prospects of reform, and the ways its public culture has historically developed.[1] The emergence of a cosmopolitan avant-garde seeking to articulate a different interpretation of the function and purpose of existing institutions and to include global justice imperatives in the commitments of ordinary citizens is after all a recent phenomenon. The movement still needs to consolidate, and the political and cultural features of its various components would need to be defined more clearly before the cosmopolitan principles we have been discussing may be reflected in fully worked-out political platforms. Yet, from an empirical perspective, at an early stage of the process the real interest of activist initiatives all over the world lies not so much in what the movement achieves but in what kind of alternative concepts and discourses of political agency it manages to create; not in what problems it resolves but in what issues it problematizes. Without taking into account the contribution of all these elements, the kind of theory of global justice we have tried to present and defend in the previous chapters would have been very difficult to articulate.

One might object at this point that, although the empirical links between poverty and inequality to which these manifestations of political agency render us alert are very important, they fail to capture other instances of absolute deprivation and consequently other requirements of political transformation. Many important episodes of extreme poverty, so one might argue, are hardly linked to the expansion of global distributive inequalities and seem conducive merely to domestic factors. So, to take one relevant case, the so-called 'failed' states, the crucial problem seems to be the absence of a central system of government and severe deficiencies in the provision of public goods rather than the unequal distribution of resources triggered by globally relevant factors. Yet, that objector might continue, an analysis of the cosmopolitan avant-garde similar to the one we have provided would be misleading here. Its different way of understanding priorities for institutional reform leaves us with very few resources to address the question of political transformation in many severely deprived regions of the world.

The answer to that critique is that, if we place emphasis on the combination of appropriate diagnostic capacity with conceptual innovation in pursuing relevant reforms, there is nothing to prevent the avant-garde conception of political agency from applying even to cases such as these. Of course, in the latter case, both the justification of fundamental principles and the analysis of agency required for political transformation would need to be conducted at a different level, with different competing theories in mind and a different set of assumptions concerning the circumstances of injustice. However, the fact that we have chosen to focus on questions of *global* rather than *domestic* injustice does not imply that the latter are deemed less important, that activist political theory is not interested in them, or that the avant-garde model of political agency could not apply to similar cases. Future work extending the same methodological premises to these and other important issues in normative political theory might be both plausible and required. The constraints of this book prevent us for going into details on how that work ought to be pursued, yet some of the more general remarks offered in earlier chapters concerning activist political theory and the avant-garde account hopefully provide a starting point.

One might also object to this normative defence of the role of avant-gardes by pointing out that a similar model of political agency may not always serve progressive ideals or that avant-garde movements risk taking politics in an elitist, manipulative, or even authoritarian direction. This is an important objection, and those who have no faith in the power of reason, and the capacity of citizens to judge and select between different (more or less appropriate) sets of normative commitments, would find it difficult to answer. Notice, however, that the objection seems too vague to be successful at this point, for it seems to challenge not so much the mode of political engagement reflected in avant-garde political agency as the substantive set of commitments promoted by avant-garde political agents. Yet that substantive set of commitments was not justified merely with reference to a certain kind of practice (e.g. the avant-garde one), it was justified by analysing; what a fundamentally appropriate account of global justice should look like and by comparing cosmopolitanism to its rival theoretical alternatives. If the arguments in defence of cosmopolitanism presented in previous chapters are sound, the objection mentioned above will appear at best empirically controversial, at worst normatively inaccurate. The sceptics we are confronting at this point should no longer dispute that the kind of cosmopolitan theory offered here represents a progressive and democratic normative ideal.[2] They might simply remind us that, notwithstanding its normative plausibility, cosmopolitanism might have very few resources to be politically effective and motivationally sustainable. It is precisely this argument that the defence of cosmopolitan political agency attempts to challenge. If the statist cosmopolitan account offered in the previous pages is sound, cosmopolitan avant-gardes need not be elitist; on the contrary they promote inclusion. They also need not be manipulative; they stand for greater accountability. And far from raising an obstacle to democracy, they defend the necessity of expanding its reach.

A final doubt at this stage might concern the relationship between normative discourse and political agency that I have constructed above. In the defence of cosmopolitan avant-gardes presented throughout this work, ideals are importantly informed by existing expressions of political agency. However, as we have already seen, the claims arising from these manifestations are not sufficient by themselves to illustrate why a particular theory is more fundamentally appropriate than another: a significant amount of work is done through pure normative argument. This should not be surprising. In the dialectical model we have been defending, political theory, if pursued in an activist mode, is both informed by existing concerns and commitments and required to further articulate these concerns in light of specific first-order values. Theory thus interacts with political action in a potentially transformative fashion. The progressive nature of this interaction accounts for the historical direction of the moral learning processes we have been trying to emphasize. These processes owe their distinctiveness to the particular associative circumstances in which they first emerge, and their emancipatory force to their ability to outperform their rivals with regard to their diagnostic, innovative, and heuristic potential.

One might argue here that the cosmopolitan avant-garde is not the only model through which to pursue transformative political projects. It is of course plausible to think that one might be able to obtain as much through other mechanisms, for example, changing international law, reforming international institutions, or cultivating mainstream politics. But the question at this stage is not who might *possibly* take initiative to change existing states of affairs. The question is: who is already out there, suffering the consequences of global injustice and showing support for cosmopolitan commitments? The answer is: the cosmopolitan avant-garde. That is the concept from which we have to start.

Justifying global egalitarianism from a fundamentally appropriate normative perspective is not enough to guarantee the political feasibility and motivational sustainability of the project in existing political circumstances. Without collective political agency animating the general will in each particular state, without historically reflected goals, cosmopolitan ideals appear unhelpfully detached from local practices and interpretations. At worst they end up nurturing political elitism, at best they construct moral utopias. Even a broadly shared moral consent on the necessity of global justice might not be able to substitute the political and cultural mechanisms of adaptation grounded on a particular collective self-understanding. It is as important to start a theory of global justice with ideal principles as it is to conclude it with at least some notion of how to cope with the nonideal dimension of politics. Debating the normative justification of global equality matters as much as reflecting on concrete political processes of hegemony construction and the political participation required for its pursuit. Without cosmopolitanism at the level of principle, statist agency is morally indefensible. Without statism at the level of agency, cosmopolitan principles are politically ineffective and motivationally unsustainable. The avant-garde is crucial to both principles and agency. To explore in what ways is to engage with political theory in an activist mode.

# Notes

## INTRODUCTION

1. The dialogue, also mentioned by Adorno in his essay 'On Commitment', was confirmed by Picasso himself in an interview with Simone Téry published on 14 March 1945 in *Les Lettres françaises.* 'That's true,' he is reported to have said, 'that's more or less true. Sometimes the Boches would come to visit me, pretending to admire my paintings. I gave them postcards of my *Guernica* picture saying: "Take them along, souvenirs! Souvenirs!" cited in Gijs van Hensbergen, *Guernica: The Biography of a Twentieth-Century Icon* (London: Bloomsbury, 2004) at 139.
2. See the interview with Simone Téry, 'Picasso n'est pas officier dans l'armée Française', 24 March 1945, *Les Lettres françaises*, 48 at 6, my translation.
3. It should be noted that not all cosmopolitans defend global egalitarianism. Many are limited to supporting a rights-based conception of global justice, others pursue needs-based accounts, and others still endorse theories of global democracy. In this book I focus only on cosmopolitan egalitarians, partly because doing so allows us to have a better grasp of the controversy with statists, and partly because if more demanding forms of cosmopolitanism can be defended, the route to integrating and reforming other versions is straightforward. In what follows I therefore use the terms 'cosmopolitanism' and 'egalitarianism' interchangeably. It is worth pointing out, however, that many of the issues concerning political agency and the normative standing of associative political relations maintain their relevance even in the case of other (less demanding) forms of cosmopolitanism.
4. A historically centred analysis of the relationship between normative principles and political agency is shared by Kant with prominent successive philosophers, including Hegel and Marx. However, examining in detail these authors' account of dialectic would take us too far afield, and is only marginally relevant to contemporary debates on cosmopolitanism.

## CHAPTER 1

1. 'We sometimes use this term, in joking, in order to refer to a man who has no fixed residence, that is to say a man who is nowhere a stranger.' Both definitions are cited in Georges Pieri, 'Raison et Cosmopolitisme au XVIIIe Siècle', in Lorenzo Bianchi (ed.), *L'Idea di Cosmopolitismo. Circolazione e Metamorfosi* (Naples: Liguori, 2002), 357–64 at 358.
2. The assumption appears frequently in normative studies emphasizing the roots of the cosmopolitan project in the philosophy of the Enlightenment, particularly the thought of Kant. See, for example, Martha Nussbaum, 'Kant and Stoic Cosmopolitanism', *The Journal of Political Philosophy*, 5/1 (1997) at 1–25.; Onora O'Neill, *Bounds of Justice* (Cambridge: Cambridge University Press, 2000) at 136–7; Kok-Chor Tan, *Justice without Borders: Cosmopolitanism, Nationalism, and Patriotism* (Cambridge: Cambridge University Press, 2004) at 33–5; Jeremy Waldron, 'What is Cosmopolitan?', *The Journal of Political Philosophy*, 8/2 (2000), 227–43 at 236 ff.

3. For good historical overviews on the Enlightenment idea of cosmopolitanism and its tensions with patriotism, see Lorenzo Bianchi and Alberto Postigliola (eds.), *Un 'Progetto Filosofico della Modernità per la Pace Perpetua di Immanuel Kant*. (Naples: Liguori, 2000); Lorenzo Bianchi (ed.), *L'Idea di Cosmopolitismo. Circolazione e Metamorfosi* (Naples: Liguori, 2002); Volker Gerhardt, Rolf-Peter Horstmann, and Ralph Schumacher (eds.), *Kant und die Berliner Aufklärung. Akten des IX. Internationalen Kant-Kongresses* (Berlin: Walter de Gruyter, 2001); Pauline Kleingeld, 'Six Varieties of Cosmopolitanism in Late Eighteenth-Century Germany', *Journal of the History of Ideas,* 60/3 (1999) at 505–24; Nicolao Merker, *L'Illuminismo in Germania. L'Età di Lessing* (Rome: Editori Riuniti, 1989); Thomas J. Schlereth, *The Cosmopolitan Ideal in Enlightenment Thought* (Notre Dame: University of Notre Dame Press, 1977).

4. See Eric Brown, 'Hellenistic Cosmopolitanism', in Mary Louise Gill and Pierre Pellegrin (eds.), *A Companion to Ancient Philosophy* (Oxford: Blackwell, 2006), 549–58 at 549; Derek Heater, *World Citizenship and Government: Cosmopolitan Ideas in the History of Western Political Thought* (New York: St. Martin's Press, 1996) at 6–8.

5. Immanuel Kant, 'An Answer to the Question: What Is Enlightenment?', in Mary J. Gregor (ed.), *Practical Philosophy* (Cambridge: Cambridge University Press, [1784] 1996), 11–22 at 11.

6. It must be noted that Socrates' commitment to Athens was not unconditional. As Plato often makes clear, Socrates appreciated Athenian democracy and its requisite respect for free speech because he recognized that only where such values were politically realized did his teaching become at all possible. See Grg. 461e1-3; Apology 37c5-e2; Meno 80b4-7, in Plato, *The Collected Dialogues of Plato Including the Letters*, eds. Huntingon Cairns and Edith Hamilton (Princeton: Princeton University Press, 1961).

7. Brown, 'Hellenistic Cosmopolitanism' at 551.

8. See his *Codex Juris Gentium* (1693) in Gottfried Wilhelm Leibniz, *Political Writings*, ed. Patrick Riley (Cambridge: Cambridge University Press, 1988) at 171, translation amended. For a discussion of these issues, see André Robinet, 'G. W. Leibniz: L'Esprit Cosmopolitique jusqu'à la Lettre', at 10 in Lorenzo Bianchi (ed.), (Naples: Liguori, 2002) at 5–26.

9. Cited in Robinet, *L' Esprit Cosmopolitique jusqu'à la Lettre,* at 10.

10. Gottfried Wilhelm Leibniz, *New Essays on Human Understanding*, eds. Peter Remnant and Jonathan Bennett (Cambridge: Cambridge University Press, [1704] 1996), esp. pp. 1–32.

11. Cited in Robinet, 'G. W. Leibniz: L'Esprit cosmopolitique jusqu'à la Lettre', at 12.

12. 22 February 1768, *Correspondance*, cited in Schlereth, *The Cosmopolitan Ideal in Enlightenment Thought* at 1.

13. Baron de Montesquieu, *Pensées et fragments inédits*, vol. 1, cited in ibid. at 47.

14. See Gita May, 'Le Cosmopolite ou Le Citoyen du Monde; La Capitale des Gaules ou La Nouvelle Babylone by Louis-Charles Fougeret De Monbron', *The French Review,* 45/3 (1972), 737–8 at 738.

15. 'All the countries are the same to me as long as I can enjoy freely the clarity of the skies and comfortably entertain my own person until the end of its days. Absolute

master of my will, and sovereign independent, changing place of residence, customs and climate according to my whim, I hold onto everything and hold onto nothing.' See Fougeret De Monbron, *Le Cosmopolite ou Le Citoyen du Monde*, ed. Raymond Trousson (Paris: Ducros, [1750] 1970) at 130. My translation.

16. 'Let my country perish, let the county where I command perish too, let both citizens and strangers perish. . .All the places of the universe are the same to me. When I will have devastated, sucked, exhausted one region there will always be another where I could bring my gold and enjoy it in peace'; see Guillaume-Thomas Raynal, *Histoire des Deux Indes* (Paris: La Découverte, [1781] 1980) at 70. My translation.

17. François Marie Arouet Voltaire, *Political Writings*, trans. D. Williams (Cambridge: Cambridge University Press, [1752] 1994) at 27–8.

18. Ibid. at 28.

19. Ibid. at 25–6.

20. Ibid.

21. Ibid.

22. See François Marie Arouet Voltaire, *Le Siècle de Louis XIV* (Paris Garnier-Flammarion, [1774] 1966).

23. See for a historical account, Istvan Hont, *Jealousy of Trade: International Competition and the Nation State in Historical Perspective* (Cambridge, MA: Harvard University Press, 2005).

24. Jean Jacques Rousseau, *The Discourses and Other Early Political Writings*, trans. V. Gourevitch (Cambridge: Cambridge University Press, [1775] 1997) at 175–80. It is interesting to notice how Kant makes use of the same term in discussing the role of civilization in his essay on universal history; see Immanuel Kant, 'Idea for a Universal History with a Cosmopolitan Purpose', in Hans Reiss (ed.), *Political Writings* (Cambridge: Cambridge University Press, [1784] 1991), 41–53 at 49.

25. Cited in G. R. Havens, *Voltaire's Marginalia on the pages of Rousseau: A Comparative Study of Ideas,* (Columbus: The Ohio State University, 1933) at 15.

26. Rousseau, *The Discourses and Other Early Political Writings* at 174.

27. Ibid.

28. Ibid. at 152.

29. Jean Jacques Rousseau, 'Of the Social Contract', in Victor Gourevitch (ed.), *The Social Contract and Other Later Political Writings* (Cambridge: Cambridge University Press, [1762] 1997), 39–161 at 158.

30. Jean-Jacques Rousseau, *Émile*, trans. Barbara Foxley (Charleston: Biblio Bazaar, [1762] 2006) at 14.

31. 'The first man who, having enclosed a piece of ground, to whom it occurred to say *This is mine* and found people sufficiently simple to believe him, was the true founder of civil society.' Rousseau, *The Discourses and Other Early Political Writings* at 164.

32. Ibid. at 173.

33. Rousseau, 'Of the Social Contract' at 40.

34. I will return to both issues in Chapter 6.

35. Rousseau, 'Of the Social Contract' at 81.

36. See for an excellent historical analysis of this problematique in Enlightenment political thought, Sankar Muthu, *Enlightenment against Empire* (Princeton: Princeton University Press, 2003).
37. Jean Jacques Rousseau, 'Abstract and Judgement of Saint Pierre's Project of Perpetual Peace', in Stanley Hoffman and David Fidler (eds.), *Rousseau on International Relations* (Oxford: Clarendon Press, [1756] 1991) at 54.
38. Ibid.
39. 'Everyone can see that what unites any form of society is a community of interests, and what disintegrates it is their conflict,' Rousseau claims. This is why 'as soon as society is founded, some coercive power must be provided to co-ordinate the actions of its members'. Rousseau, 'Abstract and Judgement of Saint Pierre's Project of Perpetual Peace' at 61.
40. Kant, 'Idea for a Universal History with a Cosmopolitan Purpose' at 47.
41. Ibid. at 44–5.
42. For a longer discussion of the systematic role of the culture of skill and the culture of discipline in Kant's philosophy of history, see Lea Ypi, 'Natura Daedala Rerum? On the Justification of Historical Progress in Kant's Guarantee of Perpetual Peace', *Kantian Review,* 14/2 (2010b) at 118–48.
43. Kant, 'Idea for a Universal History with a Cosmopolitan Purpose' at 45.
44. See on the latter issue Peter Niesen, 'Hospitality and Colonialism', *Politics and Ethics Review,* 3/1 (2007) at 90–108.
45. Kant, 'Idea for a Universal History with a Cosmopolitan Purpose' at 51.
46. Ibid.
47. For Otfried Höffe, those are pragmatic reasons; see Otfried Höffe, *Kant's Cosmopolitan Theory* (Cambridge: Cambridge University Press, 2006) at 189–203. Howard Williams, Georg Cavallar, and Pauline Kleingeld argue for a kind of mediation between normative and empirical requirements; see Georg Cavallar, *The Rights of Strangers. Theories of International Hospitality, the Global Community and Political Justice since Vitoria* (Aldershot: Ashgate, 2002) at 323–49; Pauline Kleingeld, 'Kant's Cosmopolitan Law: World Citizenship for a Global Order', *Kantian Review,* 2 (1998) at 72–90; Howard Williams, *Kant's Political Philosophy* (Oxford: Blackwell, 1983) at 253–60. Katrin Flikschuh considers the problem to create irresolvable tensions within the normative discourse of Kant's *Doctrine of Right*; see Katrin Flikschuh, 'Kant's Sovereignty Dilemma: A Contemporary Analysis', *The Journal of Political Philosophy,* 18/4 (2010) at 469–93.
48. For a longer discussion of the systematic reasons that trigger this change, especially in the light of Kant's analysis of the capacity for judgement, see my 'Natura Daedala Rerum? On the Justification of Historical Progress in Kant's Guarantee of Perpetual Peace' at 130–42.
49. Immanuel Kant, 'Toward Perpetual Peace', in Mary Gregor (ed.), *Practical Philosophy* (Cambridge: Cambridge University Press, [1795] 1996), 311–52 at 327.
50. Kant is very clear on the historical impact of similar political initiatives 'even if the end viewed in connection with this occurrence should not now be attained, even if the revolution or reform of a national constitution should finally miscarry' and even if 'after some time had elapsed, everything should relapse into its former rut'. Its influence, he argues, is 'too widely propagated in all areas of the world to not be

recalled on any favourable occasion by the nations which would then be roused to a repetition of new efforts of this kind; because then [. . .] the intended constitution, at a certain time, must finally attain that constancy which instruction by repeated experience suffices to establish in the minds of all'. See Immanuel Kant, 'The Conflict of the Faculties', in Allen W. Wood and George Di Giovanni (eds.), *Religion and Rational Theology* (Cambridge: Cambridge University Press, [1798] 2001), 233–328 at 304.

51. Kant, 'Toward Perpetual Peace' at 328.
52. Immanuel Kant, 'The Metaphysics of Morals', in Mary Gregor (ed.), *Practical Philosophy* (Cambridge: Cambridge University Press, [1797] 1996), 353–604 at 489.
53. See Kant's remarks on patriotism in Immanuel Kant, 'On the common saying: That may be correct in theory, but it is of no use in practice', in Mary Gregor (ed.), *Practical Philosophy* (Cambridge: Cambridge University Press, [1793] 1996), 273–310 at 294–5, and Kant, 'Toward Perpetual Peace' at 322–5.
54. Kant, 'The Metaphysics of Morals' at 489–90.
55. Ibid. at 482.
56. Ibid. Unfortunately I cannot discuss in more detail the justification of cosmopolitan right derived from the global extension of interactions among individuals but only mention that it may be linked to the broader 'relational' requirement of Kant's metaphysics of right. An excellent discussion of this issue is provided in Katrin Flikschuh, 'Kant's Indemonstrable Postulate of Right: A Response to Paul Guyer', *Kantian Review*, 12 (2006) at 1–39. Pauline Kleingeld has also focused on the justification of a cosmopolitan right by linking it to Kant's innate right to freedom, see Kleingeld, 'Kant's Cosmopolitan Law: World Citizenship for a Global Order' at 78–79.
57. On this issue, see Lea Ypi, 'A Permissive Theory of Territorial Rights', *The European Journal of Philosophy*, forthcoming.
58. Kant, 'The Metaphysics of Morals' at 489.
59. Ibid.
60. This 'pragmatic' argument is made by Höffe, *Kant's Cosmopolitan Theory* at 189–203.
61. Kant, 'The Metaphysics of Morals' at 487.
62. Jean Jacques Rousseau, 'Considerations on the Government of Poland', in Victor Gourevitch (ed.), *The Social Contract and Other Later Political Writings* (Cambridge: Cambridge University Press, [1772] 1997), 177–260 at 113. Kant, 'The Metaphysics of Morals' at 336.
63. Kant, 'Toward Perpetual Peace' at 336.
64. Ibid.
65. Kant, 'Toward Perpetual Peace' at 327. Katrin Flikschuh rightly emphasizes the limits of the analogy between individuals and states with regard to the question of sovereignty. As she observes the relational metaphysics of Kant's *Doctrine of Right* allows for a distinction between the former and the latter, the ability of individuals to claim rights does not precede but rather follows the existence of a sovereign authority. Unlike states, individuals are not right-enforcers; they may be compelled to enter a civil condition but an attempt to coerce states would result in the

dissolution of every relation of right. See Flikschuh, 'Kant's Sovereignty Dilemma: A Contemporary Analysis'.

66. Kant, 'Toward Perpetual Peace' at 330–1.

67. Contrary to what is usually assumed by contemporary cosmopolitans, for example, Charles Beitz, 'Cosmopolitan Liberalism and the States System', in Chris Brown (ed.), *Political Structuring in Europe* (London: Routledge, 1994) at 124–6; O'Neill, *Bounds of Justice* at 171–85; Thomas Pogge, *World Poverty and Human Rights* (Cambridge: Polity Press, 2002) at 182–95. I will return to contemporary perspectives in the third chapter.

68. Kant, 'Toward Perpetual Peace' at 340.

69. Ibid.

70. Ibid.

71. Ibid.

72. Ibid.

73. Ibid.

74. Part of the reason is historical; the agents Kant has in mind here are mostly heads of state: the kind of enlightened monarchs one might have hoped would take to heart the progressive causes of the eighteenth century in order to gradually introduce political changes. However, if we abstract from this historical limitation and consider how the range of mechanisms of political participation is now much more extended, it is possible to defend the role of similar innovating agents without identifying them with single politicians and thinking about them as citizens who are collectively organized. For more on this issue see my last chapter.

75. Kant, 'Idea for a Universal History with a Cosmopolitan Purpose' at 47.

76. See Seyla Benhabib, *Citizens, Residents and Aliens: Aliens, Residents, and Citizens* (Cambridge: Cambridge University Press, 2004); Norberto Bobbio, *L'Età dei Diritti* (Torino: Einaudi, 1990); James Bohman and Matthias Lutz-Bachmann (eds.), *Perpetual Peace: Essays on Kant's Cosmopolitan Ideal* (Cambridge, MA: MIT Press, 1997); Jürgen Habermas, *The Inclusion of the Other: Studies in Political Theory* (Cambridge, MA: MIT Press, 1998); Jürgen Habermas, *The Postnational Constellation* (Cambridge: Polity Press, 2001); Kleingeld, 'Kant's Cosmopolitan Law: World Citizenship for a Global Order'; Pauline Kleingeld, 'Approaching Perpetual Peace: Kant's Defence of a League of States and His Ideal of a World Federation', *European Journal of Philosophy,* 12 (2004) at 304–25; Martha C. Nussbaum, 'Kant and Stoic Cosmopolitanism', *The Journal of Political Philosophy,* 5/1 (1997) at 1–25. For a more balanced approach, see Katrin Flikschuh, *Kant and Modern Political Philosophy* (Cambridge: Cambridge University Press, 2000).

## CHAPTER 2

1. At one extreme of this spectrum one finds, for example, the work of G. A. Cohen, who distinguishes between fundamental principles of justice and what he calls 'rules of regulation'; see Gerald A. Cohen, *Rescuing Justice and Equality* (Cambridge: Harvard University Press, 2008). For other sympathetic discussions, also see Adam Swift, 'The Value of Philosophy in Non-Ideal Circumstances', *Social Theory and Practice,* 34/3 (2008) at 363–87; Zofia Stemplowska, 'What's Ideal about Ideal

Theory?', *Social Theory and Practice,* 34/3 (2008) at 319–40; David Estlund, *Democratic Authority: A Philosophical Framework* (Princeton: Princeton University Press, 2009) at 258–277. Notice that not all ideal theorists agree with the temporal or normative sequence presented above, but for one view that endorses it, see the Rawlsian-inspired analysis in A. J. Simmons, 'Ideal and Nonideal Theory', *Philosophy and Public Affairs,* 38/1 (Winter 2010) at 5–36.

2. See, for example, Amartya Sen's critique of what he calls 'transcendental theories of justice' in Amartya Sen, *The Idea of Justice* (London: Allen Lane, 2009) at 467. See also for defences of the nonideal approach, some more conciliatory than others, Ingrid Robeyns, 'Ideal Theory in Theory and Practice', *Social Theory and Practice,* 34/3 (2008) at 341–62; Charles W. Mills, 'Ideal Theory as Ideology', *Hypatia,* 20/3 (2005) at 165–184; Colin Farrelly, 'Justice in Ideal Theory: A Refutation', *Political Studies,* 55/4 (2007) at 844–64; David Miller (2010), 'A Tale of Two Cities; Or, Political Philosophy as Lamentation' (unpublished manuscript).

3. As Rawls puts it in *A Theory of Justice*: 'The intuitive idea is to split the theory of justice into two parts. The first, or ideal, part assumes strict compliance and works out the principles that characterize a well-ordered society under favorable circumstances. [...] Nonideal theory, the second part, is worked out *after* an ideal conception of justice has been chosen' (Rawls 1999a at 216). Notice, however, that Rawls also broadened the distinction in his recent work; for an excellent account of the development, see Simmons, 'Ideal and Nonideal Theory'.

4. For recent discussions, overviews on the literature, and different ways of making the distinction between an ideal and a nonideal approach, see Robeyns, 'Ideal Theory in Theory and Practice'; Stemplowska, 'What's Ideal about Ideal Theory?'; Laura Valentini, 'On the Apparent Paradox of Ideal Theory', *The Journal of Political Philosophy,* 17/3 (2009) at 332–55.

5. So, for example, Rawls' theory of justice starts by imagining a well-ordered society in which people have a sense of justice and are motivated by the desire to form, revise, and pursue a sense of the good. Dworkin's theory of equality of resources assumes that individuals make choices regarding resource distribution without being influenced by envy and prejudice or that society in which such decisions are made is unaffected by technological difficulties. For examples illustrating this distinction, see Valentini, 'On the Apparent Paradox of Ideal Theory' at 332–3.

6. As G.A. Cohen puts it, 'the question for political philosophy is not what we should do but what we should think, even when what we should think makes no practical difference' Cohen, *Rescuing Justice and Equality,* p. 268. For a defence of the relevance of false and idealized assumptions, and of the value of developing normative theories in counterfactual circumstances, see also Kimberley Brownlee and Zofia Stemplowska, 'Trapped in an Experience Machine with a Famous Violinist: Thought Experiments in Normative Theory' (unpublished manuscript).

7. Both assumptions are implicit, for example, in Rawls' analysis of a realistic utopia in *The Law of Peoples* (see John Rawls, *The Law of Peoples* (Cambridge, MA: Harvard University Press, 1999a) at 11–23) or in David Miller's defence of contextualist political theory (see David Miller, *Principles of Social Justice* (Cambridge, MA: Harvard University Press, 1999) at 42–61). More references to this

debate and other texts with a similar methodological approach are given in the following pages.

8. For example, this way of casting the distinction will also come as a surprise to many Rawlsians (and would have probably troubled Rawls himself). However, I believe it captures at a more appropriate level of generality various concerns raised in the literature and, as will become clearer in what follows, allows us to see better the distinctive ways in which ideal and nonideal approaches reflect on the method and aims of the normative enterprise. It also prevents the debate from degenerating into a dispute about the views of particular authors and the definition and role of ideal and nonideal approaches in the work of each (e.g. is Rawls an ideal theorist as Sen maintains? or is he a nonideal theorist as recently emphasized by Cohen?). The distinction is flexible enough to allow us to explore particular arguments whilst granting that some aspects of an author's work can be seen as contributions to an ideal approach and others to a nonideal approach (as is often the case with Rawls).

9. The most prominent recent critique along those lines can be found in Sen, *The Idea of Justice.*

10. This characterization of dialectic seems fairly uncontroversial; indeed, it is one that has been endorsed even by some of its most authoritative critics. Popper, for example, defines dialectic as the method of 'trial and error'; see Karl R. Popper, 'What Is Dialectic?', *Mind,* 49/196 (1940), 403–26 at 404. In what follows, I will keep to this uncontroversial definition and try to defend dialectic as a heuristic method, rather than in its more complicated Hegelian and Marxian versions where it characterizes the intrinsic movement of what Hegel calls 'the concept'. This not out of hostility to the authors, but because the more limited defence of dialectic as the method of 'trial and error' will both take on board critics like Popper and be sufficient for this book's purposes.

11. Here, I shall not explore the issue of how we develop these first-order principles. Some reflections on the question, as applied to the global justice debate, will be found in the chapters that follow. At this point my aim is to show simply how activist political theory combines these principles (whatever they are and however we approximate them) with an analysis of existing social practices which reconciles insights from both ideal and nonideal perspectives.

12. The final chapter of this book explores a number of concrete examples in which a similar dynamic can be observed.

13. See for empirical accounts of how a similar issue of 'problem construction' emerges in deliberative policy research the essays contained in Maarten A. Hajer and Hendrik Wagenaar, *Deliberative Policy Analysis: Understanding Governance in the Network Society* (Cambridge: Cambridge University Press, 2003).

14. In the following, I use 'theory' and 'families of theories' interchangeably. This is to leave open the possibility that the use of the same dialectical method by different interpreters might deliver different theories. However, it is important to notice that theories that are part of the same family will differ from each other in their details, not in their general outlook and understanding of a particular problem. They will be, as it were, part of the same research programme, confronting a different, more or less adequate, research programme (with different component

theories). This is not to deny that there may be a problem of adjudication in this case too but the revision of theories that are part of the same family will be more a question of degree and mutual adjustment of their premises than of radical challenge of all their assumptions. Where disagreements within the same family of theories remain outstanding, it might be possible to invoke suitable procedures for resolving them, for example, democratic deliberation or a voting procedure.

15. See for a discussion Michael Rosen, *Hegel's Dialectic and Its Criticism* (Cambridge: Cambridge University Press, 1982) at 23–54.

16. See for this critique Popper, 'What Is Dialectic?'.

17. As Habermas puts it, 'the revolutionized situation contains the one that has been surpassed, because the insight of the new consists precisely in the experience of revolutionary release from the old consciousness. [...] A state defined by both cognitive performances and fixed attitudes can be overcome only if its genesis is analytically remembered', Jürgen Habermas, *Knowledge and Human Interests* (London: Heinemann, 1972) at 17–20.

18. The distinction between idealization and abstraction, whilst significant in itself, does not matter for the larger point I am making here. For an analysis of that distinction, see Onora O'Neill, 'Abstraction, Idealization and Ideology in Ethics', in J.D.G. Evans (ed.), *Moral Philosophy and Contemporary Problems* (Cambridge: Cambridge University Press, 1987) at 55–69.

19. For a discussion of how idealizations make the world 'simpler or better' than it really is, see Valentini, 'On the Apparent Paradox of Ideal Theory'.

20. This critique is also familiar to the so-called justificationist approaches in the sciences; see, for example, Paul Feyerabend, 'How to Defend Philosophy against Science', in Nigel Warburton (ed.), *Philosophy. Basic Readings* (Abingdon: Routledge, [1975] 2005), 365–75 at 368; and Imre Lakatos, 'Falsification and the Methodology of Scientific Research Programmes', in Imre Lakatos and Alan Musgrave (eds.), *Criticism and the Growth of Knowledge* (Cambridge: Cambridge University Press, 1970) at 91–196.

21. For a discussion of the role of counterfactual premises in normative theory, see Brownlee and Stemplowska, 'Trapped in an Experience Machine with a Famous Violinist: Thought Experiments in Normative Theory'.

22. For a critique of this point, see also Robeyns, 'Ideal Theory in Theory and Practice', and David Miller, 'A Tale of Two Cities; or, Political Philosophy as Lamentation' (unpublished manuscript, 2010).

23. One might argue here that the method of reflective equilibrium is less vulnerable to these objections. However, that method also relies heavily on the relevance of intuitions and various assumptions concerning a pre-existing moral sense, making the method more or less reliable depending on whether it is possible to identify a filter that distinguishes genuine moral insight from prejudice. For a discussion of the difficulty of relying on intuitions selected in this way, even when adopting the method of reflective equilibrium, see Stefan Sencerz, 'Moral Intuitions and Justification in Ethics', *Philosophical Studies,* 50/1 (1986) at 77–94.

24. Lakatos, 'Falsification and the Methodology of Scientific Research Programmes' at 102.

25. The Beverly Hills example is in Roger Crisp, 'Equality, Priority, and Compassion', *Ethics*, 113 (2003), 745–63 at 755. However, variations of it are relatively well known and thoroughly discussed in the egalitarian literature.

26. See, for example, Michael Blake, 'Distributive Justice, State Coercion, and Autonomy', *Philosophy and Public Affairs*, 30/3 (2001), 257–96 at 290 ff.

27. For the idea that it is very difficult to know what to say about a world that is so different from ours that it simply does not track any of the concepts we are familiar with, see also Patrick Horace Nowell Smith, *Ethics* (London: Penguin Books, 1954) at 8.

28. In fact, as many committed egalitarians like to emphasize, when faced with difficulties concerning the interpretation of pure principles with reference to complex cases, it is important to be a pluralist about value.

29. For a discussion of the motivational effects of ideal theory on political action and an even more radical critique of the extent to which ideal theories facilitate or hinder engaging with issues of political change, see also Miller, 'A Tale of Two Cities; or, Political Philosophy as Lamentation'.

30. See J. G. A. Pocock, *Political Thought and History: Essays on Theory and Method* (Cambridge: Cambridge University Press, 2009) at 51–66.

31. I shall explore all these features in further detail when examining the case of global justice in the chapters that follow.

32. For discussion of this point, see Andrea Sangiovanni, 'Justice and the Priority of Politics to Morality', *The Journal of Political Philosophy*, 16/2 (2008) at 137–64.

33. See for this formulation Sangiovanni, 'Justice and the Priority of Politics to Morality' at 141. See also 'the content, scope, and justification of a conception of justice depends on the structure and form of the practices that the conception is intended to govern', ibid. at 138. See also for a similar practice-based approach to the issue of human rights, Charles R. Beitz, *The Idea of Human Rights* (Oxford: Oxford University Press, 2009) and for a critique, Pablo Gilabert, 'Humanist and Political Perspectives on Human Rights', *Political Theory*, 39 (4), 439–467 (2011).

34. For a discussion of this argument and more specific references to the literature, see the following chapters.

35. Detailed discussion is offered in the second part of this work.

36. See Ronald Dworkin, *Law's Empire* (Cambridge, MA: Harvard University Press, 1986) at ch. 2; Aaron James, 'Constructing Justice for Existing Practice: Rawls and the Status Quo', *Philosophy and Public Affairs*, 33/3 (2005) at 281–316; Sangiovanni, 'Justice and the Priority of Politics to Morality'. For a recent discussion of the position with reference to the global justice debate, see Laura Valentini, 'Global Justice and Practice-Dependence: Conventionalism, Institutionalism, Functionalism', *The Journal of Political Philosophy*, 19 (4), 375–497.

37. Dworkin, *Law's Empire* at ch. 2; James, 'Constructing Justice for Existing Practice: Rawls and the Status Quo' at 301.

38. This is precisely why for Rawls we begin our enquiry on fundamental principles of justice by focusing on what he calls 'the basic structure of society', whose effects on human lives are 'profound and present from the start'; John Rawls, *A Theory of Justice* (Rev. edn.; Cambridge, MA: Harvard University Press, 1999b).

39. John Rawls, *Political Liberalism* (New York: Columbia University Press, 1993) at 37. For discussion of this point, see also James, 'Constructing Justice for Existing Practice: Rawls and the Status Quo' at 300 ff.

40. See for this analysis Lakatos, 'Falsification and the Methodology of Scientific Research Programmes' at 98.

41. James Ladyman, *Understanding Philosophy of Science* (London: Routledge, 2002) at 113.

42. See for a reply along these lines Sangiovanni, 'Justice and the Priority of Politics to Morality' at 149, where Miller and Walzer are seen as representatives of the former, and Rawls as representative of the latter.

43. For a similar analysis of culture, see Ernst Cassirer, *An Essay on Man: An Introduction to a Philosophy of Human Culture* (New Haven: Yale University Press, 1977) at 237.

44. So, for example, Rawls' focus on the tension between freedom and equality, as reflected in the main institutions of a well-functioning democratic society, is clearly grounded on a cultural reading of the processes that led to the affirmation of such tension, including an interpretation of particular historical conflicts, the progressive emergence of foundational legal documents, and so on. Even practices embedded within institutions that one might initially think are independent from cultural phenomena, for example, the European Union or the United Nations, will appear upon closer scrutiny as the product of historical processes of expansion, integration, and transformation that are irreducible to merely political features of interaction.

45. See Sangiovanni, 'Justice and the Priority of Politics to Morality' at 147, who links this response to the distinction between conventionalism and institutionalism mentioned above.

46. So, for example, some of Rawls' observations whereby the conceptions of the person as free and equal and of society as a fair system of cooperation are embedded in the political self-representation of functioning democracies seem to go in this direction.

47. For a historically informed normative discussion of how the injustice of slavery might have contributed to its demise, and how certain ethical explanations might have normative force, see Joshua Cohen, 'The Arc of the Moral Universe', *Philosophy and Public Affairs*, 26/2 (Spring 1997) at 91–134.

48. One should not think of this process as composed of stages that are clearly, temporarily distinct from each other. Experience will often show that many elements from each stage will be present at once, and I have only distinguished them here for clarity of illustration.

49. Needless to say, what counts as 'significant' is not an issue that can be solved from a merely theoretical perspective; normative theory here needs to proceed in conjunction with empirical political science.

50. See Pocock, *Political Thought and History: Essays on Theory and Method* at 63.

51. Theories with racist/xenophobic implications could provide an example of return to regressive discourses (see also my point about slavery above).

52. See also Marx's remarks on the universal status of the working class in Karl Marx, *Critique of Hegel's 'Philosophy of Right'*, ed. Joseph J. O'Malley (Cambridge: Cambridge University Press, [1843] 1977).

53. J. G. A. Pocock, *The Machiavellian Moment: Florentine Political Thought and the Atlantic Republican Tradition* (Princeton: Princeton University Press, 2003) at 634.

54. Quentin Skinner, *Visions of Politics* (3. Hobbes and Civil Science; Cambridge: Cambridge University Press, 2002).

## CHAPTER 3

1. See David Miller, *On Nationality* (Oxford: Oxford University Press, 1997) at 49–80; David Miller, 'Against Global Egalitarianism', *The Journal of Ethics,* 9/1–2 (2005), 55–79 at 55–79; David Miller, *National Responsibility and Global Justice* (Oxford: Oxford University Press, 2007) at 23–50; Michael Walzer, *Spheres of Justice: A Defence of Pluralism and Equality* (Oxford: Robertson, 1983) at ch. II. The argument from 'common sympathies' is in John Rawls, *The Law of Peoples* (Cambridge, MA: Harvard University Press, 1999a) at 23–5, but inspired by John Stuart Mill, 'Considerations on Representative Government', in John Gray (ed.), *On Liberty and Other Essays* (Oxford: Oxford University Press, [1861] 1991), 203–470 at 391. See also Samuel Scheffler, *Boundaries and Allegiances: Problems of Justice and Responsibility in Liberal Thought* (Oxford: Oxford University Press, 2003) at 48–81.

2. For the political–associativist argument, see Michael Blake, 'Distributive Justice, State Coercion, and Autonomy', *Philosophy and Public Affairs,* 30/3 (2001) at 257–96; Thomas Nagel, 'The Problem of Global Justice', *Philosophy and Public Affairs,* 33/2 (2005) at 113–47; Mathias Risse, 'What to Say About the State', *Social Theory and Practice,* 32/4 (2006) at 671–98; Andrea Sangiovanni, 'Global Justice, Reciprocity, and the State', *Philosophy and Public Affairs,* 35/1 (2007) at 3–39.

3. See Charles Beitz, 'Rawls' Law of Peoples', *Ethics,* 110/4 (2000) at 669–96; and Martha Nussbaum, *Frontiers of Justice* (Cambridge, MA: Harvard University Press, 2006) at 245.

4. For similar critiques, see Arash Abizadeh, 'Cooperation, Pervasive Impact, and Coercion: On the Scope (Not Site) of Distributive Justice', *Philosophy and Public Affairs,* 35/4 (2007) at 318–58; Joshua Cohen and Charles Sabel, 'Extra Rempublicam Nulla Justitia?', *Philosophy and Public Affairs,* 34/2 (2006) at 147–75; A. J. Julius, 'Nagel's Atlas', *Philosophy and Public Affairs,* 34/2 (2006) at 176–92; Ryan Pevnick, 'Political Coercion and the Scope of Distributive Justice', *Political Studies,* 56 (2008) at 399–413.

5. In *Political Liberalism* and in *The Law of Peoples*, Rawls, for example, clarifies that if the sharing of 'common sympathies' depended on language, history, and political culture, 'this feature would rarely, if ever, be fully satisfied'. Nevertheless, he emphasizes, 'the Law of Peoples starts with the need for common sympathies, no matter what their source may be' for 'if we begin in this simplified way, we can work out political principles that will, in due course enable us to deal with more difficult cases where all the citizens are not united by a common language and shared historical memories'. See Rawls, *The Law of Peoples* at 25.

6. Ibid.

7. Allen Buchanan, 'Rawls' Law of Peoples: Rules for a Vanished Westphalian World', *Ethics,* 110/4 (2000) at 697–721; Simon Caney, 'Cosmopolitanism and the Law of

Peoples', *The Journal of Political Philosophy,* 10/1 (2002) at 95–123; Andrew Kuper, 'Rawlsian Global Justice: Beyond the Law of Peoples to a Cosmopolitan Law of Persons', *Political Theory,* 28/5 (2000) at 640–74.

8. See Thomas W. Pogge, 'Cosmopolitanism and Sovereignty', *Ethics,* 103/1 (1992), 48–75 at 58; and Charles Beitz, *Political Theory and International Relations* (Princeton: Princeton University Press, 1999) at 214–16.

9. I also noted (and expressed some reservations on) the attempt to distinguish between cultural conventionalism and political institutionalism in Chapter 2, Section 2.5.

10. A response similar to the one just sketched seems to characterize several recent attempts to move beyond communitarian or Law of peoples-type of arguments. See for the coercion-based argument Blake, 'Distributive Justice, State Coercion, and Autonomy'; for the cooperation-based argument, Samuel Freeman, 'The Law of Peoples, Social Cooperation, Human Rights, and Distributive Justice', *Social Philosophy and Policy,* 23/1 (2006) at 29–68; and, more ambiguously, Nagel, 'The Problem of Global Justice'. For the reciprocity-based argument, see Sangiovanni, 'Global Justice, Reciprocity, and the State', cit. The 'feasibility' criterion is literally central to Rawls' justification of a peoples-based global original position. As he puts it: 'historically speaking, all principles and standards proposed for the law of peoples must, to be feasible, prove acceptable to the considered and reflective public opinion of people and their governments'. See Rawls, *The Law of Peoples* at 49.

11. See, for example, Blake, 'Distributive Justice, State Coercion, and Autonomy', at 263–4, fn 7, where he distinguishes between institutional and non-institutional approaches to global justice arguing that forms of ideal theory exist in both cases. As he puts it, 'the mere fact of accepting political institutions does not render a theory nonideal'.

12. Beitz, *Political Theory and International Relations* at 129, Simon Caney, *Justice Beyond Borders – a Global Political Theory* (Oxford: Oxford University Press, 2005) at 107; Darrel Moellendorf, *Cosmopolitan Justice* (Boulder, CO: Westview Press, 2002) at 7; Thomas Pogge, *Realizing Rawls* (Ithaca, NY: Cornell University Press, 1989) at 254. It should be emphasized that the debate has moved on since these earlier expositions, with several authors now trying to occupy the middle ground; see, for example, Gillian Brock, *Global Justice: A Cosmopolitan Account* (Oxford: Oxford University Press, 2009) at 366; Richard Miller, *Globalizing Justice* (Oxford: Oxford University Press, 2009); Kok-Chor Tan, *Justice without Borders: Cosmopolitanism, Nationalism, and Patriotism* (Cambridge: Cambridge University Press, 2004). Moreover, even some of the pioneers of the debate have now partly modified their positions and weakened the terms of their critique to political membership; for a good overview of the debate see Simon Caney, 'Global Distributive Justice and the State', *Political Studies,* 56/3 (2008) at 487–518. However, none of these reinterpretations has cleared the ground from the methodological confusion I am interested in exploring here nor has it brought to light the positive importance of shared political relations within an avant-garde conception of political agency.

13. See for this early formulation: David A. J. Richards, *A Theory of Reasons for Action* (Oxford: Clarendon Press, 1971) at 290.

14. Pogge, *Realizing Rawls* at 247. In the cosmopolitan literature, it is possible to find countless statements along these lines.

15. Charles Beitz, 'Cosmopolitan Ideals and National Sentiments', *Journal of Philosophy*, 80/10 (1983), 591–600 at 595.

16. Of course, as we saw in the previous section, Rawls himself does not always capitalize on his own analysis of the circumstances of justice, but that is not the main point here.

17. See, for Rawls' account, John Rawls, *A Theory of Justice* (Rev. edn.; Cambridge, MA: Harvard University Press, 1999*b*) at 113.

18. David Hume, *A Treatise of Human Nature* (Oxford: Oxford University Press, [1739–40]1978) at 496–497.

19. The last expression comes from Pogge, *Realizing Rawls* at 227.

20. Beitz, *Political Theory and International Relations* at 203.

21. Jean Jacques Rousseau, 'Of the Social Contract' at 40.

22. Ibid. at 80ff.

23. Kant, 'Toward Perpetual Peace' at 336.

24. Immanuel Kant, 'Idea for a Universal History with a Cosmopolitan Purpose' at 52.

25. Beitz, *Political Theory and International Relations* at 203; Caney, *Justice Beyond Borders – A Global Political Theory* at 32–3; Moellendorf, *Cosmopolitan Justice* at 32–8.

26. How the individual moral sense of justice arises is a separate issue that I assess in the following section.

27. Rawls, *A Theory of Justice* at 112–18.

28. See, for example, Beitz, *Political Theory and International Relations* at 151, Pogge, *Realizing Rawls* at 247.

29. This would be the interpretation more in line with Beitz's statement that 'it is not the case that we begin with an actually existing basic structure and ask whether it is reasonable for individuals to cooperate in it. Rather, we begin with the idea that some type of basic structure is both required and inevitable [. . .] and work towards principles the structure should satisfy.' See Beitz, *Political Theory and International Relations* at 203; Pogge, *Realizing Rawls* at 139–41.

30. See Nussbaum, *Frontiers of Justice* at 266.

31. As Rawls clarifies at one point, 'there are no limitations on general laws and theories, since conceptions of justice must be adjusted to general systems of social cooperation which they are to regulate, and there is no reason to rule out these facts'. See Rawls, *A Theory of Justice* at 119.

32. See Brian Barry, 'International Society from a Cosmopolitan Perspective', in David Mapel and Terry Nardin (eds.), *International Society: Diverse Ethical Perspectives* (1998), 144–63; Beitz, 'Cosmopolitan Ideals and National Sentiments' at 595–6; Richards, *A Theory of Reasons for Action* at 272–82, 389–93.

33. John Rawls, 'The Sense of Justice', *The Philosophical Review*, 72/3 (1963), 281–305 at 293. The question of stability is at the heart of the third part of *A Theory of Justice* and was considered by Rawls as one of the main issues motivating the reassessment of his first major work in *Political Liberalism*. In the latter,

the problem of moral motivation is linked very clearly to the public culture of a particular political association. 'Given certain assumptions specifying a reasonable human psychology and the normal conditions of human life, those who grow up under just basic institutions acquire a sense of justice and a reasoned allegiance to those institutions sufficient to render them stable. Expressed another way, citizens' sense of justice, given their traits of character and interests as formed by living under a just basic structure, is strong enough to resist the normal tendencies to injustice. Citizens act willingly so as to give one another justice over time. Stability is secured by sufficient motivation of the appropriate kind acquired under just institution.' See John Rawls, *Political Liberalism* (New York: Columbia University Press, 1993) at 142. For a more critical appraisal of this question and of the transition from *A Theory of Justice* to *Political Liberalism*, see Brian Barry, 'Rawls and the Search for Stability', *Ethics,* 105/4 (1995) at 874–915.

34. Rawls, *A Theory of Justice* at 454.
35. Jean Jacques Rousseau, 'Considerations on the Government of Poland', in Victor Gourevitch (ed.), *The Social Contract and Other Later Political Writings* (Cambridge: Cambridge University Press, [1772] 1997), at 189.
36. As Rawls also puts it: 'what justifies a conception of justice is not its being true to an order antecedent to and given to us, but its congruence with our deeper understanding of ourselves and our aspirations, and our realization that given our history and the traditions embedded in our public life, it is the most reasonable doctrine for us'. John Rawls, 'Kantian Constructivism in Moral Theory', *The Journal of Philosophy*, 77/9 (1980), 515–72 at 519.
37. I further explore such issues in Chapters 6 and 7.
38. Onora O'Neill and Thomas Pogge, for example, discuss the question of agency in the international order only to undermine the role of states and argue for the need to replace them with other international actors, that is, NGOs, multinational corporations, regional or transnational bodies which could perform analogous functions. See Onora O'Neill, *Bounds of Justice* (Cambridge: Cambridge University Press, 2000) at 181–5; Thomas Pogge, *World Poverty and Human Rights* (Cambridge: Polity Press, 2002) at 186–95. Their arguments, moreover, hardly ever engage with the question of how political innovation and conceptual change effectively take place.
39. Simon Caney, 'Cosmopolitan Justice and Institutional Design: An Egalitarian Liberal Conception of Global Justice', *Social Theory and Practice,* 32/4 (2006), 725–56 at 752.
40. Miller, *On Nationality* at 53–65.

## CHAPTER 4

1. Rawls, for example, considers assistance to burdened societies part of the 'nonideal' theory of global justice, since the target is to help these societies overcome radical poverty rather than contribute to the reduction of global inequalities; see John Rawls, *The Law of Peoples* (Cambridge, MA: Harvard University Press, 1999) at 23–5. For another approach to global justice which advocates principles similar to

Rawls' *The Law of Peoples*, see also David Miller, *National Responsibility and Global Justice* (Oxford: Oxford University Press, 2007).

2. Karl Marx, Critique of the Gotha Program' in *Selected Writings*, ed. by Lawrence H. Simon (Indianapolis: Hackett Publishing, [1875], 1994), at 322.

3. See G. A. Cohen, *History, Labour, and Freedom. Themes from Marx* (Oxford: Oxford University Press, 1989) at 299–300.

4. The metaphor is found in Marx's *Critique of the Gotha Program*. My attention was drawn to it by Richard Arneson, 'What's Wrong with Exploitation', *Ethics*, 91/1 (1981), 207–27 at 223.

5. For a further discussion of the moral nature of this critique, see ibid. at 222–3.

6. Thomas Nagel, 'The Problem of Global Justice', at 119; Rawls, *The Law of Peoples* at 76–7. I shall return to the conceptual distinction between sufficientarian and egalitarian obligations in the next chapter.

7. See most especially Miller, *National Responsibility and Global Justice* at 111–62; Rawls, *The Law of Peoples* at 118–21; Mathias Risse, 'How Does the Global Order Harm the Poor?', *Philosophy and Public Affairs*, 33/4 (2005a) at 349–76.

8. See especially Miller, *National Responsibility and Global Justice* at 51–81.

9. See, for example, Thomas Pogge, 'Do Rawls's Two Theories of Justice Fit Together?', in Rex Martin and David Reidy (eds.), *Rawls's The Law of Peoples* (Oxford: Blackwell, 2006); Peter Singer, 'Outsiders: Our Obligations to Those Beyond Our Borders', in Deen K. Chatterjee (ed.), *The Ethics of Assistance: Morality and the Distant Needy* (Cambridge: Cambridge University Press, 2004) at 11–32. Although ultimately rejecting cosmopolitanism, Leif Wenar also notices that if Rawls had taken seriously the principle of responsibility in domestic societies, he would have ended up endorsing a typical libertarian line of thought on the distribution of wealth; see Leif Wenar, 'The Legitimacy of Peoples', in Pablo De Greiff and Ciaran Cronin (ed.), *Global Justice and Transnational Politics* (Cambridge, MA: MIT Press, 2002) at 53–76.

10. One counterargument might also be that this is a good reason to weaken distributive requirements even within domestic theories of justice. However, this is not commonly found among the kind of statists we are considering, who are usually keen to emphasize the relevance of domestic egalitarianism.

11. Rawls, *The Law of Peoples* at 114–16; Andrea Sangiovanni, 'Global Justice, Reciprocity, and the State' at 20–38.

12. In addition to Rawls' *The Law of Peoples*, see on this issue, Samuel Freeman, 'The Law of Peoples, Social Cooperation, Human Rights, and Distributive Justice', *Social Philosophy and Policy*, 23/1 (2006) at 29–68; Nagel, 'The Problem of Global Justice'.

13. For the most sophisticated versions of the argument, see Miller, *National Responsibility and Global Justice* at 51–80; Nagel, 'The Problem of Global Justice' at 138; Rawls, *The Law of Peoples* at 106–18.

14. Friedrich August Hayek, *Law, Legislation and Liberty: The Mirage of Social Justice* (London: Routledge and Kegan, 1978) at 62–106; Jan Narveson, 'Welfare and Wealth, Poverty and Justice in Today's World', *The Journal of Ethics*, 8/4 (January 2005) at 305–48.

15. For a discussion of the empirical literature on poverty and global justice see Thomas Pogge, World Poverty and Human Rights, esp. 103 ff.

16. See, for example, Pogge: 'My standard of social justice entails not, then, an open-ended duty to help the badly off, but a much narrower duty that is tightly limited in *range* (to persons subject to an institutional order you cooperate in imposing), in *subject matter* (to the avoidance of human rights deficits), and in *demanding-ness* (to compensation for your share of that part of the human rights deficit that is reasonably avoidable through an alternative institutional design).' Thomas Pogge, 'Severe Poverty as a Violation of Negative Duties', *Ethics & International Affairs*, 19/1 (2005*b*) at 55–83. Pogge 2005 at 61. Compare this to the view of someone like John Rawls or David Miller, both of whom defend not only a negative duty to avoid harming severely deprived citizens of poor countries but also a positive duty to assist those in dire need. Of course the important difference is that cosmopolitans à-la-Pogge do not follow statists in denying that more demanding principles of justice might also be valid in the global sphere – in this sense their approach is intended to be ecumenical and non-committal. However, this does not invalidate my point that the account of the circumstances of justice upon which they rely can only go as far as to justify claims that statists approaching the issue of global poverty from a nonideal perspective would happily endorse.

17. Mathias Risse, 'Do We Owe the Global Poor Assistance or Rectification?', *Ethics & International Affairs*, 19/1 (2005*c*) at 9–18, Mathias Risse, 'What We Owe to the Global Poor', *Journal of Ethics*, 9 (2005*b*) at 81–117.

18. I owe the definition of positional goods as goods with the property that one's relative place in the distribution of the good affects one's absolute position with respect to its value to Harry Brighouse and Adam Swift, 'Equality, Priority, and Positional Goods', *Ethics*, 116 (2006), 471–97 at 472. I shall return to this definition and the issue of positional goods in the next chapter.

19. See Gerald A. Cohen, *Self-Ownership, Freedom and Equality* (Cambridge: Cambridge University Press, 1995) at 198.

20. Ibid.

21. Ibid. at 199.

22. For an analysis of the criteria employed to assess the progressive potential of a theory compared to its rivals, see my discussion of dialectic in Chapter 2.

## CHAPTER 5

1. See 'Zimbabwean dies queuing for visa' on http://news.bbc.co.uk/go/pr/fr/-/2/hi/africa/7090730.stm, published on 2007/11/12, 13:30:30.

2. On egalitarianism and positional goods, see especially Harry Brighouse and Adam Swift, 'Equality, Priority, and Positional Goods'.

3. Health, for example, is typically considered a good the value of which does not depend on others' access to it. And yet there seems to be some evidence suggesting that health inequalities have an important impact on individuals' ability to compete in the labour market or in trying to obtain access to other desired goods; see for a discussion Brighouse and Swift, 'Equality, Priority, and Positional Goods' at 479.

4. I have explored the potential of this account in Lea Ypi, 'On the Confusion between Ideal and Nonideal in Recent Debates on Global Justice', *Political Studies*, 58/3 (2010) at 536–55.

5. Not all statists resist this point; see, for example, the observations in instrumental defences of egalitarianism in Miller, *National Responsibility and Global Justice* at ch. 3. What appears missing is an account of how these conclusions relate to a fundamentally appropriate analysis of the links between absolute and relative deprivation, and of how (depending on the empirical evidence available) some of these considerations might be extended to several dimensions of global interaction (not only those mediated by states).

6. For the distinction between weak and strong equalisandum claims, see Gerald A. Cohen, 'On the Currency of Egalitarian Justice', *Ethics*, 99/4 (1989), 906–44 at 908.

7. David Miller is one of the few that come to mind here. Some authors (e.g. David Reidy) have argued that Rawls' *The Law of Peoples* also allows for incorporating global egalitarianism but the textual evidence there is ambiguous, to say the least. Even leaving aside exegetical issues it is not clear that such accounts have sufficient resources to really embrace global egalitarianism. For a good exposition of the reasons (starting with the case of Rawls), see Chris Armstrong, 'Defending the Duty of Assistance?', *Social Theory and Practice*, 35/3 (2009) at 461–82.

8. Michael Blake, 'Distributive Justice, State Coercion, and Autonomy' at 265. Emphasis added. And further: 'a concern for domestic economic equality and international economic sufficiency reflects [...] a consistent and thoroughgoing concern for the liberal principle of autonomy', ibid. at 295. Andrea Sangiovanni has also recently tried to show that '*moral* equality only generates a demand for *social* equality when we share membership in a state' and that 'equality is a demand of justice only among citizens (and, indeed, residents) of a state'. See Sangiovanni, 'Global Justice, Reciprocity, and the State' at p. 4 and p. 38. A precursor argument may be found, in slightly different words in Rawls' *The Law of Peoples*, when he discusses the difference between a (sufficientarian) duty of assistance and global difference principle, see Rawls, *The Law of Peoples* at 115–16.

9. Nagel, 'The Problem of Global Justice', at 114–15.

10. Bertolt Brecht, *The Threepenny Opera*, trans. Desmond Vesey (New York: Grove Press, 1964) at 66.

11. Literally translated: eating (gobbling) comes first, morality follows.

12. I shall not go into further details on the justification of subsistence claims; for arguments to this effect see Robert E. Goodin, *Reasons for Welfare. The Political Theory of the Welfare State.* (Princeton: Princeton University Press, 1988); Rawls, *The Law of Peoples* at 38 ff; Thomas Scanlon, 'Preference and Urgency', *The Journal of Philosophy*, 72/19 (1975) at 655–69; Henry Shue, *Basic Rights: Subsistence, Affluence, and U.S. Foreign Policy* (Princeton: Princeton University Press, 1996).

13. See Joel Feinberg, 'Noncomparative Justice', *The Philosophical Review*, 83/3 (1974) at 297–338.

14. Scanlon, 'Preference and Urgency' at 658.

15. Adam Smith, *The Wealth of Nations: IV–V*, ed. Andrew Skinner (London: Penguin, [1776–83] 1999) at 465.

16. See, for one good empirical discussion, Amartya Sen, *Poverty and Famines: An Essay on Entitlement and Deprivation* (Oxford: Oxford University Press, 1983).

17. This account of justice as equality of proportions is proposed by Plato both in *Republic* (*Rep 433b*) and in *Gorgias* (508a, see also 465b/c); see Plato, *The Collected Dialogues of Plato Including the Letters*.

18. Aristotle, *Nicomachean Ethics*, trans. J. A. K. Thomson (London: Penguin, [unknown] 2004) at 118.

19. Harry Frankfurt, 'Equality as a Moral Ideal', *Ethics*, 98/1 (1987) at 21–43. For a recent restatement of the doctrine of sufficiency, see Roger Crisp, 'Equality, Priority, and Compassion', *Ethics*, 113 (2003) at 745–63. I focus here on only some aspects of these accounts. For a recent critique and an attempt to defend a mixed version of the doctrine of sufficiency, see Paula Casal, 'Why Sufficiency Is Not Enough', *Ethics*, 117 (January 2007) at 296–326.

20. This point is central to the statist analysis with which we started.

21. Sen, *Poverty and Famines* at 76–7.

22. Ibid.

23. See especially the use of the Bengal famine example in Rawls, *The Law of Peoples* at 106–18; and those who endorse Rawls' sufficientarian approach to global justice, for example, Blake, 'Distributive Justice, State Coercion, and Autonomy', at 94; Freeman, 'The Law of Peoples, Social Cooperation, Human Rights, and Distributive Justice,' at 50–2; David Miller, 'Collective Responsibility and International Equality in the Law of Peoples', in Rex Martin and David Reidy (eds.), *Rawls's The Law of Peoples* (Oxford: Blackwell, 2006) at 191–205; Nagel, 'The Problem of Global Justice', at 119; David A. Reidy, 'Rawls on International Justice, A Defense', *Political Theory*, 32/3 (2004), 291–319 at 311.

24. For some of the evidence, see 'Asian states feel rice pinch' on http://news.bbc.co.uk/go/pr/fr/-/2/hi/south_asia/7324596.stm, published on 2008/04/03; 'Riots prompt Ivory Coast tax cuts' on http://news.bbc.co.uk/go/pr/fr/-/2/hi/africa/7325733.stm, published on 2008/04/02; 'Rice prices hit Philippines poor' on http://news.bbc.co.uk/go/pr/fr/-/2/hi/business/7330168.stm, published on 2008/04/06; 'Egyptians hit by rising food prices' on http://news.bbc.co.uk/go/pr/fr/-/2/hi/middle_east/7288196.stm, published on 2008/03/11.

25 The data are drawn from *The Economist*, see 'Cheap no more', http://www.economist.com/node/10250420, published on 6 December 2007.

26. Reported in 'Riots prompt Ivory Coast tax cuts', cited fn. 24.

27. Reported in 'Cheap no more', cited fn. 25. The problem is not just India and China but also the levels of meat consumption in developed countries; see George Monbiot, 'Credit crunch? The real crisis is global hunger. And if you care, eat less meat', in: http://www.guardian.co.uk/commentisfree/2008/apr/15/food.biofuels/print.

28. See 'IMF head gives food price warning', on http://news.bbc.co.uk/go/pr/fr/-/2/hi/business/7344892.stm, published on 2008/04/13.

29. Frankfurt, 'Equality as a Moral Ideal' at 22. It should be pointed out, however, that those who apply sufficientarian principles to global relations explicitly rule out even this weaker point considering sufficientarian and egalitarian justice to have entirely different domains of application.

30. See Miller, *National Responsibility and Global Justice* at 56–67.

31. One might object here that this is what the capabilities metric developed by Sen, Alkire, Robeyns, and others aims to capture. Notice, however, that the capabilities' metric is used to measure poverty, not inequality. In other words, the capabilities' approach is helpful to discover whether people in different countries have fallen below a threshold under which they are unable to function and Sen even emphasizes that establishing such a threshold must take into account community variations; see Amartya Sen, 'A Sociological Approach to the Measurement of Poverty: A Reply to Professor Peter Townsend', *Oxford Economic Papers,* 37/4 (1985) at 669–76. But the objection mentioned above applies to the issue of inequality rather than simple poverty: it requires us to identify a currency for measuring relative goods with reference to which inequalities should be reduced rather than asking how it is possible to establish a global poverty line. Some defenders of global egalitarianism have acknowledged the force of this critique; see, for example, Charles R. Beitz, 'Does Global Inequality Matter?', *Metaphilosophy,* 32/1&2 (2001), 95–112 at 102.

32. Simon Caney, 'Cosmopolitan Justice and Equalizing Opportunities', *Metaphilosophy*, 32/1&2 (2001) 113–34 at 120. See also the discussion on 'global apartheid' at 116–17.

33. For this critique, see Miller, *National Responsibility and Global Justice* at 64 and Gillian Brock, *Global Justice: A Cosmopolitan Account* (Oxford: Oxford University Press, 2009) at 45–62.

34. Kok-Chor Tan makes a similar case, but addressed to equality between nations rather than states. See Kok-Chor Tan, *Justice without Borders: Cosmopolitanism, Nationalism, and Patriotism* (Cambridge: Cambridge University Press, 2004) at 107–34. However, Tan's defence is based on the value of self-determination, mine on the necessity of equalizing certain positional goods (such as power) in global circumstances of justice.

35. John Locke, *An Essay Concerning Human Understanding*, ed. Pauline Phemister (Oxford: Oxford University Press, [1690] 2008), 140 ff. For the 'resistance' argument, see Steven Lukes, *Power: A Radical View* (New York: Palgrave Macmillan, 2005) 192; 24 cm at 69.

36. Ibid. at 70.

37. Robert A. Dahl, 'Power' in *International Encyclopedia of the Social Science* (New York, Macmillan: 1968), vol. 12, pp. 405–414 at p. 409.

38. Thomas Hobbes, *Leviathan* ed. by R. Tuck (New York: Cambridge University Press, [1651] 1991) at 70.

39. Ibid.

40. These examples are taken from Brighouse and Swift, 'Equality, Priority, and Positional Goods' at 475.

41. Which dimension of power matters more is a complex question that I cannot explore here. There is an ongoing debate engaging scholars in IR on whether we should consider only 'hard' power (i.e. military and economic – as in the old realist fashion) or also 'soft' power (i.e. information, scientific knowledge, or cultural influence – as recently argued by liberal theorists of international interdependence). For the classical realist approach, see Hans Morgenthau, *Politics among Nations: The Struggle for Power and Peace* (2nd edn.; New York: Alfred Knopf,

1959); and for a recent powerful restatement of realism, see Robert Gilpin, *Global Political Economy. Understanding the International Economic Order* (Princeton: Princeton University Press, 2001). For the liberal discussion on 'hard' and 'soft' power, see Jr Joseph S. Nye, 'The Changing Nature of World Power', *Political Science Quarterly*, 105/2 (1990); and Robert Keohane and Joseph S. Nye Jr., *Power and Interdependence* (Boston: Little, Brown, 1977). Settling these controversies is something that I must defer to future work. Notice only that the difficulty of being more detailed on which particular aspects of the distribution of power matter more is not specific to my argument. It would be encountered by any analysis of the distribution of positional goods; e.g even in the domestic sphere saying that citizens need equal access to educational opportunities does not immediately settle the question of which particular scholastic degrees matter most.

42. Brighouse and Swift, 'Equality, Priority, and Positional Goods' at 475ff.

43. Ibid. at 476–7. As the authors go on to stress, in cases where a less than equal chance could be considered to guarantee enough of a chance, less levelling down might be required. However, similar attempts might be motivated not so much by the argument that a less than equal chance is enough of a chance but by trading off equality with other values (477).

44. Joseph Stiglitz and Andrew Charleton, *Fair Trade for All* (Oxford: Oxford University Press, 2005) at 120.

45. See John Braithwaite and Peter Drahos, *Global Business Regulation* (New York: Cambridge University Press, 2000); Gregory Shaffer, 'Power, Governance and the WTO: A Comparative Institutional Approach', in Michael Barnett and Raymond Duvall (ed.), *Power in Global Governance* (Cambridge: Cambridge University Press, 2005) at 130–61; Richard H. Steinberg, 'In the Shadow of Law or Power? Consensus-Based Bargaining and Outcomes in the GATT/WTO', *International Organization*, 2/56 (2002) at 339–74; Joseph E. Stiglitz, *Globalization and Its Discontents* (London: Penguin, 2002). For more normative discussion of some of these issues, see also Miriam Ronzoni, 'The Global Order: A Case of Background Injustice? A Practice-Dependent Account', *Philosophy and Public Affairs*, 37/3 (2009) at 229–56.

46. As with other discussions on egalitarianism, this does not mean endorsing 'simple' equality as a distributive ideal (e.g. that each state should obtain 1/Nth of the total share). The idea that equality requires taking proportions into account is already in Aristotle; Aristotle, *Nicomachean Ethics* at book 5.

47. Remember that I have assumed, only for the sake of argument, that the sufficientarian conception of justice is normatively fundamental. I have not independently argued for that conclusion. I also happen to believe that the conclusion is vulnerable to several objections. One is that most of the arguments that assign egalitarian principles purely instrumental value can be also extended to sufficientarianism by emphasizing some other (even more fundamental) conception of the person as the one that needs to be intrinsically promoted. However, I do not have space to go into this discussion here, nor is it necessary for this book's purposes.

48. See the use of such examples in Blake, 'Distributive Justice, State Coercion, and Autonomy' at 290–2; Miller, *National Responsibility and Global Justice* at 68–75; Rawls, *The Law of Peoples* at 117–18.

49. Rich and Poor here are individuals, but even if we took them to be collective agents, that is, states or other associative units, the point would remain the same.

## CHAPTER 6

1. Some of the arguments leading to the endorsement of a similar model were discussed in Chapter 3.
2. Again, this is a position that many statists of the kind discussed in Chapter 3 would happily endorse.
3. On 'political disaffection' as symptomatic of this model of society, see Claus Offe, 'Political Disaffection as an Outcome of Institutional Practices? Some Post-Tocquevillean Speculations', in T. Mariano and G. R. Montero (ed.), *Political Disaffection in Contemporary Democracies. Social Capital, Institutions and Politics* (London: Routledge, 2006) at 23–45.
4. A similar emphasis is typically found in both the conventionalist and institutionalist understandings of political community emphasized in Chapters 2 and 3.
5. Benjamin Constant, 'The Liberty of the Ancients Compared with That of the Moderns', in Biancamaria Fontana (ed.), *Political Writings* (Cambridge: Cambridge University Press, [1819] 1988), 308–28 at 327–8.
6. See, for example, Simon Caney, 'Cosmopolitan Justice and Institutional Design: An Egalitarian Liberal Conception of Global Justice', *Social Theory and Practice,* 32/4 (2006) at 725–56; Richard Falk, *Law in an Emerging Global Village: A Post-Westphalian Perspective* (Ardsley: Transnational Publishers, 1998); David Held, *Democracy and the Global Order: From the Modern State to Cosmopolitan Governance* (Stanford: Stanford University Press, 1995); Raffaele Marchetti, *Global Democracy: For and Against. Ethical, Institutional, and Social Perspectives on Political Inclusion* (London: Routledge, 2008); Pogge, *World Poverty and Human Rights* at 169–95.
7. Rousseau, 'Considerations on the Government of Poland' at 179.
8. Ibid.
9. Ibid.
10. Ibid. at 183.
11. See the discussions on empirical reactions to the European Union or NAFTA in Will Kymlicka, *Politics in the Vernacular – Nationalism, Multiculturalism, and Citizenship* (Oxford: Oxford University Press, 2001) at 320 ff.
12. See Miller, *On Nationality* at 57–8.
13. See, for example, Chapters 3 and 4.
14. For one such objection to ethical theories emphasizing the distinction between normative reasons and motivation, see Michael Stocker, 'The Schizophrenia of Modern Ethical Theories', *The Journal of Philosophy*, 73/14 (1976) at 453–66.
15. Friedrich von Schiller, *Letters Upon the Aesthetic Education of Man* (Montana: Kessinger Publishers, [1795] 2004) at 7–10.
16. Immanuel Kant, *Religion within the Boundaries of Mere Reason and Other Writings* (Cambridge: Cambridge University Press, [1793] 1998) at 39–40.

17. See for a similar response to Stocker's charge of 'moral schizophrenia' in the context of a discussion on Kantian ethics Richard Henson, 'What Kant Might Have Said: Moral Worth and the Overdetermination of Dutiful Action', *The Philosophical Review,* 88 (1979) at 39–54; and Barbara Herman, 'On the Value of Acting from the Motive of Duty', *The Philosophical Review,* 90/3 (July 1981) at 359–82.

18. So, for example, one does not need to know much about the history of socialism to realize that the same principles of social equality and collective responsibility were interpreted and applied in distinctive ways in Yugoslavia, the Soviet Union, and China, just like the way in which the basic principles of liberalism are interpreted in the United States might turn out to be quite different from Germany or France.

19. See, for example, Max Weber, *Economy and Society: An Outline of Interpretive Sociology* (Berkeley: University of California Press, [1914] 1978) at 901–40.

20. I have discussed this view in Lea Ypi, 'Justice in Migration: A Closed Borders Utopia?', *The Journal of Political Philosophy,* 16/4 (2008) at 391–418.

21. This discussion draws on John Rawls' analysis of the general principles of moral psychology and the development of associative loyalties, see Rawls, *A Theory of Justice* at 409–14, 56–64. Admittedly, Rawls does not use the vocabulary of patriotism to discuss the morality of the association. However, it would be difficult to deny that such a process of moral learning is not linked to the development of particularist loyalties. As Eamonn Callan notices, 'the only alternative interpretation is to suppose that in the morality of association individuals become attached to just schemes of cooperation in general and to all who might conceivably participate in them. But that is as absurd as supposing that within the morality of authority children become attached to loving parents in general, as opposed to the particular ones who love them.' See Eamonn Callan, *Creating Citizens: Political Education and Liberal Democracy* (Oxford: Oxford University Press, 1997) at 93.

22. Hence Rousseau's emphasis that 'there is only one law which by its nature requires unanimous consent' see Rousseau, 'Of the Social Contract', at 123.

23. See Kant, 'The Metaphysics of Morals', at 409.

24. There is an ongoing debate between scholars on whether the role of civic education is merely to train citizens to engage with public institutions regardless of their basic moral principles (the legitimacy-based view of education) or whether it must also provide them with critical knowledge and the ability to evaluate competing points of view in a way that is conducive to a specific perspective on justice (the autonomy-promoting view of education). What I say on civic education follows the latter position. However, I do not have space here to engage with a detailed critique of the former. For a defence of the legitimacy-based view of education, see Harry Brighouse, 'Civic Education and Liberal Legitimacy', *Ethics,* 108 (1998) at 719–45. For a defence of the autonomy-promoting view of education, see Amy

Gutmann, *Democratic Education* (Princeton: Princeton University Press, 1987); and Eamonn Callan, 'Liberal Legitimacy, Justice, and Civic Education', *Ethics*, 111 (2000) at 141–55.

25. For an excellent analysis of the role of schools in civic education and a more elaborate discussion of the controversies surrounding them in multicultural democracies, see Harry Brighouse, *On Education* (London: Routledge, 2006); and Callan, *Creating Citizens: Political Education and Liberal Democracy* at 46–62.

26. See William Galston, *Liberal Purposes: Goods, Virtues, and Diversity in the Liberal State* (Cambridge: Cambridge University Press, 1991) at 244.

27. For a further discussion of this issue, see Kymlicka, *Politics in the Vernacular – Nationalism, Multiculturalism, and Citizenship* at 303–20.

28. This account might be thought to resemble Michael Walzer, *Interpretation and Social Criticism* (Cambridge, MA: Harvard University Press, 1987) at 21–3. Whilst sharing Walzer's view that social criticism is much more efficacious when it engages seriously with particular social practices, I do not agree with his scepticism on the very possibility of grounding such criticism on an impartial, universalist account of morality. As I have tried to show in the previous pages, starting the process of moral learning with well-consolidated views embedded in particular traditions does not necessarily preclude questioning them from a moral perspective that is ultimately universal in its reach. For a more elaborate critique of Walzer's account along similar lines, see Brian Barry, 'Social Criticism and Political Philosophy', *Philosophy and Public Affairs*, 19/4 (1990), 360–73 at 368 ff.

29. For a discussion of the conditions of legitimacy of civil disobedience, see Rawls, *A Theory of Justice* at 319–46; and Michael Walzer, *Obligations: Essays on Disobedience, War, and Citizenship* (Cambridge, MA: Harvard University Press, 1970) at 3–76.

30. For a good overview of the controversies surrounding this issue, see Kevin McDonough and Walter Feinberg, *Citizenship and Education in Liberal-Democratic Societies – Teaching for Cosmopolitan Values and Collective Identities* (Oxford: Oxford University Press, 2003). For an excellent defence of cosmopolitan civic education, see Martha C. Nussbaum, *Cultivating Humanity: A Classical Defense of Reform in Liberal Education* (Cambridge: Harvard University Press, 1997).

31. See Benjamin Barber's essay on 'Constitutional Faith' in Martha Nussbaum (ed.), *For Love of Country?* (Boston: Beacon Press, 2002) at 36.

32. See Niccolo Machiavelli, *Discourses on Livy* (Chicago: Chicago University Press, [1517] 1996) at 60.

33. See Bentham's discussion of human rights in Jeremy Waldron (ed.), *Nonsense Upon Stilts: Bentham, Burke, and Marx on the Rights of Man* (London: Methuen, 1987).

CHAPTER 7

1. Henri De Saint Simon, *Selected Writings on Science, Industry and Social Organization*, trans. Keith Taylor (London: Croom Helm, [1825] 1975) at 281.
2. Ibid.
3. Ibid.

4. 'Qu'il sorte du sein des Académies quelqu'Homme qui descende dans les ateliers, qui y recueille les phénomènes des *Arts*, & qui nous les expose dans un ouvrage qui détermine les Artistes à lire, les Philosophes à penser utilement, & les Grands à faire enfin un usage utile de leur autorité & de leurs récompenses'; see Denis Diderot and Jean Le Rond D'Alembert, *Encyclopédie, Ou Dictionnaire Raisonné Des Sciences, Des Arts Et Des Métiers*, 28 vols. (Geneva; Paris; Neufchatel: Briasson and others, [1754–1772]) at 713.

5. My analysis of artistic avant-gardes is quite selective and has a merely illustrative function. I focus only on some significant representatives of the so-called 'historical avant-gardes', a term used to denote those movements operating between the end of the nineteenth century and the beginning of the twentieth century. I do not consider the neo-avant-gardes of the late twentieth century (e.g. Pop Art, Conceptual Art, Fluxus, etc.). This is not only because the aesthetic nature and artistic intentions of neo-avant-gardes are very different from those of historical ones but also because their production is explicitly politically disengaged. Where the historical avant-gardes tried to reinterpret the role of art in the light of important changes in society (starting from the events of the 1848 Paris Commune), neo-avant-gardes merely repeated the strategies of their predecessors but abandoned social struggle. For one pioneering analysis of this issue, see Peter Bürger, *Theory of the Avant-Garde* (Manchester: Manchester University Press, 1984). For an interesting discussion of the death of avant-gardes in the twentieth century and the relationship between art and politics, see Eric Hobsbawm, *Behind the Times: The Decline and Fall of the Twentieth-Century Avant-Gardes* (New York: Thames and Hudson, 1999).

6. Andreas Huyssen, *After the Great Divide: Modernism, Mass Culture, Postmodernism* (Bloomington: Indiana University Press, 1986) at 5–6.

7. Cited in Donald D. Egbert, 'The Idea of "Avant-Garde" in Art and Politics', *The American Historical Review*, 78/2 (December 1967), 339–66 at 341.

8. Cited in Charles Harrison and Paul Wood (eds.), *Art in Theory 1815–1900: An Anthology of Changing Ideas* (Oxford: Blackwell, 1998) at 797.

9. The first page of its first issue published a telegram sent to the International Office for Revolutionary Literature in Moscow, where the surrealists declared that they were submitting to the directives of the Second International. For an analysis of this issue, see Mario De Micheli, *Le Avanguardie Artistiche Del Novecento* (Milan: Feltrinelli, 1988) at 178. The socialist movement was not always at ease with artistic avant-gardes, however. Rosa Luxemburg, for example, had to justify herself for preferring more traditional literature and even Leon Trotsky, usually attentive to new forms of art, allegedly disapproved of the extreme subjectivism of avant-gardes. For a discussion of this issue, see Eric Hobsbawm, 'Socialism and the Avantgarde in the Period of the Second International', *Le Mouvement Social*, 111 (1980), 189–99 at 195–8.

10. Cited in Micheli, *Le Avanguardie Artistiche Del Novecento* at 178. My translation.

11. See Alan C. Birnholz, 'The Russian Avant-Garde and the Russian Tradition', *Art Journal*, 32/2 (1973) at 146–9.

12. It should be pointed out that the first experiments trying to render music accessible to the mass public had already started in nineteenth-century opera, with the

works of Wagner or Mascagni. For more on this issue, Eric Hobsbawm, *The Age of Empire* (London: Weidenfeld and Nicolson, 1987) at 220–4.

13. Hilton Kramer, 'The Age of the Avant-Garde', *Journal of Aesthetic Education,* 7/2 (1973), 35–51 at 43.

14. Ibid. On the relationship between avant-gardes (including artistic ones) and tradition, see also Göran Therborn, 'Entangled Modernities', *European Journal of Social Theory,* 6 (2003), 293–305 at 296.

15. This was the reason why Georg Lukács, for example, preferred the realism of Balzac and Tolstoj and criticized literary avant-gardes for reflecting bourgeois decadence and for their inability to be politically constructive. Unfortunately, I cannot explore in greater depth the controversy that this issue generated between defenders of the avant-gardes such as Adorno, Bloch, and more ambiguously, Brecht, on the one hand, and Lukásc, on the other. For some of the important exchanges, see Perry Anderson (ed.), *Aesthetics and Politics* (London: Verso, 1977). For a discussion of the relationship between historical and neo-avant-gardes, see Lea Ypi, 'Public Spaces and the End of Art', *Philosophy and Social Criticism,* forthcoming (2011).

16. See Hobsbawm, *The Age of Empire* at 220–32; Hobsbawm, *Behind the Times: The Decline and Fall of the Twentieth-Century Avant-Gardes.* See also Ypi, 'Public Spaces and the End of Art'.

17. Bertolt Brecht, 'Against Georg Lukács', *New Left Review,* 84 (March–April 1974), 39–53 at 41.

18. Vladimir I. Lenin, *What Is to Be Done?* (New York: International Publishers, [1902] 1929) at 85.

19. Jean Jacques Rousseau, 'Of the Social Contract', in Victor Gourevitch (ed.), *The Social Contract and Other Later Political Writings* (Cambridge: Cambridge University Press, [1762] 1997), 39–161 at 109.

20. Antonio Gramsci, *Selections from the Prison Notebooks,* ed. Geoffrey Nowell Smith and Quintin Hoare (London: Lawrence and Whishart, 1971) at 172.

21. Ibid.

22. Gramsci's idea of the modern prince applied in particular to political parties; for a further discussion of their role, see Jonathan White and Lea Ypi, 'Rethinking the Modern Prince: Partisanship and the Democratic Ethos', *Political Studies,* 58/4 (2010) at 809–28.

23. Gramsci, *Selections from the Prison Notebooks* at 193.

24. Ibid.

25. See Martha Finnemore and Kathryn Sikkink, 'International Norm Dynamics and Political Change', *International Organization,* 52/4 (1998), 887–917 at 897.

26. See Francisco O. Ramirez, Yasemin Soysal, and Suzanne Shanahan, 'The Changing Logic of Political Citizenship: Cross-National Acquisition of Women's Suffrage Rights, 1890 to 1990', *American Sociological Review,* 62/5 (1997) at 735–45. A recent example of such 'cascade' effect taking place is the ban on landmines. By May 1997, the number of states supporting the ban on anti-personnel landmines had reached sixty, or approximately one-third of the total states in the system. After that, a 'cascade occurred, and 124 states ratified the Ottawa land mine treaty within only seven months'. See Finnemore and Sikkink, 'International Norm Dynamics and Political Change' at 901.

27. See for a description of the episode and a narrative history of the British anti-slavery movement Adam Hochschild, *Bury the Chains: The British Struggle to Abolish Slavery* (London: Pan Macmillan, 2006) at 16. On the crucial role of popular mobilization for the abolition of the slave-trade in Britain, see also Seymour Drescher, 'Whose Abolition? Popular Pressure and the Ending of the British Slave-Trade', *Past & Present,* 143 (1994) at 136–66.

28. For an excellent analysis of how Enlightenment discourses on commercial society and the critique of international trade practices informed political activism, see Sankar Muthu, *Enlightenment against Empire* (Princeton: Princeton University Press, 2003) and Sankar Muthu, 'Conquest, Commerce, and Cosmopolitanism in Enlightenment Political Thought', in Sankar Muthu (ed.), *Empire and Modern Political Thought* (Cambridge: Cambridge University Press, 2011), forthcoming.

29. These were the words of Stephen Fuller, the London agent for the Jamaica planters and a central figure in the pro-slavery movement, cited in Hochschild, *Bury the Chains: The British Struggle to Abolish Slavery* at 5.

30. William Fox, 'Address to the People of Great Britain, on the Propriety of Abstaining from West India Sugar and Rum' (15th edn.; Glasgow: W. Bell, 1791), at 9.

31. My account in what follows is indebted to the discussions about human rights development in Africa and Asia in Thomas Risse, 'International Norms and Domestic Change: Arguing and Communicative Behavior in the Human Rights Area', *Politics & Society,* 27/4 (1999) at 529–59; Thomas Risse, Stephen C. Ropp, and Kathryn Sikkink (eds.), *The Power of Human Rights: International Norms & Domestic Change* (Cambridge: Cambridge University Press, 1999).

32. For definitions and discussions of civil society, see Jean Cohen and Andrew Arato, *Civil Society and Political Theory* (Cambridge, MA: MIT Press, 1992); John S. Dryzek, *Deliberative Democracy and Beyond – Liberals, Critics, Contestations* (Oxford: Oxford University Press, 2002); John Keane, *Global Civil Society?* (Cambridge: Cambridge University Press, 2003). On the difficulty of including in a definition of civil society both social movements and civic associations, see Sidney Tarrow, 'Transnational Politics: Contention and Institutions in International Politics', *Annual Review of Political Science,* 4/1 (2001) at 1–20. For a recent analysis of the role of these movements see Raffaele Marchetti, *Global Democracy: For and Against. Ethical, Institutional, and Social Perspectives on Political Inclusion* (London: Routledge, 2008).

33. See Donatella Della Porta, Hanspeter Kriesi, and Dieter Rucht (eds.), *Social Movements in a Globalizing World* (London: MacMillan, 1999); Dryzek, *Deliberative Democracy and Beyond – Liberals, Critics, Contestations*, Margret Keck and Kathleen Sikkink, *Activists Beyond Borders: Advocacy Networks in International Politics* (Ithaca: Cornell University Press, 1998); Iris Marion Young, *Inclusion and Democracy* (Oxford: Oxford University Press, 2002).

34. See for a discussion of transnational advocacy networks Keck and Sikkink, *Activists Beyond Borders: Advocacy Networks in International Politics*. See also the discussion on the role of social movements in democratizing international institutions in Luis Cabrera, *The Practice of Global Citizenship* (Cambridge: Cambridge University Press, 2010) and Marchetti, *Global Democracy: For and Against. Ethical, Institutional, and Social Perspectives on Political Inclusion* and

Carol Gould, *Globalizing Democracy and Human Rights* (Cambridge: Cambridge University Press, 2004). The latter also refers to the relevance of a dialectical approach in articulating the link between theory and practice.

35. Donatella Della Porta and Mario Diani, *Social Movements: An Introduction* (Oxford: Blackwell, 1999) at 253.
36. See Donatella Della Porta, *Globalization from Below: Transnational Activists and Protest Networks* (Minneapolis: University of Minnesota Press, 2006) at 33.
37. For several empirical discussions of transnational protest-campaigns with national targets, see Della Porta, Kriesi, and Rucht (eds.), *Social Movements in a Globalizing World*, especially the papers by Doug Imig and Sidney Tarrow, at pp. 112–32.
38. Iris Marion Young, 'Responsibility and Global Labour Justice', *The Journal of Political Philosophy,* 12/4 (2004) at 365–88.
39. See on some of these issues, Tom Mertes, 'Grass-Roots Globalism', *New Left Review,* 17 (September–October 2002), 101–10; Emir Sader, 'Beyond Civil Society', *New Left Review,* 17 (September–October 2002) at 87–99.
40. See Keck and Sikkink, *Activists Beyond Borders: Advocacy Networks in International Politics* at 128–49.
41. For various empirical examples of the relationship between global issues and grass-root activism with regard to labour movements, see the essays contained in Kate Bronfenbrenner, *Global Unions: Challenging Transnational Capital through Cross-Border Campaigns* (Ithaca: Cornell University Press, 2007).

## CONCLUSION

1. This remark seems to be confirmed by the various strategies the global justice movement has chosen to pursue in different countries, with agents in the global South of the world seeking active inclusion in state structures and introducing cosmopolitan political innovations by means of institutional reform (think of India, South Africa, and several Latin American countries) and those in the global North relying on less civil initiatives.
2. If that claim is still contested, objections should be directed to those parts of the book where points of principle were discussed, not to the idea of a cosmopolitan avant-garde in itself.

# Bibliography

Abizadeh, Arash (2007), 'Cooperation, Pervasive Impact, and Coercion: On the Scope (not Site) of Distributive Justice', *Philosophy and Public Affairs*, 35 (4), 318–58.

Anderson, Perry (ed.) (1977), *Aesthetics and Politics* (London: Verso).

Aristotle ([unknown] 2004), *Nicomachean Ethics*, trans. J. A. K. Thomson (London: Penguin).

Armstrong, Chris (2009), 'Defending the Duty of Assistance?', Social Theory and Practice, 35/3, 461–82.

Arneson, Richard (1981), 'What's Wrong with Exploitation', *Ethics,* 91 (1), 207–27.

Barry, Brian (1990), 'Social Criticism and Political Philosophy', *Philosophy and Public Affairs,* 19 (4), 360–73.

—— (1995), 'Rawls and the Search for Stability', *Ethics,* 105 (4), 874–915.

—— (1998), 'International Society from a Cosmopolitan Perspective', in David Mapel and Terry Nardin (eds), *International Society: Diverse Ethical Perspectives*, (Princeton: Princeton University Press), 144–63.

Beitz, Charles (1983), 'Cosmopolitan Ideals and National Sentiments', *Journal of Philosophy,* 80 (10), 591–600.

—— (1994), 'Cosmopolitan Liberalism and the States System', in Chris Brown (ed.), *Political Structuring in Europe* (London: Routledge).

—— (1999), *Political Theory and International Relations* (Princeton: Princeton University Press).

—— (2000), 'Rawls's Law of Peoples', *Ethics,* 110 (4), 669–96.

—— (2001), 'Does Global Inequality Matter?', *Metaphilosophy,* 32 (1&2), 95–112.

—— (2009), *The Idea of Human Rights* (Oxford: Oxford University Press), xiii, 235.

Benhabib, Seyla (2004), *Citizens, Residents and Aliens: Aliens, Residents, and Citizens* (Cambridge: Cambridge University Press).

Bianchi, Lorenzo (ed.) (2002), *L'Idea di Cosmopolitismo. Circolazione e Metamorfosi* (Naples: Liguori).

—— and Postigliola, Alberto (eds) (2000), *Un 'Progetto Filosofico della Modernità' Per la Pace Perpetua di Immanuel Kant* (Naples: Liguori).

Birnholz, Alan C. (1973), 'The Russian Avant-Garde and the Russian Tradition', *Art Journal,* 32 (2), 146–9.

Blake, Michael (2001), 'Distributive Justice, State Coercion, and Autonomy', *Philosophy and Public Affairs,* 30 (3), 257–96.

Bobbio, Norberto (1990), *L'Età dei Diritti* (Torino: Einaudi).

Bohman, James and Lutz-Bachmann, Matthias (eds) (1997), *Perpetual Peace: Essays on Kant's Cosmopolitan Ideal* (Cambridge, MA: MIT Press).

Braithwaite, John and Drahos, Peter (2000), *Global Business Regulation* (New York: Cambridge University Press).

Brecht, Bertolt (1964), *The Threepenny Opera,* trans. Desmond Vesey (New York: Grove Press).

—— (1974), 'Against Georg Lukàsc', *New Left Review,* 84, 39–53.

Brighouse, Harry (1998), 'Civic Education and Liberal Legitimacy', *Ethics,* 108, 719–45.

—— (2006), *On Education* (London: Routledge).

—— and Swift, Adam (2006), 'Equality, Priority, and Positional Goods', *Ethics,* 116, 471–97.

Brock, Gillian (2009), *Global Justice: A Cosmopolitan Account* (Oxford: Oxford University Press).

Bronfenbrenner, Kate (2007), *Global Unions: Challenging Transnational Capital through Cross-border Campaigns* (Ithaca: Cornell University Press).

Brown, Eric (2006), 'Hellenistic Cosmopolitanism', in Mary Louise Gill and Pierre Pellegrin (eds), *A Companion to Ancient Philosophy* (Oxford: Blackwell).

Brownlee, Kimberley and Stemplowska, Zofia (unpublished manuscript), 'Trapped in an Experience Machine with a Famous Violinist: Thought Experiments in Normative Theory'.

Buchanan, Allen (2000), 'Rawls's Law of Peoples: Rules for a Vanished Westphalian World', *Ethics,* 110 (4), 697–721.

Bürger, Peter (1984), *Theory of the Avant-Garde* (Manchester: Manchester University Press).

Cabrera, Luis (2010), *The Practice of Global Citizenship* (Cambridge: Cambridge University Press).

Callan, Eamonn (1997), *Creating Citizens: Political Education and Liberal Democracy* (Oxford: Oxford University Press).

—— (2000), 'Liberal Legitimacy, Justice, and Civic Education', *Ethics,* 111, 141–55.

Caney, Simon (2001), 'Cosmopolitan Justice and Equalizing Opportunities', *Metaphilosophy,* 32 (1/2), 113–34.

—— (2002), 'Cosmopolitanism and the Law of Peoples', *The Journal of Political Philosophy,* 10 (1), 95–123.

—— (2005), *Justice Beyond Borders – A Global Political Theory* (Oxford: Oxford University Press).

—— (2006), 'Cosmopolitan Justice and Institutional Design: An Egalitarian Liberal Conception of Global Justice', *Social Theory and Practice,* 32 (4), 725–56.

—— (2008), 'Global Distributive Justice and the State', *Political Studies,* 56 (3), 487–518.

Casal, Paula (2007), 'Why Sufficiency is not Enough', *Ethics,* 117, 296–326.

Cassirer, Ernst (1977), *An Essay on Man: An Introduction to a Philosophy of Human Culture* (Yale: Yale University Press).

Cavallar, Georg (2002), *The Rights of Strangers. Theories of International Hospitality, the Global Community and Political Justice since Vitoria* (Aldershot: Ashgate).

Cohen, Gerald A. (1989a), *History, Labour, and Freedom. Themes from Marx* (Oxford: Oxford University Press).

—— (1989b), 'On the Currency of Egalitarian Justice', *Ethics,* 99 (4), 906–44.

—— (1995), *Self-ownership, Freedom and Equality* (Cambridge: Cambridge University Press).

—— (2008), *Rescuing Justice and Equality* (Cambridge, MA: Harvard University Press).

Cohen, Jean and Arato, Andrew (1992), *Civil Society and Political Theory* (Cambridge, MA: MIT Press).

Cohen, Joshua (1997), 'The Arc of the Moral Universe', *Philosophy and Public Affairs,* 26 (2), 91–134.

—— and Sabel, Charles (2006), 'Extra Rempublicam Nulla Justitia?', *Philosophy and Public Affairs,* 34 (2), 147–75.

Constant, Benjamin (1988 (1819)), 'The Liberty of the Ancients Compared with that of the Moderns', in Biancamaria Fontana (ed.), *Political Writings* (Cambridge: Cambridge University Press).

Crisp, Roger (2003), 'Equality, Priority, and Compassion', *Ethics*, 113, 745–63.

Dahl, Robert A. (1968), 'Power' in *International Encyclopaedia of the Social Sciences* (New York, Macmillan: 1968), vol. 12, pp. 405–414.

Della Porta, Donatella (2006), *Globalization from Below: Transnational Activists and Protest Networks* (Minneapolis: University of Minnesota Press).

—— and Diani, Mario (1999), *Social Movements: An Introduction* (Oxford: Blackwell).

—— Kriesi, Hanspeter, and Rucht, Dieter (eds) (1999), *Social Movements in a Globalizing World* (London: MacMillan).

Diderot, Denis and D'Alembert, Jean Le Rond ([1754–1772]), *Encyclopédie, ou Dictionnaire raisonné des sciences, des arts et des métiers*, 28 vols. (Geneva; Paris; Neufchatel: Briasson and others).

Drescher, Seymour (1994), 'Whose Abolition? Popular Pressure and the Ending of the British Slave-Trade', *Past & Present*, 143, 136–66.

Dryzek, John S. (2002), *Deliberative Democracy and Beyond – Liberals, Critics, Contestations* (Oxford: Oxford University Press).

Dworkin, Ronald (1986), *Law's Empire* (Cambridge, MA: Harvard University Press).

Egbert, Donald D. (1967), 'The Idea of "Avant-Garde" in Art and Politics', *The American Historical Review*, 78 (2), 339–66.

Estlund, David (2009), *Democratic Authority: A Philosophical Framework* (Princeton: Princeton University Press).

Falk, Richard (1998), *Law in an Emerging Global Village: A Post-Westphalian Perspective* (Ardsley: Transnational Publishers).

Farrelly, Colin (2007), 'Justice in Ideal Theory: A Refutation', *Political Studies*, 55 (4), 844–64.

Feinberg, Joel (1974), 'Noncomparative Justice', *The Philosophical Review*, 83 (3), 297–338.

Feyerabend, Paul ([1975] 2005), 'How to Defend Philosophy against Science', in Nigel Warburton (ed.), *Philosophy. Basic Readings* (Abingdon: Routledge), 365–75.

Finnemore, Martha and Sikkink, Kathryn (1998), 'International Norm Dynamics and Political Change', *International Organization*, 52 (4), 887–917.

Flikschuh, Katrin (2000), *Kant and Modern Political Philosophy* (Cambridge: Cambridge University Press).

—— (2006), 'Kant's Indemonstrable Postulate of Right: A Response to Paul Guyer', *Kantian Review*, 12, 1–39.

—— (2010), 'Kant's Sovereignty Dilemma: A Contemporary Analysis', *The Journal of Political Philosophy*, 18 (4), 469–93.

Fox, William (1791), *Address to the People of Great Britain, on the Propriety of Abstaining from West India Sugar and Rum* [online text], W. Bell http://galenet.galegroup .com/servlet/MOME?af=RN&ae=U102335251&srchtp=a&ste=14&locID=oxford.

Frankfurt, Harry (1987), 'Equality as a Moral Ideal', *Ethics*, 98 (1), 21–43.

Freeman, Samuel (2006), 'The Law of Peoples, Social Cooperation, Human Rights, and Distributive Justice', *Social Philosophy and Policy*, 23 (1), 29–68.

Galston, William (1991), *Liberal Purposes: Goods, Virtues, and Diversity in the Liberal State* (Cambridge: Cambridge University Press).

Gerhardt, Volker, Horstmann, Rolf-Peter, and Schumacher, Ralph (eds) (2001), *Kant und die Berliner Aufklärung. Akten des IX. Internationalen Kant-Kongresses* (Berlin: Walter de Gruyter).

Gilabert, Pablo (2011), 'Humanist and Political Perspectives on Human Rights', *Political Theory* 39 (4), 439–467.

Gilpin, Robert (2001), *Global Political Economy. Understanding the International Economic Order* (Princeton: Princeton University Press).

Goodin, Robert E. (1988), *Reasons for Welfare. The Political Theory of the Welfare State* (Princeton: Princeton University Press).

Gould, Carol (2004), *Globalizing Democracy and Human Rights* (Cambridge: Cambridge University Press).

Antonio, Gramsci, *Selections from the Prison Notebooks*, ed. Geoffrey Nowell Smith and Quintin Hoare (London: Lawrence and Whishart, 1971).

Gutmann, Amy (1987), *Democratic Education* (Princeton: Princeton University Press).

Habermas, Jürgen (1972), *Knowledge and Human Interests* (London: Heinemann).

—— (1998), *The Inclusion of the Other: Studies in Political Theory* (Cambridge, MA: MIT Press).

—— (2001), *The Postnational Constellation* (Cambridge: Polity Press).

Hajer, Maarten A. and Wagenaar, Hendrik (2003), *Deliberative Policy Analysis: Understanding Governance in the Network Society* (Cambridge: Cambridge University Press).

Harrison, Charles and Wood, Paul (eds) (1998), *Art in Theory 1815–1900: An Anthology of Changing Ideas* (Oxford: Blackwell).

Havens, G. R. (1933), *Voltaire's Marginalia on the Pages of Rousseau: A Comparative Study of Ideas* (Columbus: The Ohio State University).

Hayek, Friedrich August (1978), *Law, Legislation and Liberty: The Mirage of Social Justice* (vol. 2, London: Routledge and Kegan).

Heater, Derek (1996), *World Citizenship and Government: Cosmopolitan Ideas in the History of Western Political Thought* (New York: St. Martin's Press).

Held, David (1995), *Democracy and the Global Order: From the Modern State to Cosmopolitan Governance* (Stanford: Stanford University Press).

Henson, Richard (1979), 'What Kant Might Have Said: Moral Worth and the Over-determination of Dutiful Action', *The Philosophical Review*, 88, 39–54.

Herman, Barbara (1981), 'On the Value of Acting from the Motive of Duty', *The Philosophical Review*, 90 (3), 359–82.

Hobbes, Thomas ([1651] 1991), *Leviathan*, ed. by R. Tuck (New York: Cambridge University Press).

Hobsbawm, Eric (1980), 'Socialism and the Avantgarde in the Period of the Second International', *Le Mouvement Social*, 111, 189–99.

—— (1987), *The Age of Empire* (London: Weidenfeld and Nicolson).

—— (1999), *Behind the Times: The Decline and Fall of the Twentieth-Century Avant-Gardes* (New York: Thames and Hudson).

Hochschild, Adam (2006), *Bury the Chains: The British Struggle to Abolish Slavery* (London: Pan Macmillan).

Höffe, Otfried (2006), *Kant's Cosmopolitan Theory* (Cambridge: Cambridge University Press).

Hont, Istvan (2005), *Jealousy of Trade: International Competition and the Nation State in Historical Perspective* (Cambridge, MA: Harvard University Press).

Hume, David ([1739–40] 1978), *A Treatise of Human Nature* (Oxford: Oxford University Press).

Huyssen, Andreas (1986), *After the Great Divide: Modernism, Mass Culture, Postmodernism* (Bloomington: Indiana University Press).

James, Aaron (2005), 'Constructing Justice for Existing Practice: Rawls and the Status Quo', *Philosophy and Public Affairs*, 33 (3), 281–316.

Julius, A. J. (2006), 'Nagel's Atlas', *Philosophy and Public Affairs*, 34 (2), 176–92.

Kant, Immanuel ([1784] 1991), 'Idea for a Universal History with a Cosmopolitan Purpose', in Hans Reiss (ed.), *Political Writings* (Cambridge: Cambridge University Press).

—— ([1784] 1996), 'An Answer to the Question: What is Enlightenment?', in Mary Gregor (ed.), *Practical Philosophy* (Cambridge: Cambridge University Press).

—— ([1793] 1996), 'On the Common Saying: That may be Correct in Theory, but is of no Use in Practice', in Mary Gregor (ed.), *Practical Philosophy* (Cambridge: Cambridge University Press).

—— ([1793] 1998), *Religion within the Boundaries of mere Reason and other Writings* (Cambridge: Cambridge University Press).

—— ([1795] 1996), 'Toward Perpetual Peace', in Mary Gregor (ed.), *Practical Philosophy* (Cambridge: Cambridge University Press).

—— ([1797] 1996), 'The Metaphysics of Morals', in Mary Gregor (ed.), *Practical Philosophy* (Cambridge: Cambridge University Press).

—— ([1798] 2001), 'The Conflict of the Faculties', in Allen W. Wood and George Di Giovanni (eds), *Religion and Rational Theology* (Cambridge: Cambridge University Press).

Keane, John (2003), *Global Civil Society?* (Cambridge: Cambridge University Press).

Keck, Margret and Sikkink, Kathleen (1998), *Activists Beyond Borders: Advocacy Networks in International Politics* (Ithaca: Cornell University Press).

Keohane, Robert and Nye, Joseph S. (1977), *Power and Interdependence* (Boston: Little, Brown).

Kleingeld, Pauline (1998), 'Kant's Cosmopolitan Law: World Citizenship for a Global Order', *Kantian Review*, 2, 72–90.

—— (1999), 'Six Varieties of Cosmopolitanism in Late Eighteenth-Century Germany', *Journal of the History of Ideas*, 60 (3), 505–24.

—— (2004), 'Approaching Perpetual Peace: Kant's Defence of a League of States and his Ideal of a World Federation', *European Journal of Philosophy*, 12, 304–25.

Kramer, Hilton (1973), 'The Age of the Avant-Garde', *Journal of Aesthetic Education*, 7 (2), 35–51.

Kuper, Andrew (2000), 'Rawlsian Global Justice: Beyond the Law of Peoples to a Cosmopolitan Law of Persons', *Political Theory*, 28 (5), 640–74.

Kymlicka, Will (2001), *Politics in the Vernacular – Nationalism, Multiculturalism, and Citizenship* (Oxford: Oxford University Press).

Ladyman, James (2002), *Understanding Philosophy of Science* (London: Routledge).

Lakatos, Imre (1970), 'Falsification and the Methodology of Scientific Research Programmes', in Imre Lakatos and Alan Musgrave (eds), *Criticism and the Growth of Knowledge* (Cambridge: Cambridge University Press).

Leibniz, Gottfried Wilhelm (1988), *Political Writings*, ed. Patrick Riley (Cambridge: Cambridge University Press).

—— ([1704] 1996), *New Essays on Human Understanding*, ed. Peter Remnant and Jonathan Bennett (Cambridge: Cambridge University Press).

Lenin, Vladimir I. ([1902] 1929), *What is to be Done?* (New York: International Publishers).

Locke, John ([1690] 2008), *An Essay Concerning Human Understanding*, ed. Pauline Phemister (Oxford: Oxford University Press).

Lukes, Steven (2005), *Power: A Radical View* (New York: Palgrave Macmillan).

Machiavelli, Niccolo ([1517] 1996), *Discourses on Livy* (Chicago: Chicago University Press).

Marchetti, Raffaele (2008), *Global Democracy: For and Against. Ethical, Institutional, and Social Perspectives on Political Inclusion* (London: Routledge).

Marx, Karl ([1843] 1977), *Critique of Hegel's 'Philosophy of Right'*, ed. Joseph J. O'Malley (Cambridge: Cambridge University Press).

—— ([1875] 1994), 'Critique of the Gotha Program' in *Selected Writings,* ed. Lawrence H. Simon (Indianapolis: Hackett Publishing), 315–331.

May, Gita (1972), 'Le Cosmopolite ou Le Citoyen du Monde; La Capitale des Gaules ou La Nouvelle Babylone by Louis-Charles Fougeret de Monbron', *The French Review,* 45 (3), 737–8.

McDonough, Kevin, and Walter Feinberg (2003), *Citizenship and Education in Liberal-Democratic Societies – Teaching for Cosmopolitan Values and Collective Identities* (Oxford: Oxford University Press).

Merker, Nicolao (1989), *L'Illuminismo in Germania. L'Età di Lessing* (Rome: Editori Riuniti).

Mertes, Tom (2002), 'Grass-Roots Globalism', *New Left Review,* 17, 101–10.

Micheli, Mario De (1988), *Le avanguardie artistiche del Novecento* (Milan: Feltrinelli).

Mill, John Stuart ([1861] 1991), 'Considerations on Representative Government', in John Gray (ed.), *On Liberty and Other Essays* (Oxford: Oxford University Press).

Miller, David (1997), *On Nationality* (Oxford: Oxford University Press).

—— (1999), *Principles of Social Justice* (Cambridge, MA: Harvard University Press).

—— (2005), 'Against Global Egalitarianism', *The Journal of Ethics,* 9 (1–2), 55–79.

—— (2006), 'Collective Responsibility and International Equality in the Law of Peoples', in Rex Martin and David Reidy (eds), *Rawls's Law of Peoples* (Oxford: Blackwell), 191–205.

—— (2007), *National Responsibility and Global Justice* (Oxford: Oxford University Press).

—— (2010), 'A Tale of Two Cities; Or, Political Philosophy as Lamentation' (unpublished manuscript).

Miller, Richard (2009), *Globalizing Justice* (Oxford: Oxford University Press).

Mills, Charles W. (2005), 'Ideal Theory as Ideology', *Hypatia,* 20 (3), 165–184.

Moellendorf, Darrel (2002), *Cosmopolitan Justice* (Boulder, CO: Westview Press).

Monbron, Fougeret de ([[1750] 1970), *Le Cosmopolite ou Citoyen du Monde,* ed. Raymond Trousson (Paris: Ducros).

Morgenthau, Hans (1959), *Politics Among Nations: The Struggle for Power and Peace* (New York: Alfred Knopf).

Muthu, Sankar (2003), *Enlightenment against Empire* (Princeton: Princeton University Press).

—— (2011), 'Conquest, Commerce, and Cosmopolitanism in Enlightenment Political Thought', in Sankar Muthu (ed.), *Empire and Modern Political Thought* (Cambridge: Cambridge University Press), forthcoming.

Nagel, Thomas (2005), 'The Problem of Global Justice', *Philosophy and Public Affairs,* 33 (2), 113–47.

Narveson, Jan (2005), 'Welfare and Wealth, Poverty and Justice in Today's World', *Journal of Ethics*, 8 (4), 305–48.

Niesen, Peter (2007), 'Hospitality and Colonialism', *Politics and Ethics Review*, 3 (1), 90–108.

Nussbaum, Martha (1997a), *Cultivating Humanity: A Classical Defense of Reform in Liberal Education* (Cambridge, MA: Harvard University Press).

—— (1997b), 'Kant and Stoic Cosmopolitanism', *The Journal of Political Philosophy*, 5 (1), 1–25.

—— (ed.) (2002), *For Love of Country?* (Boston: Beacon Press).

—— (2006), *Frontiers of Justice* (Cambridge, MA: Harvard University Press).

Offe, Claus (2006), 'Political Disaffection as an Outcome of Institutional Practices? Some Post-Tocquevillean Speculations', in Mariano Torcal and José R. Montero (eds), *Political Disaffection in Contemporary Democracies. Social Capital, Institutions and Politics* (London: Routledge), 23–45.

O'Neill, Onora (1987), 'Abstraction, Idealization and Ideology in Ethics', in John D. G. Evans (ed.), *Moral Philosophy and Contemporary Problems* (Cambridge: Cambridge University Press), 55–69.

—— (2000), *Bounds of Justice* (Cambridge: Cambridge University Press).

Pevnick, Ryan (2008), 'Political Coercion and the Scope of Distributive Justice', *Political Studies*, 56, 399–413.

Pieri, Georges (2002), 'Raison et Cosmopolitisme au XVIIIe siècle', in Lorenzo Bianchi (ed.), *L'Idea di Cosmopolitismo. Circolazione e Metamorfosi* (Naples: Liguori), 357–640.

Plato (1961), *The Collected Dialogues of Plato Including the Letters*, eds. Huntingon Cairns and Hamilton, Edith (Princeton: Princeton University Press).

Pocock, J. G. A. (2003), *The Machiavellian Moment: Florentine Political Thought and the Atlantic Republican Tradition* (Princeton: Princeton University Press).

—— (2009), *Political Thought and History: Essays on Theory and Method* (Cambridge: Cambridge University Press).

Pogge, Thomas (1989), *Realizing Rawls* (Ithaca: Cornell University Press).

—— (2002), *World Poverty and Human Rights* (Cambridge: Polity Press).

—— (2005), 'Severe Poverty as a Violation of Negative Duties', *Ethics & International Affairs*, 19 (1), 55–83.

—— (2006), 'Do Rawls's Two Theories of Justice Fit Together?', in Rex Martin and David Reidy (eds), *Rawls's Law of Peoples* (Oxford: Blackwell).

Pogge, Thomas W. (1992), 'Cosmopolitanism and Sovereignty', *Ethics*, 103 (1), 48–75.

Popper, Karl R. (1940), 'What is Dialectic?', *Mind*, 49 (196), 403–26.

Ramirez, Francisco O., Soysal, Yasemin, and Shanahan, Suzanne (1997), 'The Changing Logic of Political Citizenship: Cross-National Acquisition of Women's Suffrage Rights, 1890 to 1990', *American Sociological Review*, 62 (5), 735–45.

Rawls, John (1963), 'The Sense of Justice', *The Philosophical Review*, 72 (3), 281–305.

—— (1980), 'Kantian Constructivism in Moral Theory', *The Journal of Philosophy*, 77 (9), 515–72.

—— (1993), *Political Liberalism* (New York: Columbia University Press).

—— (1999a), *A Theory of Justice* (Rev. edn; Cambridge, MA: Harvard University Press).

—— (1999b), *The Law of Peoples* (Cambridge, MA: Harvard University Press).

Raynal, Guillaume-Thomas ([1781] 1980), *Histoire des deux Indes* (Paris: La Découverte).

Reidy, David A. (2004), 'Rawls on International Justice, A. Defense', *Political Theory*, 32 (3), 291–319.

Richards, David A. J. (1971), *A Theory of Reasons for Action* (Oxford: Clarendon Press).

Risse, Mathias (2005a), 'How Does the Global Order Harm the Poor?', *Philosophy and Public Affairs* 33 (4), 349–76.

—— (2005b), 'Do We Owe the Global Poor Assistance or Rectification?', *Journal of Ethics*, 9, 81–117.

—— (2005c), 'What We Owe to the Global Poor *Journal of Ethics*, 9, 81–117.

—— (2006), 'What to Say about the State', *Social Theory and Practice*, 32 (4), 671–98.

Risse, Thomas (1999), 'International Norms and Domestic Change: Arguing and Communicative Behavior in the Human Rights Area', *Politics & Society*, 27 (4), 529–59.

—— Ropp, Stephen C., and Sikkink, Kathryn (eds) (1999), *The Power of Human Rights: International Norms & Domestic Change* (Cambridge: Cambridge University Press).

Robeyns, Ingrid (2008), 'Ideal Theory in Theory and Practice', *Social Theory and Practice*, 34 (3), 341–62.

Robinet, André (2002), 'G. W. Leibniz: L'Esprit Cosmopolitique Jusqu'à la Lettre', in Lorenzo Bianchi (ed.), *L'Idea di Cosmopolitismo. Circolazione e Metamorfosi*, (Naples: Liguori), 5–26.

Ronzoni, Miriam (2009), 'The Global Order: A Case of Background Injustice? A Practice-Dependent Account', Philosophy and Public Affairs, 37/3, 229–56.

Rosen, Michael (1982), *Hegel's Dialectic and its Criticism* (Cambridge: Cambridge University Press).

Rousseau, Jean-Jacques ([1756] 1991), 'Abstract and Judgement of Saint Pierre's Project of Perpetual Peace', in S. Hoffman and D. Fidler (eds), *Rousseau on International Relations* (Oxford: Clarendon Press).

—— ([1762] 1997), 'Of the Social Contract', in Victor Gourevitch (ed.), *The Social Contract and Other Later Political Writings* (Cambridge: Cambridge University Press).

—— ([1762] 2006), *Émile*, trans. Barbara Foxley (Charleston: Biblio Bazaar).

—— ([1772] 1997), 'Considerations on the Government of Poland', in Victor Gourevitch (ed.), *The Social Contract and Other Later Political Writings* (Cambridge: Cambridge University Press).

—— ([1775] 1997), *The Discourses and Other Early Political Writings*, trans. V. Gourevitch (Cambridge: Cambridge University Press).

Sader, Emir (2002), 'Beyond Civil Society', *New Left Review*, 17, 87–99.

Sangiovanni, Andrea (2007), 'Global Justice, Reciprocity, and the State', *Philosophy and Public Affairs*, 35 (1), 3–39.

—— (2008), 'Justice and the Priority of Politics to Morality', *The Journal of Political Philosophy*, 16 (2), 137–64.

Scanlon, Thomas (1975), 'Preference and Urgency', *The Journal of Philosophy*, 72 (19), 655–69.

Scheffler, Samuel (2003), *Boundaries and Allegiances: Problems of Justice and Responsibility in Liberal Thought* (Oxford: Oxford University Press).

Schiller, Friedrich Von ([1795] 2004), *Letters upon the Aesthetic Education of Man* (Montana: Kessinger Publishers).

Schlereth, Thomas J. (1977), *The Cosmopolitan Ideal in Enlightenment Thought* (Notre Dame: University of Notre Dame Press).

Sen, Amartya (1983), *Poverty and Famines: An Essay on Entitlement and Deprivation* (Oxford: Oxford University Press).

Sen, Amartya (1985), 'A Sociological Approach to the Measurement of Poverty: A Reply to Professor Peter Townsend', *Oxford Economic Papers,* 37 (4), 669–76.

—— (2009), *The Idea of Justice* (London: Allen Lane).

Sencerz, Stefan (1986), 'Moral Intuitions and Justification in Ethics', *Philosophical Studies,* 50 (1), 77–94.

Shaffer, Gregory (2005), 'Power, Governance and the WTO: A Comparative Institutional Approach', in Michael Barnett and Raymond Duvall (eds), *Power in Global Governance* (Cambridge: Cambridge University Press).

Shue, Henry (1996), *Basic Rights: Subsistence, Affluence, and U.S. Foreign Policy* (Princeton: Princeton University Press).

Simmons, A. J. (2010), 'Ideal and Nonideal Theory', *Philosophy and Public Affairs,* 38 (1), 5–36.

Simon, Claude Henri de Saint ([1825] 1975), *Selected Writings on Science, Industry and Social Organization,* trans. Keith Taylor (London: Croom Helm).

Singer, Peter (2004), 'Outsiders: Our Obligations to those Beyond our Borders', in Deen K. Chatterjee (ed.), *The Ethics of Assistance: Morality and the Distance Needy* (Cambridge: Cambridge University Press), 11–32.

Skinner, Quentin (2002), *Visions of Politics* (vol. 3; Hobbes and Civil Science; Cambridge: Cambridge University Press).

Smith, Adam ([1776–1783] 1999), *The Wealth of Nations: IV–V,* ed. Andrew Skinner (London: Penguin).

Smith, Patrick Horace Nowell (1954), *Ethics* (London: Penguin Books).

Steinberg, Richard H. (2002), 'In the Shadow of Law or Power? Consensus-Based Bargaining and Outcomes in the GATT/WTO', *International Organization,* 2 (56), 339–74.

Stemplowska, Zofia (2008), 'What's Ideal about Ideal Theory?', *Social Theory and Practice,* 34 (3), 319–40.

Stiglitz, Joseph E. (2002), *Globalization and its Discontents* (London: Penguin).

Stiglitz, Joseph and Charleton, Andrew (2005), *Fair Trade for All* (Oxford: Oxford University Press).

Stocker, Michael (1976), 'The Schizophrenia of Modern Ethical Theories', *The Journal of Philosophy,* 73 (14), 453–66.

Swift, Adam (2008), 'The Value of Philosophy in Non-Ideal Circumstances', *Social Theory and Practice,* 34 (3), 363–87.

Tan, Kok-Chor (2004), *Justice without Borders: Cosmopolitanism, Nationalism, and Patriotism* (Cambridge: Cambridge University Press).

Tarrow, Sidney (2001), 'Transnational Politics: Contention and Institutions in International Politics', *Annual Review of Political Science,* 4 (1), 1–20.

Therborn, Göran (2003), 'Entangled Modernities', *European Journal of Social Theory,* 6, 293–305.

Valentini, Laura (2009), 'On the Apparent Paradox of Ideal Theory', *The Journal of Political Philosophy,* 17 (3), 332–55.

—— (2011), 'Global Justice and Practice-Dependence: Conventionalism, Institutionalism, Functionalism', *The Journal of Political Philosophy*, 19 (4), 375–497.

Van Hensbergen, Gijs (2004), *Guernica: The Biography of a Twentieth-Century Icon* (London: Bloomsbury).

Voltaire, François Marie Arouet ([1752] 1994), *Political Writings*, trans. D. Williams (Cambridge: Cambridge University Press).

—— ([1774] 1966), *Le Siècle de Louis XIV* (Paris: Garnier-Flammarion).

Waldron, Jeremy (2000), 'What is Cosmopolitan?', *The Journal of Political Philosophy*, 8 (2), 227–43.

—— (ed.) (1987), *Nonsense Upon Stilts: Bentham, Burke, and Marx on the Rights of Man* (London: Methuen).

Walzer, Michael (1970), *Obligations: Essays on Disobedience, War, and Citizenship* (Cambridge, MA: Harvard University Press).

—— (1983), *Spheres of Justice: A Defence of Pluralism and Equality* (Oxford: Robertson).

—— (1987), *Interpretation and Social Criticism* (Cambridge, MA: Harvard University Press).

Weber, Max ([1914] 1978), *Economy and Society: An Outline of Interpretive Sociology* (Berkeley, CA: University of California Press).

Wenar, Leif (2002), 'The Legitimacy of Peoples', in Pablo De Greiff and Ciaran Cronin (eds), *Global Justice and Transnational Politics* (Cambridge, MA: MIT Press).

White, Jonathan and Ypi, Lea (2010), 'Rethinking the Modern Prince: Partisanship and the Democratic Ethos', *Political Studies*, 58 (4), 809–28.

Williams, Howard (1983), *Kant's Political Philosophy* (Oxford: Blackwell).

Young, Iris Marion (2002), *Inclusion and Democracy* (Oxford: Oxford University Press).

—— (2004), 'Responsibility and Global Labour Justice', *The Journal of Political Philosophy*, 12 (4), 365–88.

Ypi, Lea (2008), 'Justice in Migration: A Closed Borders Utopia?', *The Journal of Political Philosophy*, 16 (4), 391–418.

—— (2010a), 'On the Confusion between Ideal and Non-ideal in Recent Debates on Global Justice', *Political Studies*, 58 (3), 536–55.

—— (2010b), 'Natura Daedala Rerum? On the Justification of Historical Progress in Kant's Guarantee of Perpetual Peace', *Kantian Review*, 14 (2), 118–48.

—— (forthcoming), 'A Permissive Theory of Territorial Rights', *The European Journal of Philosophy*.

—— (2011), 'Public Spaces and the End of Art', *Philosophy and Social Criticism*, forthcoming.

# Index

Abizadeh, Arash 73n4
absolute deprivation 6, 91, 95–104, 107–29
activist political theory 35–6, 40–5, 63, 71, 74–5, 78–9
Adorno, Theodor 1n1, 160n15
advocacy networks 165, 170–1
agricultural trade agreements 126
Alkire, S 121n31
*amour propre* 16–20
anarchy 15, 29, 143
Anderson, Perry 160n15
Anthony, Susan B 164
Aragon, Louis 158
Arato, Andrew 167n32
arbitrariness
    circumstances of justice 76–86
    cosmopolitanism 3, 6, 76–80, 85, 138
    moral arbitrariness 3, 51, 108, 120
    place of birth 51, 108, 120
    political membership 6, 19, 76–7, 80, 86, 134, 142–4, 149
Aristotle 53, 64, 115, 126n46, 159, 161
Armstrong, Chris 112n7
Arneson, Richard 90n4
art, politics as 155, 156
Asia 171
associative relations 4, 6–7, 12, 21, 104
    background circumstances 134, 141
    civil society model 133–5, 140–1
    coercion and cooperation 73
    cosmopolitanism 6, 28, 30, 34, 72–3, 76, 87, 90, 92, 140, 154–5
    dialectical method 133, 140, 154
    family model 136, 140–1
    ideal and nonideal 72–6
    joint citizenship 51
    loyalty 135–6, 145
    morality 25
    particularism 137
    politics 71–87, 133–41, 148
    relevance 104, 133
    statism 71, 92, 131–2
ATTAC (Action for a Tobin Tax to Aid Citizens) 168
autarchy 47, 128
autonomy 28, 92, 128, 146
avant-garde 13–14, 18–21, 31, 36–67, 75, 154–73
    artistic avant-gardes 156–65

cinema 159
creative interpretation in art and politics 1, 160–72
jazz 159
musicians 157
painters 1–2, 8, 157–60
suprematism 158–9
Surrealism 158
theatre 159

Balzac, Honoré de 160n15
Barber, Benjamin 151n31
Barnett, Michael 126n45
Barry, Brian 83n32, 83n33, 148n28
basic material goods, access to 108, 112–13, 116–17, 119–20, 174–5
Bauhaus 157
Beitz, Charles 30n67, 51n33, 72n3, 73n8, 77n12, 77n15, 78n20, 80n25, 81n28, 82n29, 83n32, 121n31
Bengal famine 1943 116–17
Benhabib, Seyla 33n76
Bennett, Jonathan 13n10
Bentham, Jeremy 152n33
Bianchi, Lorenzo 11n1, 11n3, 13n8
Birnholz, Alan C 159n11
Blake, Michael 47n26, 72n2, 74n10, 74n11, 112, 117n23, 128n48
Bloch, Ernst 160n15
Bobbio, Norberto 33n76
Bohman, James 33n76
Braithwaite, John 126n45
Brazil 172
Brecht, Bertold 113, 157, 159, 160
Breton, André 158
Brighouse, Harry 98n18, 109n2, 124n40, 125n42, 146n24
Brock, Gillian 77n12, 121n33
Bronfenbrenner, Kate 171n41
Brown, Eric 12n4, 13n7
Brownlee, Kimberley 38n6, 46n21
Buchanan, Allen 73n7
Bürger, Peter 137n5
'Burial at Ornans' 157–8

Cabrera, Luis 168n34
Cairns, Huntingon 13n6, 115n17
Callan, Eamonn 144n21, 146n24, 147n25

campaigns 154, 167–70, 176
Caney, Simon 73n7, 77n12, 80n25, 87n39,
    121n32, 135n6
Casal, Paula 115n19
Cassirer, Ernst 54n43
categorical imperative 34
causal claims 6, 99–103, 109–20
Cavallar, Georg 26n47
Cervantes, Miguel de 49–50
Charleton, Andrew 126n44
Chatterjee, Deen K 92n9
cheap labour 169
child labour 169
China 117–18
circumstances of injustice 4, 7, 44, 118–27,
    137, 148, 155
  absolute deprivation 102, 107, 109
  arbitrariness 76–86
  conflicts 61, 94–7
  cosmopolitanism 60, 80, 99, 102
  distributive justice 86–7, 102, 104, 123
  egalitarianism 44, 88, 95, 97, 99, 103, 112,
    118–20
  ideal and nonideal 47, 81–6, 108
  interpretation 76–7, 80–1, 94, 100, 104,
    109, 119
  morality 77, 79, 86, 94
  political agency 27–8, 48
  positional goods 110–11, 123–4
  relative deprivation 97, 102, 107
  statism 102, 119
  sufficientarianism 103, 111
citizen of the world 12–23, 26
civic education 7, 19–20, 23, 29, 124–5, 133,
    145–51, 153
  schools 146–7, 151
civil disobedience 149–50, 164
civil society model of political community 20,
    25, 132–6, 141–4
coercion 29, 72–3, 126, 145
Cohen, Gerald A 36n1, 38n6, 38n8, 89,
    100n19, 111n6
Cohen, Jean 167n32
Cohen, Joshua 47n56, 73n4
collective goods 132, 135
colonialism 21–2, 25, 129
commercial relations 17–18, 24, 25, 28, 59–60
common good 14, 20–1, 73, 134, 145
comparative principles 113–15, 119–21, 124
compassion 13–14, 18–19, 21
conflicts 17–20, 23–30, 58–67, 129–32, 144–5
  causes 23, 81
  circumstances of injustice 61, 94–7
  culture 162
  distributive justice 19, 102, 130, 148
  institutions 5, 20, 23–4, 29, 31, 35, 44, 61

interpretation 26, 40–1, 44, 58–9, 67, 79,
    102, 109, 144
  politics 5, 13, 63–7, 79, 154, 163, 168
  positional goods 109
  private property 19–20
  social practices 40–1
  state of nature 29–30
Constant, Benjamin 134
constitutions 23, 29, 31–3, 79, 135
conventionalism 54, 72–3, 76
cosmopolitanism 11–23, 59–60 , 96, 147–58
  agency 7–8, 147–55, 166–70
  arbitrariness 3, 6, 34, 76–80, 85, 138
  art, politics as 155, 156
  associative relations 6, 28, 30, 34, 72–3, 76,
    87, 90, 92, 140, 154–5
  avant-garde 7–8, 154–8, 166–73, 176
  basic material goods, access to 174–5
  campaigns 167–73, 176
  circumstances of injustice 60, 80, 99, 102
  civic education 133, 148–9, 151, 153
  civil disobedience 150
  civil society model of political
    community 134–5
  conflicts 17–19, 26, 154, 168
  definition 7–8, 11–15, 26, 155
  dialectical method 6, 104
  distributive justice 72–3, 89, 167
  egalitarianism 6, 7, 12–13, 88–93, 95–6,
    98–104, 166
  global justice 7, 13–14, 26–7, 29, 33, 60,
    72–3
  globalization 166–72
  ideal and nonideal 71–2, 81–6, 88, 108
  individualism 15, 17, 23, 27, 30, 59
  institutions 7, 12–13, 16, 133, 140, 151–3,
    167–70, 173, 176
  morality 51, 79–80, 121
  motivation 148–9, 152–5, 171–2, 178
  negative cosmopolitanism 11–15, 19–21
  patriotism 4, 7, 18
  philanthropy 4
  politics
    activism 4, 7, 27, 35–67
    agency 7, 30–1, 131–2, 153, 166–9, 172
    community, dialectic account of 140–1,
      154
    obligations, theory of 59–60
  popular sovereignty 133, 148–50, 153
  positional goods 109, 124–5
  positive cosmopolitanism 11–15, 19–21
  poverty 110–11
  power between states, inequalities
    of 110–11
  principles and agency, relationship
    between 7–8, 12, 30, 71, 154–5, 174–5

relative deprivation 108
sceptics 11–12, 60
selfishness 15
social movements 167–8
security guarantees 170
statism 4–8, 11–12, 28–31, 71–3, 90–9, 102, 104, 131–3, 153, 179
Courbet, Gustave 157–8, 159
Crisp, Roger 47n25, 115n19
Cronin, Ciaran 92n9
culture 54, 56, 63–4, 71–3, 95, 134–5, 151–3, 156–62, 176, 179

Dadaism 159
Dahl, Robert 123n37
D'Alembert, Jean Le Rond 11, 157
De Greiff, Pablo 92n9
Declaration of the Rights of Man 1789 163
decolonization 129
Della Porta, Donatella 168n33, 168n35, 168n36, 169n37
deprivation
  absolute deprivation 6, 91, 95–104, 107–29
  relative deprivation 6, 97–103, 107–30, 175
developing countries, international trade and 126
Di Giovanni, George 27n50
diagnostic method 44–5, 58–9, 61, 75, 91, 102, 177
dialectical method
  absolute deprivation 102–3
  activism 35
  associative relations 133, 140, 154
  avant-garde agency 36–7, 61–4, 66–7, 156
  cosmopolitanism 6, 104
  global justice 40–1, 72, 75, 107, 109
  heuristics 61–2
  ideal and nonideal 5–6, 37–8, 40–50, 55–61, 67, 71, 88–9
  learning process 42–3
  particularism 133
  politics 4, 23, 35, 40–50, 55–67, 79, 103, 133, 140–5, 154–5, 178
  preservation and innovation 145
  principles and agency, relationship between 3–4, 7–8, 41, 82, 155–6, 174
  statist cosmopolitanism 6, 104
  universalism 133
Diani, Mario 168n35
Diderot, Denis 11–12, 14, 157
Diogenes the Cynic 12–14
distributive justice 85–92
  absolute deprivation 103, 110
  circumstances of injustice 86–7, 102, 104, 123
  collective will 28
  conflicts 19, 102, 130, 148

cosmopolitanism 72–3, 89, 167
egalitarianism 89–92, 97–100, 103, 108, 115–18, 121–3, 127–9
  existing state of affairs 47
  food prices 117
  morality 78, 80, 119
  poverty 71, 90–2, 104, 176–7
  power distribution between states 109–11, 124–8
  private property 19
  production level 89
  relative deprivation 108, 110
  security 26
  starvation 108, 129
  statism 72–3, 98
*Don Quixote* 49–50
Drahos, Peter 126n45
Drescher, S 164n27
Dryzek, John S 167n32, 168n33
Duvall, Raymond 126n45
Dworkin, Ronald 38n5, 52n36, 52n37

education 7, 19–20, 23, 29, 124–5, 133, 145–51, 153
egalitarianism 8, 21, 47–8, 60, 89–97
  absolute deprivation 91, 95–104, 112, 115–20
  birth, moral arbitrariness of place of 51, 108, 120
  causal claims 99–103
  circumstances of injustice 44, 88, 95, 97, 99, 103, 112, 118–20
  civil society 20, 25
  commercial relations 24
  conflicts 94–7, 129
  cosmopolitanism 6, 7, 12–13, 88–93, 95–6, 98–104, 166
  distributive justice 89–92, 97–100, 103, 108, 115–18, 121–3, 127–9
  emerging political project, as 148
  global justice 3, 8, 44, 89–97
  ideal and non–ideal 71, 88–94, 103–4
  institutions 6, 92–5, 97, 99, 175
  motivation 154, 178–9
  normatively fundamental and causally fundamental principles 99–103
  positional goods, unequal distribution of 98
  poverty 6, 88–104, 176–7
  power of states 109–11, 109–11, 124
  relative deprivation 97–8, 100–3, 108, 110, 115, 121–3
  statism 3, 6, 12, 88–99, 102–4 , 112, 174
  sufficientarian justice 6, 89–92, 96–8, 101, 103, 107–8, 112–21, 129
  universal idea of equality 11–12

Egbert, Donald D 158n7
egoism 24
El Greco 159
Eluard, Paul 158
Engels, Friedrich 89n2
English Civil War 64–5
Enlightenment 4, 7, 11, 17, 25, 35, 59–60,
    157, 164
environment 170–1
equality *see* egalitarianism
Estlund, David 36n1
estrangement 159
European federation project 22
Evans, JDG 46n18
existing practices 39, 50–6, 60

failed states 176–7
Falk, Richard 135n6
famines 116–17
Farrelly, Colin 36n2
Fawcett, Millicent Garrett 164
Feinberg, Joel 113n13, 151n30
Feyerabend, Paul 46n20
Fidler, D 22n37
Finnemore, Martha 164n25, 164n26
first–order principles 34, 41–2, 45–8, 55–6,
    60, 84–5, 96, 101–3, 109, 147–9
Flikschuh, Katrin 26n47, 28n56, 29n65, 33n76
Fontana, Biancamaria 134n5
food prices, increase in 117–18
Fougeret de Monbron, Louis–Charles 14–15
Fourier, Charles 157
Fox, William 165
Foxley, Barbara 19n30
Frankfurt, Harry 115n19, 119n29
free movement of capital 170
freedom 17, 20, 24–5, 30–2, 60, 145–7, 159, 162
Freeman, Samuel 92n12
French Revolution 26–7, 139
Fuller, Stephen 165n29
Futurism 159

Galileo 53
Galston, William 147n26
Gerhardt, Volker 11n3
Gilabert, Pablo 51n33
Gill, Mary Louise 12n4
Gilpin, Robert 125n41
global *see* egalitarianism
global justice
    absolute deprivation 108
    arbitrariness 76–81
    associative relations 71–81
    birth, arbitrariness of place of 51, 108, 120

circumstances of injustice 4, 7, 27–8, 44,
    47–9, 60–2, 75–111, 118–27, 137,
    155, 166
civil society model of political
    community 134–5
collective political practices of
    deliberation 30
compassion 21
conflicts 80, 94–7
cosmopolitanism 7, 13–14, 26–7, 29, 33,
    60, 72–3
dialectical approach 40–1, 72, 75, 107, 109
egalitarianism 3, 8, 44, 89–97
historical controversy 23–7, 11–34
ideal and non–ideal 39, 47–8, 81–6
*ius gentium* and *ius cosmopoliticum* 28
moral psychology 83–4
political membership 81–5
relative deprivation 108
slavery 57
statism 4, 28, 44, 72
sufficientarianism 97
unsocial sociability 25
globalization 166–72, 175
good citizens 11–12, 16
Goodin, Robert E 113n12
Gough, JW 123n35
Gourevitch, Victor 17n24, 19n29, 78n21,
    84n35, 135n7, 146n22, 161n19
Gramsci, Antonio 161–2
Gray, John 72n1
Gregor, Mary J 12n5, 26n47, 27n53, 146n23
Guernica 1–2

Habermas, Jürgen 33n76, 43n17
Hajer, Maarten A 42n13
Hamilton, Edith 13n6, 115n17
Harrison, Charles 158n8
Havens, GR 17n25
Hayek, FA 93n14
Heater, Derek 12n4
Hegel, GWF 4n4, 40n10, 43
hegemony 150–1, 158, 179
Held, David 135n6
Henson, Richard 139n17
Herman, Barbara 139n17
heuristic potential 44–5, 58, 60, 75
Hoare, Quintin 161n20
Hobbes, Thomas 16, 18, 64, 123n38
Hobsbawm, Eric 137n5, 158n9, 159n12,
    160n16
Hochschild, Adam 164n27, 165n29
Höffe, Otfried 26n47, 29n60
Hoffman, S 22n37

homeland, definition of 15–16
Hont, Istvan 17n23
Horstmann, Rolf-Peter 11n3
human rights 129, 152, 163, 164–5
humanism 64
Hume, David 14, 77, 78
Huyssen, Andreas 157n6

ideal and nonideal 36, 38–50, 71–6
  abstraction and idealization 45–6
  activist political theory 71
  arbitrariness 77–80
  associative relations 72–6
  avant-garde political agency 36, 38, 40–51,
    63, 66
  circumstances of injustice 47, 81–6, 108
  cosmopolitanism 71–2, 88, 108
  dialectical approach 5–6, 37–8, 40–50,
    55–61, 67, 71, 88–9
  division of labour 39
  egalitarianism 71, 88–94, 103–4
  existing practices 50–6
  first-order principles 34, 41–2, 45–8, 55–6,
    60, 84–5, 96, 101–3, 109, 147–9
  generalizations 45–6
  global justice 39, 47–8, 71–6, 81–6
  interaction 55–6
  irrelevance 45–50, 55
  method, issue of 50–3
  poverty 128
  principles and agency, relationship
    between 36, 76, 87
  relevance 40–50, 63, 66
  statism 71–2, 88, 91–4, 108
  status-quo bias 38, 50–7, 66
  sufficientarianism 128
  thought experiments 47–8, 81–3
Imig, Doug 169n37
India 116–18, 172
indigenous people 25, 168, 170–1
individualism 15–16, 23, 30, 59, 95
innovation 3, 44–5, 58, 61, 102, 145, 159–62
institutions
  associative relations 72–5, 79–80, 131–2, 154
  civic education 150–1, 153
  civil society model of political
    community 134–5
  coercion and cooperation 72–3
  conflicts 5, 20, 23–4, 29, 31, 35, 44, 61
  cosmopolitanism 7, 12–13, 16, 133, 140,
    151–3, 167–70, 173, 176
  culture 54
  diagnostic task 44–5, 58–9, 75
  dialectical approach to political
    activism 40–1, 58–9

  egalitarianism 6, 13, 92–5, 97, 99, 175
  existing institutions 62–4, 66
  family, political community as a large 132,
    136
  function and purpose 44, 52, 61–2, 64,
    75, 129–30, 150–6, 162–3
  global justice 72–4
  heuristic potential 44–5, 58, 60, 75
  innovating task 44–5, 58
  *ius gentium* and *ius cosmopoliticum* 28
  legitimacy 140
  means through which goods are
    acquired 114
  particularism 137
  patriotism 16
  politics 26, 31–2, 73, 131–3, 141–2, 154
  popular sovereignty 146, 150
  socially-discredited institutions 57–8
  thought experiments 82
  transformation 23, 40, 43, 162–3
international law 126, 128
international trade 21–2, 25
intuitions 46–7, 50, 62–4, 138
*ius gentium* and *ius cosmopoliticum* 28–30

James, Aaron 52n36, 52n39
Julius, AJ 73n4
justice *see* global justice

Kant, Immanuel 4, 11n2, 12n5, 12–13, 17,
  22n39, 23–33, 35, 41, 59–61, 78–9,
  139, 146
Keane, John 167n32
Keck, Margret 168n33, 168n34, 171n40
Keohane, Robert 125n41
Kleingeld, Pauline 11n3, 26n47, 28n56, 33n76
Kramer, Hilton 159n13
Kriesi, Hanspeter 168n33, 169n37
Kuper, Andrew 73n7
Kymlicka, Will 136n11, 147n27

Ladyman, James 53n41
Lakatos, Imre 46n20, 47n24, 52n40
large family model of political
  community 132, 134–6, 142, 144–5
learning process 4–8, 31, 40–3, 147
legitimacy 20, 22, 62, 64–5, 127, 137, 140, 145,
  150, 153, 163–5
Leibniz, Gottfried 12, 13–15, 18, 26–7, 80
Lenin, VI 160
Lissitzky, Lazar 158–9
Locke, John 123n35
Louis XIV, king of France 17
loyalty 11–13, 15, 25, 73, 135–6, 144–5, 148
Lukács, Georg 160n15, 160n17

Lukes, Steven 123n35, 123n37
Lutz-Bachmann, Matthias 33n76
Luxemburg, Rosa 158n9

Machiavelli, Niccolò 64, 151
Malevich, Kazimir 158–9
Mandeville, Bernard 18–19
Mapel, David 83n32
Marchetti, Raffaele 135n6, 167n32, 168n34
Mariano, T 132n3
Martin, Rex 92n9, 117n23
Marx, Karl 4n4, 40n10, 64n52, 89–90, 157
Mascagni, Pietro 159n12
May, Gita 14n14
McDonough, Kevin 151n30
means through which goods are
        acquired 116–17
meat consumption, increase in 117–8
media 151
Mendes, Chico 171
Merker, Nicolao 11n3
Mertes, Tom 170n39
Micheli, Mario de 158n9, 158n10
migrants 169–70
military power 125
Mill, John Stuart 72n1
Miller, David 36n2, 38n8, 46n22, 49n29,
        54n42, 72n1, 77n12, 87n40, 89n1,
        91n7, 92n8, 93n13, 96n16, 111n4,
        112n7, 117n23, 121n30, 121n33,
        128n48, 137n12
Mills, Charles W 36n2
Moellendorf, Darrel 77n12, 80n25
Monbiot, George 117n27
money 125
Montero, GR 132n3
Montesquieu, Charles de 14, 20
morality
    activist political theory 79
    arbitrariness 3, 51, 108, 120
    autonomy 146
    basic material goods, access to 113
    circumstances of injustice 77, 79, 86, 94
    cosmopolitanism 79–80, 121
    distributive justice 78, 80, 119
    egalitarianism 60
    individual moral agency 76–80
    learning process 5
    motivation 136–9
    particularism 136–7
    politics 31–2, 35, 61, 131–2
    poverty 6
    progress 12
    universalism 136–9
motivation 136–40, 148–55, 169, 172, 178

multinational companies, campaigns to
        boycott 169
Musgrave, Alan 46n20
Muthu, Sankar 22n36, 164n28

Nagel, Thomas 72n2, 73n4, 74n10, 91n4,
        92n12, 93n13, 112, 117n23
Nardin, Terry 83n32
Narveson, Jan 93n14
natural laws 49
natural rights theory 153
negative cosmopolitanism 11–15, 19–21
neoliberalism 168
networks 165, 167, 170–1, 176
Newtonian physics 46–7
Niesen, Peter 25n44
non-comparative claims 113, 115, 119–21, 127
nonideal approaches *see* ideal and nonideal
normative principles and political agency
        distinguished 3–5
Nowell Smith, Geoffrey 161n20
Nowell Smith, Patrick Horace 48n27
Nussbaum, Martha 11n2, 33n76, 72n3,
        151n30, 151n31
Nye, Joseph S 125n41

observation 1, 53–4, 56–7, 62, 65
October Revolution 158
Offe, Claus 132n3
O'Malley, Joseph J 64n52
O'Neill, Onora 11n2, 46n18, 87n38

Pankhurst, Emmeline 164
Paris Commune 157
particularism 132–3, 136–40, 147, 152
patriotism 4, 7, 14–23, 25, 27, 29, 59, 136, 147
peace, project of perpetual 22, 33
peasants' unions 171
Pellegrin, Pierre 12n4
Peter the Great, tsar of Russia 14
Pevnick, Ryan 73n4
philanthropy 4, 13–14, 27
Picasso, Pablo 1n1, 1–2, 8, 157, 158, 159
Pieri, Georges 11n1
Pissarro, Camille 158
place of birth, arbitrariness of 51, 108, 120
Plato 13, 115
Pocock, JGA 49n30, 62n50, 64n53
Pogge, Thomas 30n67, 73n8, 77n12, 77n14,
        78n19, 82n29, 87n38, 92n9, 96n16,
        135n6
pointillism 158
Poland 135–6
politics
    activism 2, 4, 27–8, 35, 40–50, 55–61

agents 7, 30–3, 36–57, 61, 75, 131–3, 149, 153, 156–7, 160–2
arbitrariness of political membership 6, 19, 76–7, 80, 86, 134, 142–4, 149
art, as 1, 155, 156, 160–72
associative relations 71–87, 133–41, 148
community 6, 19, 86–7, 80–6, 134, 140–5, 149–50, 154
conflicts 5, 13, 63–7, 79, 154, 163, 168
cosmopolitanism 4, 27
dialectical approach 4, 23, 35, 40–50, 55–67, 79, 103, 133, 140–5, 154–5, 178
disaffection 132–3, 175
moral politicians, intervention of 31–2, 61
obligations 20–1, 24–6, 28, 30, 59–60
participation 146, 149, 164
Popper, Karl 40n10, 43n16
popular sovereignty 7, 19–20, 23, 29, 145–50, 153
positional goods, access to 98, 109–11, 121–30, 149
positive cosmopolitanism 11–15, 19–21
Postigliola, Alberto 11n3
poverty 6, 71, 88–104, 110–11, 114, 118–20, 128, 176–7
absolute deprivation 6, 91, 95–104, 107–29
absolute poverty 96, 119
relative deprivation 6, 97–103, 107–30, 175
power distribution between states 109–11, 124–8
practical reason 24
Prévert, Jacques 158
prices, increase in food 117–18
principles and agency, relationship between 3–8, 35–8, 61, 137
cosmopolitanism 7–8, 12, 30, 71, 154–5, 174–5
dialectical method 3–4, 7–8, 41, 82, 155–6, 174
first-order values 34, 41–2
ideal and nonideal 36, 76, 87
state of nature 29
statism 5–6, 36, 71, 174
private property 19–20
progression 26–7, 32–3, 61, 63, 66, 160–5, 176–8
Proudhon, Pierre-Joseph 157
public awareness of social issues 157–9, 162–5, 169–70

Ramirez, Francisco O 164n26
Rawls, John 36n1, 38, 54n44, 56n46, 72n1, 72n3, 73n5, 73n7, 74n10, 77–8, 81, 82n31, 83, 84n34, 89n1, 91n6, 91n7, 92n9, 92n11, 92n12, 93n13, 96n16, 112n7, 117n23, 128n48, 144n21, 150n29
Raynal, Guillaume-Thomas François 14–15
reason and motivation, normative 136–40
Reidy, David 92n9, 117n23
Reiss, Hans 17n24, 79n24
relative deprivation 6, 97–103, 107–30, 175
religion 13, 64, 150
Richards, David AJ 77n13, 83n32
Riley, Patrick 13n8
Rio Tinto 171
Risse, Mathias 72n2, 91n7, 97n17, 165n31
Robeyns, Ingrid 36n2, 38n3, 38n4, 46n22, 121n31
Robinet, André 13n8, 14n11
Rodchenko, Alexander 159
Ronzoni, Miriam 126n45
Ropp, Stephen C 165n31
Rosen, Michael 43n15
Rousseau, Jean-Jacques 12, 17–25, 28–30, 78–9, 84, 135–6, 146, 161
Rubens, Peter Paul 159
Rucht, Dieter 168n33, 169n37
Russia 135–6, 158

Sabel, Charles 73n4
Sader, Emir 170n39
Saint-Pierre, Charles-Irénée Castel de (Abbé de Saint-Pierre) 22, 28
Saint Simon, Claude Henri de 156–7, 156n1
Sangiovanni, Andrea 51n32, 51n33, 52n36, 54n42, 54n45, 72n2, 74n10, 92n11, 112n8
Scanlon, Thomas 113n12, 113n14
Scheffler, Samuel 72n1
Schiller, Friedrich 139, 139n15
Schlereth, Thomas J 11n3, 14n11
Schoenberg, Arnold 157
Schumacher, Ralph 11n3
science 46–7, 156–7
security 16, 22, 26, 170
self-determination 149
self-interest 21, 134, 165
selfishness 19–20, 24, 30–1, 33, 78
Sen, Amartya 36n2, 39n9, 114n16, 116n21, 121n31
Sencerz, Stefan 47n23
Shaffer, Gregory 126n45
Shanahan, Suzanne 164n26
Shue, Henry 113n12
Signac, Paul 158
Sikkink, Kathryn 164n25, 164n26, 165n31, 168n33, 168n34, 171n40
Simmons, AJ 38n3
Singer, Peter 92n9

single political body with coercive powers, idea for 26, 28–9
Skinner, Andrew 114n15
Skinner, Quentin 64n54
slavery 57, 90, 163, 164–5
Smith, Adam 113, 114n14
social contract 19–21, 161
social practices 40–1, 55–8, 63
Socrates 12–13
South America 170–1
Soysal, Yasemin 164n26
Stalinism 158
Stanton, Elizabeth Cady 164
starvation 107–8, 115–18, 129
state of nature 19–20, 22, 25, 27, 29–30
statism
  agency 131–3, 153
  associative relations 71, 92, 131–2
  circumstances of justice 102, 119
  cosmopolitanism 4–8, 11–12, 28–31, 71–3, 90–9, 102, 104, 131–3, 153, 179
  dialectical method 6, 104
  distributive justice 72–3, 98
  egalitarianism 3, 6, 12, 88–99, 102–4, 112, 174
  global justice 4, 28, 44, 72
  ideal and nonideal 71, 88, 91–4, 108
  political obligations 54–5
  positional goods 109, 122, 129, 149
  principles and agency, relationship between 5–6, 36, 71, 174
  relative deprivation 109
  selfishness 30–1
  sufficientarianism 44, 112, 119
status–quo bias 38, 50–7
Steinberg, Richard H 126n45
Stemplowska, Zofia 36n1, 38n3, 38n6, 46n21
Stiglitz, Joseph 126n44, 126n45
Stocker, Michael 138n14, 139n17
subsistence claims 108, 112–13, 116–17, 119–20, 174–5
sufficientarian justice 6, 44, 89–92, 96–103, 107–8, 111–21, 127–9, 150
Swift, Adam 36n1, 98n18, 109n2, 124n40, 125n42

Tan, Kok-Chor 77n12, 122n34
Tarrow, Sidney 167n32, 169n37
Taylor, Keith 156n1

territorial expansion 29
Téry, Simone 1n1, 2n2
Therborn, Göran 160n14
Thomson, JAK 115n18
Titian 159
toleration 95
Tolstoy, Leo 160n15
trade union organizations and activists 171–2
tradition 8, 52, 62, 64, 84, 91, 133, 135, 151, 155, 159–62, 174
transnational advocacy networks 165, 170–1
trial and error 31, 43, 56, 63
Trotsky, Leon 158n9
Trousson, Raymond 14n15

United States 118, 169, 172
universalism 11–12, 32–3, 132–3, 136–40
unsocial sociability 17, 25, 78
utility maximization 22

Valentini, Laura 38n3, 38n4, 38n5, 46n19, 52n36
Van Hensbergen, Gijs 1n1
veil of ignorance 81
Velásquez, Diego 159
virtue, science of 64
Voltaire 12, 14, 15–18, 26

Wagenaar, Hendrik 42n13
Wagner, Richard 157, 159n12
Waldron, Jeremy 11n2, 152n33
Walzer, Michael 54n42, 72n1, 148n28, 150n29
Warburton, Nigel 46n20
Weber, Max 142n19
Wenar, Leif 92n9
White, J 162n22
will for power 19
Williams, Howard 26n47
women's movements 163–4
Wood, Allen W 27n50
Wood, Paul 158n8
Worker's Party Government of Acre 171
World Trade Organization (WTO) 126

Young, Iris Marion 168n33, 169n38
Ypi, Lea 24n42, 28n57, 111n4, 143n20, 160n15, 160n16, 162n22

Zola, Émile 157

Printed and bound by CPI Group (UK) Ltd, Croydon, CR0 4YY